The Passing of the Night

To the American fighting men who died defending beliefs that we POWs were imprisoned for.

To the wives of the POWs who suffered and who gave much more than we.

And to the youth of America whose honesty and integrity make me confident and optimistic about the future of our nation.

The
Passing
of the Night My Seven Years

As a Prisoner of the North Vietnamese

by Robinson Risner

Random House : New York

Library of Congress Cataloging in Publication Data
Risner, Robinson.
   The passing of the night.
    1. Vietnamese Conflict, 1961–   —Prisoners and
prisons, North Vietnamese. 2. Vietnamese Conflict,
1961–   —Personal narratives, American. 3. Risner,
Robinson. I. Title.
DS557.A675R57 1974   959.704 37   73-9094
ISBN 0-394-48967-5

Manufactured in the United States of America

9 8 7 6 5 4 3 2

First Edition

Introduction

The distinctive character of imprisonment in a North Vietnamese prison camp was the suffocating monotony . . . the pervasive sameness of the routine, over and over, day in and day out.

Bodies built for movement were confined to closetlike boxes. Active minds were forced to be idle within the numbing nothingness of four walls in a dingy little cell.

Men trained to fly sophisticated machines at incredible speeds and breath-taking heights were caged like animals. No more horizons to scan, no more clouds to soar above, no more barriers to break through.

But worse than that, no people to be close to. No wife to kiss, no child to hold, no friend to embrace nor hand to shake.

Conditions varied in North Vietnam for different prisoners. Sometimes this was due to rank, the time of shoot-down or individual reaction to our captors. But for most of us, the events described in the pages that follow were typical.

Seven and a half years is a long time—especially to be in a prison cell. One thing for sure, it gave me a lot of time for reflection—something I did too little of before I was shot down on September 16, 1965. Days dragged into weeks, weeks finally became months, and unbelievably, months eventually became years—one, two, three, four, five, six, seven, and finally release.

Not only did I spend much time in reliving the significant events of my life but I also began to sift out those things that were most important—to reduce a lifetime to what really matters. The perspective of a prison cell gives a unique dimension to the past and the present. Hopefully, it can contribute to the future.

I have known the feeling of being away from America and returning. But there's no feeling comparable to that of returning home after an enforced separation of seven and a half years.

Since I missed out on a lot of important events, my perspective is diminished by that absence. Yet, I can still see so much to be grateful for. Things I had taken for granted—removed for a time—are now so much more precious to me.

Forgive my idealism. Believe me, it has been tested. It's not superficial. I'm glad to be an American. With all its warts and sores, its lack of perfection, America is still the greatest place in the world to me. In prison, the shortcomings of America were constantly paraded before us. They're there, for sure, but we are working on them and they're slowly changing. Too slowly sometimes, but nevertheless changing.

We have a great future ahead of us in this country. I want to have a part in it, and if possible, make some small contribution to a better tomorrow.

Special thanks are due many people who assisted in the preparation of this book. Gerald Pope negotiated arrangements with the publishers. Wayne A. Robinson prepared the manuscript for submission to the publishers. Scores of others gave advice, offered services and were helpful in untold ways.

Someone asked me why I was writing this book and my honest answer is this: I believe that today's young people are searching for a dragon to slay. I want to help them find the right dragon. I want our young people to be proud of the things that count. I want to show that the smartest and the bravest rely on their faith in God and our way of life. I hope to show how that faith has been tried by fire—and never failed. I would like to say, "Don't ever be ashamed of your faith, nor of your wonderful heritage. Be proud of those things which made America great and which can, with our help, be even greater."

R.R.

Contents

Contents

The Passing of the Night

I

Premonitions

It was a muggy night in Okinawa and the air conditioners chugged in protest against the unequal match. The next morning, August 19, 1965, I would be moving forward on TDY (temporary duty) to Korat Air Force Base in central Thailand. But for the first time in twenty-two years of flying, I had a strange premonition about leaving that would not go away. To relieve it I took out all of my papers—insurance policies, investments and obligations—and thoroughly briefed Kathleen.

We talked about the children's schooling, and I mentioned that I hoped one or more of them would go to the Air Force Academy. Even though we had lived in Okinawa since 1963, she said that if anything happened to me, she wanted to go back home to Oklahoma City to live. They had a good school system, and our neighbors and friends from the 1940s were still there. And many of our relatives still lived in Oklahoma City and Tulsa.

After Kathleen had gone to bed and the house was quiet, I pulled out my little tape recorder. I had never done it before, but I felt it important to leave a message. Ironically, I failed to tell any of my family about it, and they did not discover it until nearly a year after my shoot-down. This is what they heard me say that night:

"Kadina, Okinawa, August 18, 1965—I wanted to say a few words before I left. Kathleen, I am sure that you know how much I love you, but this is to tell you again.

"Rob, son, I have told you many times and I am asking you again. Please help take care of things. Be the man of the house and be responsible . . . for me. Be like you think I would like for you to be.

"Jeff, son, Daddy's talked to you so many times. You know how much I love you. I am asking you to be an up-standing young gentleman. Mold yourself into a fine young man. Walk straight. Be a good boy.

"Paul, son, Daddy loves you, too. Be a sweet boy. Always do the things that you know are right and stick up for them.

"Tim, Daddy loves you, ol' pardner. Try to be a sweet boy for Daddy. Grow up into a young man that I would be proud of.

"Danny doodle, Daddy loves you an awful lot. You are so sweet and I hope you will always stay that way. Be a fine young man. Stay away from bad habits.

"All of you, please help your mother. She needs it very much. Remember all of you that I love you very much, that I will pray for you. I don't expect anything to happen to me ever, but you never know. If anything should, you all will know that I was prepared and you all will know, also, that I have had a very rich and rewarding life. I do not begrudge a minute of it.

"If something should happen that I should be reported missing, you know what kind of a person I am. If there's any chance at all, you know I will be back. So never give up hope. But then, if something should happen, don't live in the past. Live for tomorrow. Let yourself enjoy life. Don't mourn over something that was meant to be. For you know that I have had a very happy life and I will think of all of you. Just remember how much I love each one of you. Bye now."

The next morning at five-thirty the alarm went off. I jumped out of bed and connected the coffeepot while Kathleen brushed her teeth and then went into the kitchen. After I dressed in my flight suit, I carried my bags into the front room.

Breakfast was not quite ready, so I went into the three rooms where the children were sleeping. I leaned over and kissed my boys without awakening any of them except Rob, the eldest, who murmured sleepily, "Good-bye, Daddy." As I kissed them, the strange feeling came back. I walked back through again. Tim and Danny were sleeping in one room, Jeff and Paul in another, and Rob in another. I stood and looked at each one. They seemed so peaceful and innocent. We had had a lot of great times together. Hopefully, there would be more.

As soon as we finished breakfast, Kathleen drove me to base operations where Colonel Bob Cardenas, my wing commander, was waiting in a T-39. At the gate I kissed Kathleen good-bye in the car, and told her not to worry.

As I walked through the gate I turned and saw her sitting there watching. I set down one of my bags and waved. She waved back and drove away. I was to remember that scene many, many times. I did not see her again until the twentieth of February, 1973. My little three-and-a-half-year-old would then be in the sixth grade, and my seventeen-year-old would be studying for his master's degree.

At Korat I began flying an average of one mission a day over North Vietnam. For some reason I was getting hit a lot and once I even had to bail out. The crew chiefs hated to see me coming. During one week I was hit four missions in a row out of five. This was a typical mission. After completing one of our bombing missions we were reconnoitering a road and found a tank alongside the river, camouflaged with brush. I made three different tries on it, but the sky was so overcast that by the time I would go up through the clouds and come back down again, I was just far enough off so that I could not get my guns on him before I passed him. I finally had to give it up for a truck that was camouflaged which I blew up.

One of the fellows in the other squadron had just been shot down and I started over to cap him (circle overhead, call rescue helicopter, etc.), but before I could get there, some of his own squadron mates had arrived and taken over.

I was at 17,000 feet and working back down the highway in the mountain passes, watching the road with my binoculars. Suddenly I saw a great big truck come out of one of the passes. We had standing orders when reconnoitering to hit trucks, trains and bridges. Evidently our planes were so high that he did not know we were around. As he hurried along the mountain road I made a 270-degree descending turn and met him head-on. I was almost supersonic when I gave him a good long burst and he exploded. As I pulled out I was hit three times, once by a 23-millimeter round in my gas tank right behind the cockpit. There were a lot of fumes but no explosion. I pulled up and went home.

The next day I received a call from Second Air Division in Saigon saying that General Joseph Moore wanted to see me right away. I put a crew chief in the back of an F-105-F and left Korat in a hurry. I landed at Saigon, and as I started walking into base operations, I met General Moore coming out. He said, "Come on, Robbie." I didn't even go inside.

We took off in a T-39 and I still didn't know what was happening. After we were airborne he came back and sat down. "I'm going to take you with me to Clark." I was a little surprised that we were going all the way back to the Philippines, but I figured it must be something important. "Will we get back today? We have a big mission tomorrow that I want to fly." He said, "Don't worry about the mission. I am taking you over to cool off for a few days. You are getting hit too often." So for three days I stayed in an air-conditioned room or played golf.

Back in Korat, on September 9 I received a note from General Harris, commander in chief of the Pacific Air Force. "Robbie, be careful. Don't get shot down again. I have plans for you."

The next day we attacked a North Vietnamese headquarters and ammunition-storage area. They had a lot of guns, so we had decided to use one man out of each four-ship flight to go in and bomb the gunners and make them keep their heads down.

That was my assignment on this mission. At the very second I released the bombs, they shot my canopy off on a head-on pass. One round burned my shoulder, and a piece of canopy glass about four times as big as my hand impaled itself in the headrest. With the canopy off, I couldn't go very fast, nor could I climb very high because of the cold. I needed some fuel to reach friendly territory and I hollered for help. An emergency tanker came up from Laos to refuel me, and I made it back to Korat okay.

On September 15 the missions were laid on. My operations officer picked up the operations order the evening before and posted the schedule. When I saw I was not on it, I scratched one of the men and put my name in his place. It was to be a late mission, about nine o'clock in the morning, September 16.

The alarm went off at about five. Another Air Force squadron commander and I bunked together. To keep from waking him I turned on a little light over the sink, shaved with a safety razor, put on a flight suit and combat boots, and went over to the officer's club to have breakfast.

The other three members from my flight were already there. We utilized some of the time to brief while we were ordering and eating breakfast. After we had gone over the usual procedures we went down to the flight line (the aircraft parking area) for our knee boards, on which were the cruise control cards, with mission data, code words, call signs, frequencies, rendezvous points, route in and out, and timing.

We saw the weatherman, had a flight briefing, took our maps which had been drawn up by one of the flight members, and received some data on the target. Intelligence gave us detailed information and some more maps and photographs. We sat down and went through the whole mission together, then went back to squadron operations for a final once-over.

After a cup of coffee and a doughnut, we picked up our guns out of the gun locker. Most of us had .38 Combat Master Pieces.

We exchanged our wallets for what we called our "blood chit," packages which had some pieces of gold bullion in them for barter and pieces of silk cloth that had printed on them, in three or four different languages, "I AM AN AMERICAN FIGHTING MAN." It promised a reward for returning the bearer to friendly hands. We also had some barter material such as watches, and a detailed map put on waterproof silk cloth.

We turned in our personal items, which were put in a small bag, and checked out our parachutes and helmets. Around the base, most of us wore Australian bush hats, broad-brimmed and turned up flat on one side. Each time we flew a mission we would mark it down on the outside band with a red felt-tip pencil. After five we would make a hash mark across them.

A truck with benches along each side was ready to drive us to the airplanes, where our crew chief met us. (In a letter after my release, he told me of his terrible depression when I failed to return. He was afraid I might have had aircraft trouble.) He put my parachute and helmet in the cockpit while I inspected the aircraft and the ordnance. At the designated time we started our engines.

We had four two-ship flights going out. For maneuverability, we wanted only two-ship flights because were were looking for SAM sites. The lead aircraft in each of the two-ship flights was loaded with napalm and the other with 750-pound bombs. As lead, when we found the SAM sites, I would go in and drop napalm on the control trailer from where they launched the missiles. Then the other man would go to afterburner (which gave him half again as much power), climb to the proper altitude and dive-bomb the SAM missiles with those 750-pound bombs.

This morning our mission was to hit a SAM site about ten miles north of the provincial capital of Thanh Hoa. Just as we came in over Highway 1, I heard one of my flight commanders, leading another flight about fifteen miles to my left, say, "Heads up. They're shooting." I knew we were going to get ground fire.

As we approached we turned left to go right up the highway. It was cut through a little hill perhaps a hundred feet high. We were right down on the deck. I had to lift to go over the hill, and as I topped it, the first thing I saw were tracers. I was hit immediately. My engine shuddered, followed by several quick explosions in the cockpit, which immediately filled with smoke. Fire was coming in behind me from the right side, and I couldn't see anything else.

As soon as I was hit I said, "Oak Lead—I'm hit." Within a second or two my wing man was shouting, "Get out, Lead! Get out, Lead! You're burning! You're burning all over!" He kept hollering, but I did not intend to get out. I was staying with the airplane until I was either over the water or blown out. I had no intention of being captured. I went to afterburner and got a surge of power. As I did, I hit the "Jettison All" button, thinking maybe since I wouldn't be able to get the control trailer I could get the ordnance off in time to hit the gun emplacements.

I was already in a right pull up and only two or three miles from the ocean. The nose was coming up when the engine quit, but I had about 550 knots by then because I had gone to afterburner. Suddenly my stick came right back into my lap and the aircraft pitched forward, throwing me up against my shoulder straps toward the canopy. My options were gone—I was out of control. I reached for the handle to eject the canopy. After it went, I squeezed the trigger and ejected.

I had never heard such a thunder of gunfire in all my life. It was a constant, awesome roar. I grabbed for my emergency radio that was stored under my right arm in a survival vest pocket and pulled out the aerial. I tried calling my wing man, Mike Stevens, to tell him to get moving. I was sure they were going to knock him down, too, for he was circling at about 9,000 or 10,000 feet. Before I realized it, I was almost ready to hit the ground. I frantically shoved the radio back in the pocket. I was headed for a rice field between two hamlets. I could see the people running toward me.

I hit on the side of a dike around one of the rice paddies. I had not had time enough to deploy my survival kit, which was a part of my seat in the airplane. It was filled with about 45 pounds of survival equipment hooked against the back of my thighs. I was supposed to have deployed it on a 20-foot strap before reaching the ground. I hadn't, and when I hit the ground I took a good tumble down the dike with the kit tied tight to me, and pulled the ligaments in my right knee.

The man who had said he would never be captured was down in enemy territory. And I had just dropped a load of napalm on them.

II

A Prisoner of the North Vietnamese

When I hit the ground I squeezed the emergency quick-release switch to my parachute, took off the harness and started to run. I had only taken a couple of steps when I was jerked down. The electric cord between the battery and the emergency radio in my pocket was wrapped around a parachute strap.

I reached down for my knife, which was in a scabbard on the back of my right calf. It was fastened in with a snap, but secured further by a piece of parachute cord that I had tied in a bow knot around my leg. When I jerked the bow, it knotted and I could not get it loose. I tried prying the knife out, and when I did, I jammed the tip of it through the scabbard into my calf.

Someone was very close. I grabbed my pistol, cocked it and started to stand up. Peering over the shoulder-high rice, I suddenly stared right into a gun barrel. For a fraction of a second I hesitated; I had always said that rather than be captured I would fight it out. But the Vietnamese already had his rifle lined on me, and my pistol was pointed up at a 45-degree angle. He must have read my thoughts, for he took one hand off his gun and motioned around me in a circle. I was covered from everywhere. I dropped my pistol and mashed it in the mud, hoping to hide it. The rest of my captors moved in close and began stripping me.

My radio was still intact. To get me disentangled, they cut the cord between the battery and the radio. They thought they were only getting me out of the parachute. Although the radio still had a homing beacon, it was now useless.

After stripping me down to my flight suit, they had me kneel and tied my hands behind me. A one-eyed civilian searching in the mud found my pistol. He put it against my forehead and held it there. I was looking right down the gun barrel into his good eye. The trigger pull was real light and I wondered if I could hear the sound before the bullet hit me. I kept watching his trigger finger to see if it would turn white.

The man was trembling and sweat was running off his forehead. I am sure it was a unique situation for him. He had probably never seen an American before, and from the stories he must have heard about us, he probably expected me to be "Mandrake the Magician." When an airplane came over so high that you could not even see it, they would hide; they thought the pilot could see them from 30,000 feet!

Mike, my wing man, was out over the water. As he made another pass they grabbed me and rushed me to a ditch half filled with water where they buried me up to my neck. I guess they were afraid that he was coming down to strafe us. As soon as he had made his pass and left again, they rushed me to a cane grove and hid me. I could hear some other airplanes coming to join the cap as they took me into the little courtyard of one of the hamlets.

They were treating me pretty well. I groaned when they bound my arms quite tightly. An old man, probably the village chief, said something to them and they loosened the rope a little. They did not appear to be trying to hurt me, although some old ladies with sticks tried to hit me. The men pushed them back and again the old man said something and they left me alone but stood glaring.

Now they stripped me down to my shorts, with the whole village watching. I was quite muddy. They drew some water from the well in the courtyard and sloshed me down. They had taken off my canvas combat boots as well as my socks. They gave me back the boots but no socks. Everything else they kept. Some peasant clothes were brought out, which were ragged and threadbare and came just below my knees. At least they were clean.

I was impressed by their curiosity. They tried to talk to me, but of course it was almost impossible. They used some French and I could get a little meaning from their gestures. In pantomime they kept asking, "Why did you come? Why did you bomb?"

They tried to talk to me about rank. How many ranks did I have? Through a combination of the similarity of English and French and counting with their fingers to indicate rank, they finally understood that I was a lieutenant colonel.

They had some photographs of Vietnamese military people to which they kept pointing with pride. Some sort of medal was hung from the neck of one of them. He was evidently a member of the household that had been awarded a decoration.

They took me into a hut and had me lie down on a wooden platform. It was the old chief's bed, I think. They put a mosquito net over me and I lay there watching them as they made an inventory of my stuff. Though it was only noontime, I went to sleep. When I woke up they were still busy with my things. I heard some airplanes, and I could hear an SA-16 offshore, circling, waiting to see if he could get in to rescue me. When somebody made a pass or two across the hamlet at about 10,000 or 12,000 feet, it really scared them. They blindfolded and hustled me out to a little stream under some heavy growth. I could not be seen at all.

They tied me to a tree and left me there during all the air activity, which lasted about an hour or so. My squadron was really trying to find me. I knew it was no use. I began to hope they would go away so I could be untied. The insects were eating on me, ants were biting, and I was tied too tightly. When the airplanes finally left, my captors took me back to the hamlet.

Later they brought me a can of sweet thick condensed cream from Czechoslovakia. They poured about half of it into a little bowl with sugar. It was so sweet that I could not get it down. They kept wanting to know if I was hungry. I finally asked for rice by pantomime. They brought me rice covered with sage. I couldn't eat that, either.

Someone brought me a bottle of what seemed to be soda pop. I drank only a few swigs, but it followed me the rest of the day. Everywhere they took me, the soda pop appeared.

At dusk we started to leave, but when we came to the edge of the hamlet we discovered there were lots of people along the sides of the road, and they were murmuring rather ominously. When my escorts noticed it we turned around and went back to another hut, where we stayed until after dark.

At our second departure, we went by another route and walked for hours. There were four civilians escorting me—two men and two women. One of the men held a spear in one hand and led me with a rope around my arm while the other followed with a rifle. The two women were carrying all of my belongings, including my parachute and guns in a basket on a shoulder pole.

Several times they had to move me to the middle of the road to keep oncoming people from hitting me. Occasionally we stopped, backtracked or took a side road to get away. The minute we heard loud voices we would shoot off the main trail and hole up for a while.

My right leg was almost incapacitated. Evidently I had pulled the ligaments in my knee pretty badly. Every step sent pain shooting up my leg. The kneecap was swollen and discolored. To top it off, my feet were killing me. At first I had tried to wear my combat boots. But they were wet, and without any socks the stiff canvas simply ate the flesh off the top of my feet. Finally I had to take them off and go barefooted. The rocky roads now chewed up the bottoms of my feet.

There was a thin, pale moonlight as we shuffled along. It became so quiet, as we did nothing but walk, walk, walk. The two women with the pole hanging between them went along at a half trot. Every hour, bells in the churches would toll. You could hear them for miles.

While marching along, I started thinking about my family. It was kind of strange—I was almost able to detach myself from where I was and what I was doing. I could see my family, the lights, where they all slept, how many doors were open. I could hear their breathing and the air conditioning. I could see the car parked in the driveway. I wondered if Kathleen's eyes were red and how she had told the boys. Did they know that I was alive? I wondered if Kathleen was lying awake, and if Rob, my seventeen-year-old, would shoulder some of the load, help pack and get ready to go home to Oklahoma. Would he help his mother with the children? I felt sure he would.

Suddenly we stopped and I snapped back to reality. We turned off at a side road and came to a little bridge. I was so tired that I lay down on the bridge and went to sleep. In a few minutes they woke me up and we moved on across into a village not far from there. We backtracked a ways and finally stopped on the patio of a large house. It was dark and the house was far enough from the road so people couldn't see us. I was so tired that I went to sleep again.

When I woke up there were people passing. We were very quiet. No one even whispered. After they were gone we left and retraced our steps back onto the main road.

About two o'clock in the morning we stopped at a hut. My escorts asked if I wanted something to eat. I made a motion of peeling a banana and they brought me ten or twelve. I ate a couple of them and carried the rest. We waited for a little while; then a truck came with a low-ranking military driver and guard. My escorts left me with them.

I boarded the truck and we rode until daylight. Then the driver pulled off the road near a small hut, whose sides were lifted up. We drove in and the sides were let down—and the truck was totally camouflaged. We climbed out and walked for about a mile to a hamlet.

People in the hamlet were very curious and passed by all day long to look at me. The two doors to the hut I was placed in were both open. The crowds became so large that the guards had to lock and bar the doors. Then people would come around behind and try to look through the window. Finally that was boarded up, too. The villagers were so curious that they even tried to pull cracks open and look in through the walls, but no one ever made a threatening gesture or committed a hostile act. When the doctor arrived, the doors were left open to allow the people to watch him treat me. I think he wanted to give me a shot for the pain in my leg, but I would not let him because I didn't know for sure what the shot was.

I had a guard at all times. Sometimes it would be a young boy or girl, at other times an older person. Once I asked to go outside and relieve myself. Going out the door, I wondered what reaction I would get. A path opened and they let me through. A soldier followed to show me where to go. When I returned to the hut, the guard pulled the doors to and locked them so that I would not be bothered.

When nighttime came we prepared to leave again. My feet were really in bad shape by this time. One of the local militia saw them and gave me his shoes to wear. They were Ho Chi Minh sandals, made out of tires with inner tubes forming the straps. His were too small for me, so he took a pair of pliers and adjusted them. I wore them to the truck about a mile away over rocky ground, and then he took them back.

On the cratered road again, I bounced around in the truck like a loose ballbearing. It was unbelievably rough. One of the bridges was out, and we had to cross on bamboo poles laid across a wooden frame. We stopped at another point along the road where we were sandwiched in with long lines of trucks halted by what was evidently a commando raid. I heard a lot of machine-gun firing, pistol and rifle shots. It was a real fire fight that went on for about six or seven minutes.

By daybreak it got to be too stinking rough for my guard in

the back of the truck, so he untied me and put me up front between him and the driver. I rode in the cab the rest of the way, blindfolded but not bound. The blindfold was fairly transparent, though, and by watching the road signs, I could tell where we were going: Highway 1 into Hanoi!

At about eight or nine in the morning we arrived in downtown Hanoi. The driver parked, and he and the guard got out, leaving me sitting in the truck. Pretty soon a crowd gathered around me—a Caucasian with a blindfold on. A young man who looked college age came up close to me and said in English, "Yankee, go home!" I replied very quietly, "I wish I could." I don't know whether I would have answered as calmly if I had known that home for the next seven and a half years would be the infamous Devil's Island of Southeast Asia—Hoa Lo Prison in Hanoi.

III

Welcome to the Hanoi Hilton

After a while my driver and guard came back, and we drove for a few minutes and then stopped again. They honked the horn and someone came out to get me. He led me, still blindfolded, through a side door into a small room. He removed the blindfold, closed the door and left.

I was in the Hoa Lo Prison—the Hanoi Hilton—built by the French over forty years before, only a few miles from downtown Hanoi. Many of the high-ranking Vietnamese government officials had been there for ten to twelve years themselves, imprisoned by the French and Japanese. Naturally, they knew it inside and out.

I looked around my cell; suspended from the ceiling was an ominous-looking hook. The floor was dirty and there were some bloody bandages in one corner, a desk, and a cloth curtain in the middle of the room. I pulled the curtain aside; behind it were stacks of records and old Vietnamese newspapers. There was a double door at the back with bars over it and curtains covering them. I pulled back the curtains and looked out into a courtyard. It had cobblestones wide enough for a truck, and on each side was an elevated flower garden, about seventy-five feet long and twenty-five feet wide. In it were some fir trees and palms. An old Vietnamese was working in the flower beds. Over the whole courtyard were the oldest grapevines I had ever seen, four to five inches thick at the base. It seemed pretty peaceful in the Hanoi Hilton. I heard what sounded like ping-pong, so I thought, "Oh, the boys are playing ping-pong. This is not going to be too bad. They must be treating them okay."

It was about ten o'clock now. After waiting for another twenty or thirty minutes, I decided to see if there was anybody else around. I sang a song to the tune of "MacNamara's Band":

> *"My name is Robbie Risner.*
> *I'm the leader of the group.*
> *Listen to my story and*
> *I'll give you all the poop."*

After a couple of verses I heard a voice say, "Hey, Robbie, this is Bob Peel. Where are you?" I told him. He wanted to know how long I had been captured. He said he was in with two other guys. "One has broken arms, and the other one has broken legs. I'm their nurse." He was an Air Force captain, but I had not known him before. He was right around the corner from me in New Guy Village. He told me the names of others in the prison, and then he said he had to sign off.

As I walked around the cell I would occasionally pull back the curtain and look out into the courtyard. The guard caught me looking out and shook his finger at me. But I did not feel too badly at the moment. I thought, "I'm a prisoner of war. According to the Geneva Convention, I am entitled to certain privileges. I'll get to write letters and receive Red Cross packages. We'll have games, and there will probably be a big compound."

I began planning what I was going to do. We would need an executive officer, operations officer and certain committees. If I was the senior officer, and as far as I knew I was, I would have a lot to do. I thought back through the books I had read. I was really chagrined that I had not been more interested in what had happened in Korea. A close friend, who was a POW there, had been in a sister squadron for a couple of years. (He was busy shooting down a MIG when another MIG hit him from behind. He got his MIG, though, and made "ace" on the mission he went down. His first question when he came out was, "Did I get credit for that MIG?")

I remembered him laughing about his capture in Korea. He said he had been shot down over the Yalu River and picked up by the Koreans in a boat. The airplanes that were with him came down and strafed them two or three times. "Every time they did, the Koreans would just beat the stuffings out of me with the oars."

I had never asked him if he had been tortured or had gotten enough to eat. I remembered him saying that the Koreans had given the POWs some padded or quilted clothes in the winter but that it had not been sufficient. That was all I could remember. I had been so caught up in my daily activities that I had not bothered to find out more. Now I sat thinking, "You're really stupid not to have inquired further." All my information had come through the survival schools and from what I had read in fiction.

As I reviewed this in my mind, I thought my captors would probably be cruel because they were Asians. But I had not been treated cruelly yet, so maybe not. I knew that since we were prisoners of war, they would try to get some information from us, and if they did not get it, they would most likely put us in a compound. Then they would give us the treatment we were supposed to get.

Anyway, none of us would be there later than June of the next year. I had been told that Secretary of Defense Robert McNamara had passed the word down: "Do not make any long-range plans and do not start any new buildings. The war will be over by June 1966."

I felt confident that this was correct. (Later I sent this out to the other POWs as top-secret information from the highest level. Boy, did my credibility go down!) Really, I was not too awfully concerned about my current situation. I had not had any sleep in a long while, though, and I was getting kind of tired.

After about three hours, a Vietnamese who could speak fair English came in to interrogate me. He claimed to be a lieutenant colonel and was the one we would call the Eagle. (We nicknamed everyone so we could have a common reference. They would not tell us their Vietnamese names.) He was dressed in a khaki uniform with the sleeves rolled up. It looked rather rumpled, as though he had been wearing it for several days, and he had on Ho Chi Minh sandals.

I was dressed in the reddish-brown peasant clothes, which were knee-length and shredded at the bottom. The jacket had two pockets down low, like an apron, and was too small, and I was barefooted. But I wanted him to know I was military. So when he came in, I snapped to attention and popped him a salute, and he returned it. Then he went around the desk and told me to be seated on a small, low interrogation stool.

When I did I crossed my legs just as the guard was walking by. He came in, uncrossed my legs, and shook his finger at me. Evidently this was not a polite thing to do.

My interrogator was about forty-five years old. He looked intelligent, squinted his eyes quite often, and smiled a lot. Where he held his cigarette, his fingers were black from chain-smoking. He would light one right after the other. When he offered me cigarettes, I told him I did not smoke. There was tea on the desk and I drank a little out of a big white porcelain cup.

I later found out that the Eagle was the ranking military interrogator. To each of his questions I would say, "I can't answer that."

"Guess."

"I can only give you my name, rank, serial number and date of birth. I cannot guess."

He kept asking questions. To keep from continually telling him I could not answer, I asked him some. "How long am I going to be at this prison?" Sometimes he would answer and at other times he would not. Some of his answers I knew were lies, but at least it got him off the subject.

He showed me maps and circles he had drawn. He would say,

"Now the way I have it planned, the Americans are going to do this: they are going to have Phase I, which is this. I figure then they are going to bomb here, after which they will continue to escalate." (I discovered later that some other POW had told him this to throw him off. As a result, he had some of the wildest ideas I had ever heard.)

He seemed very pleasant. When I did not answer, he would smile, inhale on his cigarette or go to another question. He never got really harsh. I took it for granted that this was standard procedure. From the treatment I had received up to that point and since nobody had leaned on me, my impression was that things were going to be okay.

The Eagle left after about an hour and a half. I was alone again for another thirty minutes or so. My next visitor was the Rabbit, who was younger and spoke a little better English. He was the interpreter for the Cat, a major on the Joint Staff who ran the whole American POW system.

The Rabbit's approach was totally different: if I did not talk, I would never see my family again. Then he told me that I was not a prisoner of war but a criminal. I laughed out loud and said, "You call me what you want. I know I'm not a criminal. You're being ridiculous. Nobody believes that."

He went on to tell me that I had violated the sovereign air space of the Democratic Republic of Vietnam. I was considered in the same way as those who used to prey on their coasts. "You are the same as a pirate. You are going to have to talk."

"No, I am not!"

He made some threats about being tried as a criminal. As an additional scare tactic, he told me that the Vietnamese people would like nothing better than to get their hands on me. "We may turn you over to the people!" He did not lean on me too hard, though, and then he left.

Next came a Vietnamese officer who could not speak

English, and his interpreter. He got somewhat heated. "You will talk! You have information that we need, and you are going to give it to us! Do you want to be executed?"

"No, I don't want to be executed."

"Well, if you do not talk, you will be."

I still refused, and he became more animated. "We will take you back to Thanh Hoa, where you bombed them. We will let them deal with you. Do you remember what happened to Mussolini?"

"No, I can't remember."

"He was hung upside down. How would you like that? How would you like to be burned at the stake?"

I realized that maybe I would be executed as an example, but I did not take him too seriously.

After that a man came in with a woman who was young and spoke fairly good English. They both took a turn at me. The woman said, "Do you love your wife?"

"Sure I do."

"Do you love your children?"

"Naturally."

"Do you ever want to see them again?"

"Yes. I expect to see them again."

Threateningly, she said, "If you do not talk, you will never see them again. Your only hope is to answer our questions and to cooperate with us."

After a while she left and the man stayed on and kept trying some more. They ran several other interrogators through that day with no luck. Finally, late in the evening they took me to Heartbreak Hotel, one of the cellblocks in the huge Hanoi Hilton. They opened the door of one of the cells, and I was so exhausted I hardly looked at the little room that would be my new home for the next two weeks. My leg was throbbing. I had not slept for hours, and I was exhausted from the hours of intensive interrogation. I lay down on the concrete bunk with my head on a rolled-up mosquito net and was asleep in minutes.

IV

First Day in a North Vietnamese Prison Cell

Early the next morning a loudspeaker's blaring woke me. In a sing-song cadence, *"Mot, ha, ba, bon, nom, sow"* was repeated over and over. Vietnamese music accompanied the count, which to my Western ears was terribly discordant. I could not imagine what it was.

After around five minutes a woman instead of a man did the singsong counting. Then they interchanged back and forth. It was the daily exercise period for the Vietnamese civilian prisoners. The music stopped only momentarily before starting another exercise. Then it would begin again. Same old count with an increase in the rhythm occasionally. The exercise lasted for about twenty minutes (in Hanoi the church bells rang every fifteen minutes, so we could tell the time fairly accurately), but the music did not stop for an hour and a half. I was so emotionally drained after my capture that before it was over, I wanted to strangle whoever was doing it.

By the time it stopped, the sun had begun to shine. My mind was in such a whirl that I could not remember much of what had happened the day before. The newness of my surroundings, the abrupt change in my life were crowding in upon me.

Now, on this first morning, I began to look around at my new "home." I stepped it off; the cell was seven feet by seven feet. On opposite sides were cement bunks that ran the length of the cell.

That left a walking space of approximately two and a half by seven feet.

The bunks were built at an angle so that any liquids would run toward the foot of the bunk. About a foot and a half from the end of the bunk was a set of leg stocks hinged against the wall. A heavy piece of iron about two feet long with two half-moon shapes in them could be raised and lowered at will. Underneath, set in wood, was an identical piece. These pieces of steel formed two small holes—one for each ankle. They had been built for Vietnamese ankles, and so were in many cases too small.

On the end of the bunk opposite me was a bunch of blankets and also a stack of old grass bed mats. Apparently my cell had been used as a storage room. The walls looked as if they had been whitewashed a few years before. Below the leg stocks, the paint had been worn away by feet rubbing against it. The bunk was slick where human bodies had lain.

The floor was broken and the cracked cement had not been repaired since it had been laid. At the wall, leading into the courtyard, was a drain hole about three inches square to let water run out of the room. As I found out later, the drain led to an open sewer—an open hole down into a big accumulator filled with the wastes of those who had lived there before.

A ceramic water pot had been brought in along with a rusty gallon-and-a-half bucket which was to be my private commode. The bucket had a loosely fitting wooden cover with a little piece of board nailed to the top of it. To urinate, you picked up the bucket and held it. Since the rim was somewhat sharp, sitting was a more delicate operation. (Later when we were issued sandals, one option was putting a sandal on either side.) The toilet paper was almost the texture of a brown paper bag.

The windows were covered with board, but by peeking through a nail hole, I could look into the courtyard. The transom over my cell door had bars over it and had been covered with wood. There was a peephole in the door about four inches square covered by a hinged piece of metal which could be opened to permit the guard to look in and check on me.

I felt as if someone had put me in a clothes closet, locked the door and said, "See you in six months, buddy." I already hated that stinking small cell. Long flying cockroaches were everywhere. Rats were running back and forth at random under the door and through the drain hole at the bottom of the wall. The mice were profuse, and spiders were all over. Since I had failed to put up my mosquito net the night before, the insects had nearly carried me off. My feet looked like pincushions.

At about seven o'clock I sang "MacNamara's Band" and from the response discovered that the place was full. There was somebody in every cell but one—six besides myself.

Across the hall from me was Wes Schierman, one of my assistant flight commanders as well as safety officer. He was a captain when he was shot down and would have been a lot higher in rank had he not been out of the service for a while. He was an outstanding officer and pilot and had been a member of an Air National Guard unit that was recalled to active duty during the Berlin crisis.

Not too long before his shoot-down, Wes had received a letter from the airline company that he had worked for asking him his intentions, for his obligatory tour of three years was now drawing to a close. His seniority was still going on in the airlines and he would have to apply for separation from the service in order to keep his position. He came to me to talk about what he should do. He decided to separate but when he applied, it was turned down because he was so badly needed.

He had not been injured to any extent when he was shot down, and his radio was intact. The Vietnamese had tried for some time to get him to call the rescue planes in and he had refused. They threatened to kill him, and he still refused. He was to prove later on just how tough a cookie he was.

Now that we were in prison together, I could bring him up-to-date on his family. After his shoot-down a few months before, Kathleen and I had put his wife and family on the plane to fly home. I told Wes they were okay and that everyone believed he was alive. This cheered him, of course.

In the next cell up was Major Ray Merritt, who was one of my flight commanders. Ray's daughter and Jeff, my second son, were in grade school together. I remember Jeff was always coming home frustrated because she was the fastest member on the track team. Doris, Ray's wife, was a good friend of Kathleen's. We had spent a lot of time together.

Ray said he had sprained his ankle when he hit the ground. The Vietnamese had been rather rough with him and dragged him through the fields for a while because he had grabbed his pistol and destroyed his radio. He seemed to be in good spirits.

Next to him was Navy Lieutenant Commander Wendell Rivers, whom I was to get to know better. I talked to Wendy awhile. He had only recently been captured.

The next man on the same side of the hall was Major Ron Byrns, also one of my flight commanders. He had been a prisoner for about a month. His face and hands had been burned in the aircraft before he ejected. He was trying to make it to a mountain range and stayed with his plane longer than he should. He was healing nicely, though, and in good spirits.

I was able to tell him a little about his wife, Jo. I had been in frequent communication with Kathleen by letter while on my last TDY, and she had given me a running account of how the gals were getting along. Jo was continuing to help in the squadron. She intended to stay in Okinawa until October or November and do her Christmas shopping before she returned to the States. Ron was encouraged at this. Everyone felt sure that he was alive because he had been spotted on the ground.

As we started to sign off, he said, "Hey, Robbie, just remember. The first year is the hardest." I wanted to go over there and slug him. I could not bear the thought of being in there a whole year.

On my right was Navy Commander Bill Frank, who had been a squadron commander when he was shot down. We were to spend long hours of the day occupying ourselves by talking about our families and our backgrounds by tapping through the two-foot wall.

Beyond him was Navy Lieutenant Commander Rod Doremus. He became involved in the first Vietnamese attempt to punish me.

After I had talked to everyone, they said, "We better not talk any more. It's time for the guard to come." Before we signed off, they told me what to do: "You'll be taken out and put into the shower to empty your waste bucket. Every time you are put in there, wash. You won't get many opportunities." They told me that if I had any food left, to be sure to cap my dishes one over the other to keep the rats out. If I had any bread left, not to leave it where the rats could get at it but tie it on the wall, or wrap it and hang it high.

They added, "Be sure to take all your food. If you turn any back, they may figure we are getting too much and reduce the amount." They were not getting enough as it was.

The rest of the events of that day are very distinct. I heard the guards opening other cell doors for the men to take showers. When my turn came, I was ready. The shower head was gone, leaving only a pipe. I did not have a towel or soap, but I jumped right under the pipe as quick as I got in and dried off on part of my peasant's uniform.

Rod Doremus called to me through his window, and while I was talking to him the guard came in and caught us. He took me back to my cell, opened up the leg stocks and started to put me in them. I really made a big fuss saying, "Don't put me in those stocks!" He could not understand English but made a sign that I had been talking. I said, "No! No! I was singing," and began to sing for him. He stood there perplexed. He was a civilian medic and evidently not too hard-nosed. But I had been talking and he was supposed to do something to make me uncomfortable, so he was going to put me in stocks. Luckily, I argued him out of it.

As soon as he left, the guys wanted to know what had happened. They told me that Wes Schierman had had a similar problem when he was in the end cell. He had been very uncooperative, the Vietnamese felt, so when they caught him on the lookout for guards, they put him in stocks for three days. "You'd better be careful." Right then I decided I did not want any stocks. I was already tied down enough just being in that seven-foot cell.

About nine-thirty the guard opened my door and motioned me to come out. Down the hall the cook was waiting with some small stack-type dishes. He offered me one filled with a kind of mulligan stew. Then he gave me a little dish with a boiled vegetable of some sort, and a piece of bread.

Back in the cell I set my food down, holding the bread in my lap because I did not want it to touch anything. The rats and cockroaches had come right out of the sewer. I felt dirty and filthy every time I touched something because I knew they had walked on it.

Almost mechanically, before eating I bowed my head to say grace, a habit since I was a child. The memories of my family flooded me so that I could not eat. I recalled the last time I had sat at a table surrounded by my wife and five sons. I could see little Danny, my youngest, only three and a half, asking the blessing. I had helped him as he prayed:

> *"For all we eat and all we wear,*
> *For all we have everywhere,*
> *We thank you, Father."*

Finally I picked up the bowl and began to say thanks. I had food and I had not been tortured. I still had life before me. Those were things to be thankful for.

After I had finished eating I capped my dishes one on top of the other so the rats would not get into them and tied my leftover bread to the wall. That was it. There was nothing now to do. A sickening reality began to sink in on me. In my forty years I had lived a richer life than most people experience in a full lifetime. But that was changed now.

I sat down, leaning my back against the wall. I could hear the chatter of the Vietnamese outside. But nothing was happening inside. I was a prisoner in enemy hands and there was not anyone who could help me.

I began to think about what I could do to pass the time. Although I was not a musician, I liked music. I began to whistle all the songs that appealed to me. Sometimes I would sing one. Later that morning when the guard had left, I lay on the floor to talk through the crack under the door. Someone said, "Hey! We enjoyed your serenade, but you had better keep it quiet or they'll put you in stocks."

I was learning the first lessons of life in a Vietnamese prison. One was that you had to be silent—no whistling, no singing, no talking. Another was that the Vietnamese always liked to find an excuse to punish you.

The first day, though, I forgot a lot of things I was told. My mind was so crowded that I could not seem to assimilate very much. No sooner did one of the men tell me names of people already in prison than I would forget them and would have to be told again.

But some things I remembered quite well. None of them jibed with my concept of a prisoner-of-war camp. I also found out that the prisoners were being interrogated frequently, and that some of them had been mistreated on the way in. Things were not rosy, to say the least.

I still was laboring under the misconception that we were going to be treated as prisoners of war. I felt Hoa Lo was only a processing center; as soon as the Vietnamese realized that we were not going to give them any information, we would be moved to a compound to start the life of a regular prisoner of war. In fact, one of the men had said, "You won't stay here more than two or three weeks. This is just a processing center, and they'll move you to another camp." I asked, "What is the other camp like?" Since none of them had ever been to another camp, nobody knew.

That afternoon I was having trouble hearing under the door and someone said, "Hey! Can you take off your transom cover?" I reached up and jiggled the wooden cover back and forth and was finally able to pull it off. "Get ready to put it back on. If the guard comes in and catches you, you're in bad shape." Now I could see Wes. He looked rather drawn but he was a beautiful sight to see. And I could get a glimpse of a couple of the other men.

They started teaching me the tap code. Captain Carlisle (Smitty) Harris had brought it in about six months before. It was almost our life's blood. I took a nail that I had found and imprinted the code into the wall very deeply, never thinking it would show to the Vietnamese.

That night when the gong went off at almost nine-thirty, I was ready for bed. I had rigged my net, taken off all of the blankets, unfolded them and put them so that they would cover my bunk. It was a stack about three inches thick. Then I put my mat on top of these. (The guard took all but two blankets the next day.)

My guard opened the peephole to look in on me. I was filled with envy for this little brown guy who could come and go as he pleased. He could lock me in, put me in stocks, and seemingly could decide if I should live or die. I was no longer a proud American from a rich and powerful country. I was nothing . . . at their disposal.

With all the power of America behind me, all the technology, all the brains and the riches, here I was in a seven-foot cell, eating food hardly fit for consumption . . . in dirt and filth that we would not have raised our pigs in. I had never envisioned this as the climax to a career I had begun over twenty-two years before as an Air Force cadet in World War II.

V

Shaping of the Future

As a strapping 125-pound seventeen-year-old, my dream in 1942 was to be a pilot in the United States Air Force. Consequently, when my eighteenth birthday rolled around, January 16, 1943, I wasted little time in joining. The biggest hurdle was my birth certificate. The old country doctor in Mammoth Springs, Arkansas, had been so busy delivering babies—there were ten Risners alone!—that he had failed to write my full name. The birth certificate read simply, "Robinson Risner," instead of *James* Robinson Risner. In my impatience I decided to forgo getting a correct one. It would take too long. Soon, instead of "James," "Jamey" or "Jim," I was "Robbie."

My first assignment as an Air Force cadet was a toughie. I was sent as a part of a training detachment to Iowa State Teachers College. The population of the campus was 2,300 women, 50 men and 300 cadets!

Before long I was in Florida, ready to ship overseas. In the interim I had been to preflight, primary and advanced flight-training schools and was gung-ho to get into combat.

We arrived in Miami with sealed orders and were immediately cloistered in a hotel for three days. There were to be no phone calls or letters—absolutely no communication with the outside. Early the third morning we pulled out in trucks on our way to the airport. Halfway out, a big band appeared and played for us all the way to the airport.

It was a big send-off—the secrecy, the band, the sealed orders. There was little doubt that we were headed for combat. The only question was where. The Pacific? Europe? Africa? A few hours out when we opened the orders and discovered our destination, we could not believe it—Panama!

I spent World War II in Panama flying mostly P-38s and P-39s. When it was over, a mass exodus of personnel began. The squadron I was in was deactivated and I became assistant base operations officer and tower officer. Now I was flying all kinds of airplanes—the L-1, C-45 and C-47. And due to lack of personnel, the five or six of us pilots had to become our own mechanics.

We did little to endear ourselves to the local populace. Most of us flew at least five half days a week. A favorite pastime was to blow the roofs off the little native huts. The P-39 was ideal for this. You could stick the nose in the air and it would "mush," the tail sticking close to the ground. At full throttle it would not start climbing for a while. You could mush along blowing the roofs off one at a time. And if the huts were not available, sailboats were fair game. Hardly a sailboat ever escaped.

While there, through an accident, I met the woman who was to become my wife, Nurse Kathleen Shaw from Ware Shoals, South Carolina. It happened when a buddy of mine bought a motorcycle upon my promise to teach him how to ride it. One day, impatient with the speed with which he was learning, he insisted on his driving and my riding as we headed out of Panama City.

When we met a bus on the corner, he went too far to the outside and he dumped us. I landed on my stomach and hands; he landed on my back. It tore all my clothes off, smashed my right wrist, rammed it out of socket and splintered the bones. He did not even get his clothes dirty.

In the hospital a cute little blond day nurse was extra good to me. I was in pain and could not write, so she wrote letters for ters for me, rubbed my back, washed my hair and shaved me.

When I began feeling well enough to be restless, Kathleen, who was the night supervisor, let me out on a pass to date the day nurse. We went to a party at the squadron and did not make it back to the hospital until daylight. Kathleen was very put out!

A friend of mine wanted a date, so I fixed him up with Kathleen and we double-dated. After I was released from the hospital, I bought a motorcycle of my own. I was on the convalescent list for ten weeks, since my right arm was in a cast. I began dating Kathleen in the daytime and her girl friend at night. I can remember on one occasion taking them both on the motorcycle carrying their formals on the arm to change into later.

But I soon discovered it was Kathleen I really cared for. Since I flew days and she worked nights, she would go with me on DDT spray missions and the like. Several times aircraft trouble or failure to disclose flight plans resulted in her being late or my being disciplined.

One day I was able to even the score with my friend who had dumped me on the motorcycle. We rounded a corner at a fair speed with him riding "shotgun" behind me and I laid the motorcycle over so that the footboard dragged, but he said, "That wasn't so hot." As we approached Coffee Avenue, where most of the civil service girls lived, I really poured it on. It laid over so far that the wheels came out from under us. The motorcycle roared down the street ahead of us and we went sliding along in its path.

Luckily for me I had fallen on my right side and was sliding on my cast. But my buddy was on his stomach sliding feet first. If he put his hands down, the cement burned the skin off. When he took the weight off his hands, his chin would drag.

The cycle hit the curb and jumped halfway up the steps of some girls' quarters. My cast had ground through, but the skin was not even broken. However, my buddy was raw all over. I figured we were even when he refused to go to the doctor and let me bathe him in Merthiolate.

Administratively I was no ball of fire, since all I wanted to do was fly. But in the eighteen months since being commissioned, I had managed to make first lieutenant. When I had served my time, the ship I was scheduled to ride home on had several thousand troops on it. A good friend was the general's aide and he arranged for both of us to have our girl friends return with us on the ship.

Lying on the deck under the moonlight with the breeze blowing across our bodies did it. Kathleen and I became engaged on the ship and were married in September 1946, shortly after both of us were discharged.

A short time later I joined the Oklahoma Air National Guard, based in Oklahoma City, flying P-51 Mustangs. One day my friends and I decided to have a party and for it we needed some shrimp. The best place we knew of to buy it was Brownsville, Texas. I was designated to fly down on the day of the party and bring back the required amount for that night.

I took off fairly early in the morning with the normal charts. The Mustang had pretty poor navigational equipment as far as radios were concerned—a "detrolla" with a range of about twenty-five miles maximum. It was very unreliable. Most of the time we navigated by visual reference to the ground, using maps.

As I came in over Texas, there was heavy cloud coverage. I did not know it, but there was a hurricane lying just off the Gulf Coast. Although I did not have an instrument flight clearance and the sky was almost overcast, I climbed above the clouds. At the time I did not know much about jet streams—a strong wind in which the flow of air runs as high as 200 knots.

When the time ran out according to my estimated time en route, I started to let down through the clouds. Shortly after I broke out, I saw the coast. It was not recognizable and I could not place it on the map. I turned east and started flying up the coast, thinking I was west of Brownsville. I flew for quite a while and never ran into a town at all. I decided I was going in the wrong direction. (Actually I had been bucking a strong headwind.) I concluded I was actually between Brownsville and Houston. So I turned around and went back in the other direction.

Meanwhile I had run out of gas in all tanks but one. Flying down the beach at low altitude, I looked for any sort of identification mark. I saw an old man riding down the beach on a donkey. I buzzed him and rocked my wings trying to get him to stop. He looked up once and waved, then pulled his hat down over his eyes and continued on down the beach.

I flew until my fuel tank indicated empty. I knew now that I would have to find a place to land. The beach was too narrow and had some debris and driftwood on it. I looked just inland and found a dry lake bed. I circled, lowered my landing gear, descended and rolled the wheels on the lake bed without landing, to see how smooth it was. It appeared smooth enough, so I pulled up preparing to land.

I had been on empty for so long that I figured my engine would quit any minute, so I loosened my shoulder straps and prepared to bail out if necessary. But the engine kept running and I had sufficient fuel to make my landing pattern and land the aircraft. I turned the plane toward the ocean and chopped the engine.

That afternoon several airliners passed over and I tried unsuccessfully to contact them on the emergency frequency of my radio. I also used a signal mirror. At dusk, I prepared to spend the night. I had done some exploring and I knew there was a small stream nearby, but other than that, only jungle, perhaps a hundred yards away.

I decided to sleep on the wing because it was quite hot but the mosquitoes became so intense that I had to wrap myself in my parachute, despite the heat.

Sometime during the night, the hurricane hit. When I awakened, the rain came pouring down. I jumped into the cockpit with my parachute. For the remainder of the night I would periodically shine my flashlight on the air-speed indicator. Sometimes it would go up to 70 knots, enough to get airborne.

The water came up over my wings and the sound of the surf against the beach was so thunderous that I imagined I had been washed out to sea and was afloat. But the next day when the storm had passed and the sun had begun to shine, I could see that I was still in the middle of the lake and that the water was receding. By midmorning it was down enough so that I could wade out.

When I did, I noticed a bunch of huge longhorn cattle. I later found out that the Mexican government had imported Brahman cattle and turned the bulls loose on the range to upgrade their native longhorns. They had certainly been successful, for these cattle stood almost as high as my head. They were the largest I had ever seen and my predicament did not make them seem any smaller.

They were unaccustomed to seeing a man on foot, and as I approached the edge of the lake they charged at me. I ran for my life and scrambled up on the aircraft. They encircled it and I could not get down. In coon-hunter's language, they had me treed.

Finally I took my parachute in my arms and edged off the plane. When the cattle started to charge, I threw the silk out into the wind, holding on to the parachute pack. The wind caught it and made it billow, frightening the cattle. They ran, I gathered up my parachute and walked some more, repeating my matador act several times. Finally I reached the stream and they left me alone.

I spent half that day walking up the beach and half a day back without sighting anything. I tried unsuccessfully to kill some birds, for I was getting pretty hungry. I became so thirsty that I drank some water from the lake which the cattle were standing in. I spent the next night in the plane.

The following morning I started west. About midday I saw what appeared to be something moving up the beach. It turned out to be an old tree trunk lying in the edge of the water with one limb sticking up. When the surf came in, it turned the tree and made it appear as though it were a man moving.

A little while later I saw something moving about a quarter of a mile up the beach. By now I was starved and a little nauseated. I started running and praying that this would be someone who could help. It was a man on a donkey. When he saw me coming, he appeared to be frightened and turned off into the jungle. As he took off, so did I, trying to intercept him. I ran through cactus and vines, my clothes were being torn and I was scratched. But I came to the trail before he had passed.

He was quite surprised when he found me waiting for him. He pulled out a huge horse pistol and held it in his hand. The barrel must have been eighteen inches long. He was an old man with a white goatee and white hair. He was wearing white pants with a loose shirt hanging over them.

Since I had been stationed in Panama, I knew a little Spanish. I used it all now. I told him I was a friend, hungry and sick. He evidently understood, for he became very friendly. He put me on his donkey and he walked. We traveled the rest of the day and arrived just after nightfall in what appeared to be a small village. There were ten or twelve huts with thatched roofs, and the walls made of slender trees about an inch or two in diameter. In the middle was a larger hut, which belonged to the old man who had picked me up.

That night I slept on his bed, while he and his wife spent the night on the floor with the pigs, chickens and dogs. Otherwise predators—leopards, jaguars and mountain lions—would have killed their animals.

My Spanish had been good enough to obtain shelter and food but not to find out where I was. I was sure I was somewhere in Texas. For a couple of days I tried to tell them I must get to a telephone. It finally seemed to get through. The old man had a son about my age who brought us two mules, and the son and I left, presumably to find a telephone.

As evening approached, we heard a shot fired ahead. We arrived at a house where the young man knew the residents. They had a friendly meeting, and then we walked around the house. There, hanging in a tree by its hind legs, was a jaguar. It was still warm.

A man came by while we were there and in the course of conversation, I thought he was asking me if I wanted him to guard the airplane. I said, "Yes," not knowing for sure what he was saying. Later I found out that he had indeed guarded the plane for me.

We proceeded the following day on our search for a telephone. Before nightfall we had discovered the "telephoneyo." It was an old telegraph station. The wires had been cut and taken down a long time ago, but the poles were still standing. I was very disappointed, to say the least.

We camped that night alongside a road. In the middle of the night we heard a terrible clanking noise and a roar and running of engines. The lights soon pierced the darkness. When they came abreast, it turned out to be a Caterpillar tractor. Behind it was a large semi-flatbed trailer, carrying a big house trailer. Following it were a couple of big trucks followed by a jeep. All of these were chained together. I later discovered that the roads were so rutted and filled with water that all the equipment was dragging on high center a good part of the time. The only way vehicles could make it over the roads was to be pulled by the Caterpillar tractor. Under the jeep and trucks there were steel plates, so that most of the time they were sliding with the Caterpillar pulling.

As luck would have it, this was an American seismograph crew, contracted for by the Mexican government to try to reopen some of the oil wells that had been closed when Mexico nationalized U.S. oil. And even more fortunate, there was a young geologist my age whose father I had known in Oklahoma City!

I told my Mexican friend good-bye and gave him the money I had intended to buy shrimp with. I crawled into the jeep with Steve, the geologist, and we spent the next day traveling. We finally reached a road good enough for the four-wheel-drive jeep to continue by itself.

We proceeded the rest of the way into Tampico. At the hotel I immediately made a phone call home. My sister answered it and when I identified myself, she screamed my name. It seems they had conducted a nationwide search for three days, using all the facilities of the Air Force and National Guard. They had given me up for dead, thinking I had gone down in the Gulf during the hurricane.

Kathleen was seven months pregnant and the doctor had put her to bed. She could not come to the phone, but they told her I was okay. My family had come together during the search, and most of them were at the house. (When I called, my brother was mowing my lawn, which had a tremendous growth of Bermuda grass. He was perhaps one third of the way through. When I returned home, there my lawn mower sat. He had not pushed it another foot when he found out that I was alive.)

I was quite dirty and still wearing a flight suit. Steve loaned me some of his clothes and said he would like to show me the town that night. Of course I had no passport, and I had flown into Mexico with an armed fighter without permission. After calling home, I had contacted the American embassy in Mexico City to let them know where I was. They cautioned me not to get into any sort of trouble, nor do anything to bring myself to the attention of the authorities until the embassy had had an opportunity to work things out.

It was Sunday in Tampico and there was a promenade in the town square. We went down to watch. Many young women were walking around and around in the one-block square. Going in the opposite direction were young men. On the inside of the sidewalk were benches. The custom was that if one of the young men saw a young lady that pleased him, he would turn and go in her direction. If she liked him, she would talk to him. Then it was possible for them to sit down and visit on a bench in the circle.

We watched this for quite some time, then decided to go up to a restaurant that someone had told us about.

We found a taxi and the driver drove and drove. We finally ended up at the edge of town. The taxi driver let us out, we paid him, and he left. By now it was quite late. We went to the door and the door was locked. We knocked and they would not let us in. We heard someone inside say something about "gringos."

We could not get to a telephone, but we finally found out that there was a streetcar line about a mile down the beach. We started walking toward it.

Since there was no moon, it was very dark, but both of us had on white shirts. Suddenly we heard some Spanish being spoken up ahead, and it sounded like several men talking. When their voices started increasing in volume, we stopped because it seemed rather ominous. Then they started coming toward us. They had evidently heard us talking because we kept hearing the word "gringos." We started to walk inland and they followed. We began running, and so did they, screaming in Spanish.

We did not know it, but there was probably half a mile or more of sand dunes before we could reach the first house. We started running in heavy sand, up and down those dunes. More Mexicans were joining the chase all the time. They began to get close enough to throw rocks at us. Steve started huffing and puffing and said he could not go on any more. Our lungs were on fire, we had been running in deep sand, and we were scared to death.

I had been running behind Steve until he slowed down, but now I started to pass him. I looked back over my shoulder and I saw the glint of a knife blade quite close to Steve. I hollered, "Look out! He's got a knife!" When I said this, Steve sped past me like an express, leaving me trailing.

We came to a small lake, dived in and started swimming. Most of the guys chasing us went around the shore. We beat them to the other side because it was not as wide as it was long. Once out, though, we could hear them coming. We saw a light and ran between some houses but were afraid to stop for fear some of the men chasing us lived there.

Finally we came to an abrupt incline and scaled it on all fours because it was so steep. At the top we were face to face with the streetcar line. On the other side was a police station. It looked beautiful.

We ran in and began to tell the man on duty what had happened. Steve could speak some Spanish, too. The man behind the desk went to get the sergeant. We told the story again. Each time we told it, the number of estimated *bandidos* increased. The sergeant began to roust the soldiers, and every time the story was retold, they would get another ammunition clip. By the time we were finished, they were loaded down as if we were going to war. They each had twin bandoleers, a bayonet and a flashlight.

Led by an officer, we crossed the streetcar track and went down the banks. We found something like thirty-five sets of footprints, most of them of bare feet. When we got to the lake the lieutenant split the force and made part of his men wade and the others walk around. There was *mucho* cussing.

Before long we flushed a couple of guys out from under a warehouse building. Steve had been so scared that now he was really very mad. When he saw them start to run, he took after one of them, caught him at an angle and tackled him. When he knocked him down, the guy rolled over and pulled a knife out of his sleeve. I shouted a warning but by that time the soldiers had arrived. They beat this guy mercilessly with their gun butts.

We backtracked to where they had come from. Underneath the old warehouse was a hollowed-out place where they lived. There were two more guys underneath with two good-looking Mexican girls they had kidnapped. The men had been arguing; one wanted to kill the girls and one just wanted to rape them. Because of their arguing, they had not done anything.

We all went back to the station, where the police asked us to file charges. Both girls, who spoke good English, were from substantial families—one was the daughter of the senior judge of Tampico, and the other's father was very wealthy. When the girls learned that we were going to file charges, they were terrified. If their names appeared in the paper, their reputation would be ruined, they said.

I asked how long it would be before a trial; I thought maybe we could prefer charges and still protect the girls. They told me they would put it on the docket in a few weeks, but I would have to remain in town. We dropped the charges.

They turned the kidnappers loose, and they carried off their buddy who had been beaten up. We waited until a streetcar came by and we hopped on it along with the two girls, who were returning to the city. At one of the stops, the same four bandits got on and took a seat behind us. We had a very eerie ride the rest of the way into town.

When we got off to escort the girls home, those four guys followed us. We thought we were going to have trouble again, but we managed to get the girls to one of their houses and then we made it back to our hotel. Safely in our room, we barricaded the door, stacked the furniture clear to the ceiling, and slept with one eye open the rest of the night.

The next day I caught an airliner out to Brownsville, where a National Guard buddy was waiting with a B-26 to fly me home. En route he told me that my wife was in the hospital and that she had lost the baby.

VI

Korea

I had put in a lot of flying time since becoming a cadet, and while in the Air National Guard in Oklahoma City, I had maintained a high state of proficiency. But since I had never seen combat, I felt like a highly trained prize fighter who has never had a bout. When the Korean conflict broke out, I very much wanted to be in the middle of it.

That does not mean I was eager for a war. In fact, I never personally knew any veteran eager for war. But there were plenty of men, once war was under way, eager to do their part. For me, that meant flying combat. I was tickled to death when my squadron was routinely activated. We had been flying P-51s; now we were given F-80s.

When it appeared that we would not be going over, I began to search for ways to make it. I learned there were openings in photo reconnaissance, in which I had been trained for a year. Only one hundred jet hours were required to qualify.

In twenty-five days I put in ninety-five hours and met the time element. I received my orders and stopped over in Tulsa for three days to see my family. Since I had always fancied myself a pretty good horseman and had done some amateur rodeo riding, it was not hard for my brother to get me to accept his challenge to break a mare he had. I wound up with a cast on a broken hand and finger, but I could not let this stop me. When I got to San

Francisco, it was raining intermittently. By keeping my raincoat over my hand, I made it through all of the inspections without detection.

In Korea, passing inspection was another matter. I knew they would never let me in the air with a cast on. I convinced the doctor that the arm had been in a cast for a long time, and he agreed to take off the cast and x-ray the arm. When he took the x-ray too high, I thought I had it made. They called back later and said the picture was foggy and to come back in for another x-ray. This one revealed that the healing had not even really started, since the breaks were only two weeks old. I pleaded, begged and cajoled the doctor until he agreed to put a leather cover on instead of a cast.

I slipped out, put on my flight suit and reported for duty. The officer on the desk asked if I had seen the flight surgeon. When I answered yes he processed me through and I began flying.

My next concern was to get out of photo recon and into fighters. My hopes went up when I discovered that my former National Guard exec was the executive officer at the 4th Fighter Wing. I began to prevail on him to work it out. They actually needed some experienced fighter pilots. I had over a thousand flying hours and was a fighter pilot at heart and by training. Before long I was in the 336th Fighter Squadron, 4th Fighter Wing.

It is hard to describe the exuberance with which I transferred across the field and checked out in the F-86. From the very first, the Sabre Jet felt like an old trusted friend. In seven hours of air time, I was ready for combat.

I had made captain during my National Guard days and I was now a flight commander in the 336th. Although I was a senior fighter pilot by rank and flying time, when we went into combat I did not lead the flight for several missions due to my lack of experience. That lack was never more apparent than the first time we engaged MIGs. On this particular day I was standing alert when an RF-80 photo reconnaissance plane, unprotected and unarmed, reported that the Chinese had scrambled some MIGs from across the Yalu River and that they were hot on his tail. We were sent up to intercept them.

I was flying number two in the flight, or wing, position. As wing man my assignment was to keep my leader clear all the time by clearing his rear from his right wing around to his left wing, making sure that nobody came in on his tail. During a fight I was supposed to say, "You are clear," about every thirty seconds, telling him I was in position doing my job.

As soon as we were airborne at about 10,000 feet, Lead called in, "Diamond, this is John Red, scrambled four." They gave us a vector on the RF-80: "Little Friend—one hundred and ten miles at twelve o'clock and twenty thousand feet"; and on the enemy: "Bogies—one hundred and thirty miles at twelve o'clock." As we approached, it became, "Little Friend, now forty-eight miles at twelve o'clock; bogies now fifty-three at twelve o'clock." Then: "Little Friend—now twenty-eight miles; bogies—thirty miles." They were gaining on him. Finally Little Friend was only about eighteen or twenty miles away, and the MIGs were about a mile or a mile and a half behind him. Little Friend could stand it no longer: "Hey, you guys, can't you hurry?" We were wide open, and so was he.

As he passed under us, a voice said with much feeling, "Thanks a lot!" I rocked up to look at him and as I rolled back level, I saw six MIGs straight ahead. They spotted us at about the same time and turned northeast. Our element of two aircraft which was flying on our right fell in behind them, with my element trailing about a mile.

One of the MIGs made a split-S toward home. Another one went straight up into the sun and out of sight. The other four turned, pulling the second element in close behind. In about a minute or two, they made another turn toward the Yalu River.

As they did, our element leader started shooting. I was so excited—it was the first MIG I had ever seen—that I forgot my assignment as wing man to keep my leader clear. My radar gun sights indicated I was locked onto one of those MIGs. I was out of range but closing fast. The first thing I knew, big red golf balls started coming across my wing—cannon shells! The MIG that had gone into the sun had come down and locked onto my tail. I yelled, "Break left! We've got a MIG on our tail!"

Red lead and I went into a tight spiral to the left and started really pulling the Gs. I ran into a little rough air and the slats on the wings which come out to give you more lift at slow airspeed came out with a bang. I said, "I think I'm hit." The G force was so great that it had almost pulled the oxygen masks, containing the microphone, off our faces. When number one responded, all I heard was a gurgle. I thought maybe he, too, was hit and gurgling in his own blood.

I really honked her in then. I went through another couple of 360-degree spirals before we could clear ourselves. When we broke out and looked around, the whole fight had gone. There was not a single airplane in sight. I returned to the base chagrined and determined that I would not forget my assignment again.

I had been in Korea a couple of months when it was time for a three-day R and R to Japan. I had been in Japan one night when someone from the outfit came in and said, "The MIGs are flying!" I caught the next plane back, arriving around three in the morning.

My flight was on alert and it was almost time for them to be awakened. I waited for about thirty minutes before I roused them. My assistant flight commander prevailed on me to take a nap, which I did. Then I went out to the alert pad, took over as flight lead, switched the parachutes and equipment, rigged my airplane, put on my helmet, and laid down on the wing.

I had almost dropped off to sleep when the horn sounded. That particular day we were the hot-shot flight. That meant we were "clean" (no fuel tanks attached to the wings) and ready for quick reaction.

We scrambled and went whipping down the runway two at a time. I was still getting my equipment on and closing my canopy on the roll. On my wing was a kid making his first combat mission. He had a big handlebar mustache and was just fresh out of combat training school. He was really eager.

We had just leveled off at 35,000 feet when I saw eight MIGs cross about a thousand feet below us, going from left to right—the perfect setup. One high side pass and we could really cream them. I had learned, though, that after spotting one formation always check six o'clock high because they normally had somebody watching over them. I said, "Check six." My number-three man said, "We've got six at three o'clock high. They're starting in." As they came in firing, two of them overshot. I whipped back over on their tail only a thousand feet behind them.

I laid the bright red circle of the gun sight on the tailpipe of one of them and gave him a good long burst. He lit up like a Christmas tree. (We were using armor-piercing incendiaries. Every time they hit a piece of metal, you would get a flash.) He had just started to make a right climbing turn when his engine evidently quit. I must have knocked it out, because he seemed to stop in the air. I chopped my throttle back to idle and threw my speed brakes out. I was doing everything I could to stay behind him. As he stalled, he fell off his left wing and started to go into a spin. My aircraft stalled too, and I kicked the left rudder unconsciously. It looked for a second as if my gun sight would fall right through him.

I thought to myself, "This is my first MIG!" I held down the trigger and all six caliber fifties started chugging away. I could smell the powder smoke. I was only three hundred feet from him when I cut his tail off just above the fuselage. The tail went one way and the fuselage spun in the other direction. We were at 32,000 feet. He panicked, bailed out and opened his chute. I imagine he was frozen as stiff as a poker by the time he hit the ground because it was awfully cold up there.

. . .

I saw a lot of great flying while in Korea, but the best pilot I came across was not an American. Our encounter happened while I was on close escort for fighter-bombers that were hitting a chemical plant in North Korea right at the mouth of the Yalu River, the border between China and North Korea. Normally we did not go across the river into China. But on this day as a part of my screen, I had to do a three-sixty (360 degrees) turn between the bombers and potential MIG forces. This carried me right over mainland China, near Antung. Here was what we called the Antung Air University—a big MIG field.

We had not even made one orbit when I met four MIGs head-on. We saw one another about the same time. The MIGs carried bathtub-type fuel tanks which sat up close to the belly, and we carried a tank on each wing. We dropped ours and they theirs. The MIGs were not eager to engage and made a 180-degree turn, heading toward Fen Chen, an airfield beyond Antung and down the coast.

I was afraid that if I lost sight of them, they might make a descending turn and come back at the bombers, so I stayed with them. When they did, my radar locked onto the tail-end Charlie. Although I was at maximum range, I fired a short burst. I knew I had hit him in the canopy because the glass began to fly. He made a hard turn into me, and the other three made a right descending turn away from me.

I told my number-three and -four men to go after the other three and I would take this one because I had already hit him. He came hard into me and I turned inside him. When I rolled out —I was not over 1,500 feet from him—I leveled down on him again and gave a short burst. It sparkled him a little bit. When I did, he did a half roll and hung upside down, then did a complete roll and ended upside down again.

Meanwhile, we were descending, making about .95 Mach, almost as fast as we could go. We were getting real low when he rolled it the second time and started a split S for the ground. He appeared to be much too low for this.

I did not think he would make it, so I widened my turn slightly to have a little more room between the ground and me. I said over the radio. "Two! This is going to be the easiest kill I ever had." I knew he was going to splatter.

But as I watched, he pulled out down a dry river bed! The dust billowed up and he stayed right on the deck. He was so low that he was throwing up small rocks. I dropped down to get him, but to hit him I had to get down behind him in his jet wash. There was so much turbulence that I couldn't do anything in it. It bounced me around like a cork in a rough sea and then spit me out.

This guy was one fantastic pilot. When I did get down in his jet wash he would chop his throttle and throw his speed brakes out so I would overshoot him. I would coast up right beside him— just wing-tip clearance—looking him right in the eye. When it looked as if I were going to overshoot him, I would have to pull up and do a roll over the top of him and come back around the other side behind him. When I did this, he would throw the coal to it and go into a hard turn, pulling all the Gs he could. About the time that I got my pipper on him, he would push the stick forward and go into an inverted turn, which is extremely difficult and hard on the body and eyes. He would turn right out of my windshield. I could not duplicate his maneuver. I had to roll into an opposite turn and start to catch him again.

One time he actually flipped upside down, went up the side of a small mountain, over the top and pulled it down on the other side. I was right side up, so when I went over the top of the mountain I had to do a half roll to go down the other side.

I was having a real difficult time, but I was hitting him occasionally. I had shot away part of his tail, his canopy was missing, and he was burning out of the left side. He was not in very good shape, but he was a great pilot—and he was fighting like a cornered rat!

We were down in the river bed again and Joe, my wing man,

who'd been sticking with me all this time, was hollering, "Hit him, Lead. Get him, Lead." Believe me, I was doing my best.

Charlie chopped the throttle, threw his speed brakes out, I coasted up and was afraid I'd overshoot him. I did a roll over the top of him, and when I came down on the other side I was right on his wing tip. We were both at idle with our speed brakes out—just coasting.

He looked over at me, raised his hand and shook his fist. I thought, "This is like a movie. This can't be happening!" He had on a leather helmet and I could see the stitching in it. His oxygen mask had evidently been sucked off when I shot away his canopy.

Then he made a left 90-degree turn and a 90-degree turn back to the right. Before I realized what was happening, he went between two hangar buildings. He had led me right on to Tak Tung Kau Airfield!

Joe began shouting, "Lead, they're shooting at us!" The flak was bursting all around. In fact, you could see the gun barrels flashing because we were right on the deck, thirty-five miles inside China. He had gone up and down this river and taken me to the airfield, figuring the flak would chase me off. He made a turn and went down the runway.

He seemed to be trying to force his aircraft down for a landing, but he hadn't lowered his gear and was doing about 300 knots. He went so low that he was blowing dust off the runway. I was not down low enough to hit him, so I just stayed where I was, knowing that he was going to have to pull up or make a turn. When he pulled up, I really hammered him. I blew about four feet off his left wing. It just exploded. When that happened he made a hard right chandelle, then a right turn back down and paralleled the runway. He may have been aiming for the grass growing alongside. I fired all the rest of my ammunition into him. He leveled off, making about 350 knots. He touched the ground and came unglued. Little pieces flew everywhere.

As Joe and I started climbing out, we had to pass over Antung.

We had been told they had about 250 radar-controlled heavy guns in this area. Joe's aircraft got hit in the belly and began losing fuel. When he was down to five minutes remaining, I told him to shut down and I would try to push him to Cho Do Island, where we had a rescue operation. He made it with room to spare, but the nose of my plane was all boogered up. Just before he bailed out he said, "I'll see you at the base tonight."

I was in radio contact with the rescue helicopter. They told me Joe landed close to shore. His parachute was still open and they decided to use the propeller to blow him into shore. The last word I caught was that he seemed to be in trouble and they were putting a man in the water.

Physically, Joe was the typical All-American boy. Six feet tall, blond, a fine swimmer, and, in fact, a one-time lifeguard. I was out of radio range but I felt sure he was okay. That evening we went to the plane to meet him. When they opened the doors, Joe did not get off. They said he had drowned.

I was the twentieth pilot to shoot down five MIGs in air-to-air combat—the requirement to become an ace. We were required to fly 100 missions, but I flew a total of 109 and shot down eight MIGs.

Korea was probably the high point of my whole career as far as real gratification is concerned. To be able to participate in air-to-air combat was a thrill. When you are in personal combat with another individual in a similar type of aircraft, the difference is going to be your training, your abilities, your motivation and sometimes guts. Then again, air-to-air warfare is a clean, impersonal type of thing. It's not dirty, like down in the trenches, and there is no hand-to-hand combat. When people die, you don't see it. I saw a few of my buddies go down, and I saw the MIG pilots go down, but you're not aware of the blood and pain.

In February 1953 I came home. I had been in Korea since May of 1950.

VII

From Korea to Vietnam

After returning from Korea I was reassigned to Clovis, New Mexico, and from there to a new fighter base at Hahn, Germany, for three years. Then, in 1956, after returning to the States to George Air Force Base in California, I had what turned out to be the most serious mishap of my career.

My squadron had been given the task of evaluating the high-altitude air-to-air capability of the F-100. This necessitated wearing a nylon partial pressure suit. It required a suit of sheer long underwear underneath to minimize blood blisters on the body when the suit inflated. The helmet, sealed to the suit prior to flight, gave the appearance of a streamlined deep-sea diver.

We would climb to 40,000, plug in the afterburner, pushing the aircraft to 1.2 times the speed of sound before starting our zoom to reach maximum altitude. The F-100 was not intended for work at these altitudes; consequently, all our personal pressure equipment was jury-rigged. Neither were the engines designed for the altitudes we were reaching.

As a result, we were getting violent compressor stalls as we passed through 50,000 feet. We melted a couple of engines before we started watching the tailpipe temperature gauge. We were soon "stop-cocking" or shutting down our engine at about 55,000 feet and coasting on up to 59,000 or 60,000 feet. We were declaring an "emergency," in accordance with flying regulations, each time we shut down the engine or it quit on us for the first few days. It was driving "Mother"—our Flying Safety Officer—right up the wall, so we discontinued this procedure.

One day as I passed through 57,000 feet on the way up, the canopy pressurization diaphragm blew, causing explosive decompression. It felt as if someone had poleaxed me. I barely remember my canopy frosting over. The tiny heating elements in my face plate malfunctioned and my instruments frosted over. My chase pilot later told me of my plane stalling, then falling past him from about 60,000 feet.

When I regained consciousness, I began to try to reach the lanyard to release my face plate because I still couldn't see. My suit had inflated and my arms stuck out in front of me like balloons. I couldn't bend them, nor reach my face plate. But by using both hands, I finally managed to reach the cord hanging below my chin and gave it a jerk.

My face plate flew up, but no air pressure escaped to ease the tremendous pressure on my body. This meant my regulator valve had also malfunctioned. My nylon shoulder straps were locked tight, and even though I could see my instruments, I couldn't reach the starter switch. I lunged again and again as my plane passed through 23,000 feet.

At last my nylon shoulder straps slipped and I gropingly flipped my air start switch. The orange and red warning lights started going out as the engine snapped to life. My chest was killing me and I couldn't bend my arms enough to disconnect the pressure hose. The valve to my helmet had failed shut, channeling all the emergency air to my body.

I finally pressed my mike button, declaring an emergency and asking for a flight surgeon to be standing by the runway to meet me. My canopy and windshield had defrosted as I approached the field, but the pressure felt as if it were crushing the life out of me. As the main gear touched the runway, I quit fighting and the nose came down with a rattling thump. I just sat there while the runway flashed by at 140 knots. Then I saw the meat wagon at the last intersection with fire trucks waiting.

I had only one thought—get that pressure off my chest. I crammed on the brakes and ground to a shuddering halt beside the ambulance. The physician was on the wing running toward me. I was content to let him do all the work. It was only a short ride to the hospital where my torn heart valve could be heard with the bare ear. It sounded like the lonely cry of a sea gull. Fortunately, though, it was not serious enough to do permanent damage.

The following year I was lucky enough to be chosen to fly the thirtieth commemoration of Charles Lindbergh's nonstop solo flight across the Atlantic. I took off from California and went nonstop to New York, setting an unofficial speed record. From New York to Paris, I made it in 6 hours and 37 minutes, an official record. It did not stand too long, though. The weather was lousy that day with visibility only a quarter of a mile. But I had no real problems and landed at Le Bourget, the same airfield where Lindbergh had landed. When I taxied up, there were hundreds of Frenchmen to welcome me. While I was in Paris, the movie *The Spirit of St. Louis* had its premiere.

From George, which was the longest tour of my career—outside of North Vietnam!—I went to Air War College, then to Hawaii. With the outbreak of hostilities in Southeast Asia, I was transferred to Kadina Air Force Base in Okinawa. It was from Kadina that I would be moved forward on TDY to Korat in Thailand for my missions over North Vietnam.

The Gulf of Tonkin Resolution, passed by Congress in August 1964, was broadly interpreted as giving congressional approval to increased military involvement in Southeast Asia. During the following months, the tempo increased considerably for those of us in Southeast Asia.

On March 2, 1965, we hit North Vietnam for the first time. This was a much more sophisticated war than Korea. And in no place was it more evident than in rescue operations.

In Vietnam, when you had a man down, they would call in a C-54 (four-engine plane), which was almost a control tower in flight. It had all the facilities for contacting headquarters, scrambling aircraft to help suppress ground fire and calling for extra choppers. Also, the downed pilot had a small emergency radio and a homing beacon that emitted an emergency signal. In addition, there were the Sandys, the ex-Navy A-1s or AD-6s. They carried a whole wad of ordnance and some armor plating to protect the pilot. They were slow enough so that they could stay right over a target, and they were great for locating downed pilots. While the support aircraft were suppressing the ground fire, the chopper would come in and sneak the pilot out. I saw this work beautifully several times.

One time, in particular, we had been after a SAM site and did not find it. On the way back we found a good-sized bridge in a strategic position on a mountain road with no way around it. We had some new ordnance on board number three and four of our four-plane flight, and we wanted to try it out.

We went in on the target, and number three was hit real bad. He was out of control, but his aircraft had its nose up. He went to afterburner and was making about 550 knots. He was trying to get to the top of a mountain nearby. Due to broken clouds, his wing man lost him as he ejected right beside the cloud. I happened to be in a position where I could see his parachute, and I orbited him while he came down. He landed right on top of the mountain in a rain forest. I could see his parachute hanging in the top of one of those huge trees that grow there.

I had number two and four climb to 20,000 feet and call for a rescue. We were not too far from the Laos border at that time. It was getting late in the afternoon. Before long a C-54 showed up and I indicated where the parachute was. By now we were getting enemy ground fire. We strafed it. Then the Sandys arrived. They began to strafe and rocket the ground positions and suppressed the fire. My flight was so low on fuel it was getting critical. We had to pull out.

The helicopter came in and lowered a sling. The downed pilot managed to get part of the way into the sling and then fell out of it and caught himself in one of those big trees. The chopper lowered the sling again and on this try they pulled him out. As we were proceeding home, they called and said he was okay. I was so emotionally involved, I had to wink back the tears of relief. I guess that is one thing that makes combat-flying buddies so close to one another.

I appreciated the rescue capabilities even more when I myself was shot down the first time. I was on a mission with twelve aircraft in early April to destroy a radar site. We really hammered away. We bombed, rocketed and strafed it. Part of the mission was to also destroy the gun positions defending it. We had dumped the dirt right in on top of them, and really wiped them out—we thought! I wanted to make sure, so I flew past fairly close in, looking it over with my binoculars. Suddenly a gun emplacement that we had actually blown the dirt in on began firing. They hit me immediately.

We were right on the coast, and I was headed inland. My plane caught fire and the engine started winding down. I was flying at about 2,500 feet. I managed to make a 180-degree turn to get out over the water when the controls went and the plane snapped inverted.

While it was inverted, I ejected downward. Although we were at 1,500 feet, the ejection system was a good one and I had no problems. I sustained a cut chin and lip from the parachute strap, but other than that, no injuries at all. I had just been through the water-survival training, so I was all set. I felt confident that I knew all the procedures and the right thing to do at the right time.

On the way down some of my guys flew by and I waved at them as they rocked their wings. I deployed my life raft, which was open and dangling twenty feet below me. It hit the water first. When my feet touched the water, I dumped my parachute, and when I came up, I needed only a couple of strokes to my raft. I was in such a hurry that I almost went over it. Altogether I was only in the water for about ten seconds. The Geneva Convention card in my pocket hardly got damp.

I dug out my emergency radio and started talking to my wing man. When I saw some North Vietnamese boats coming out from shore, I hollered, "Hey! How about those boats?" He answered, "Don't worry. We'll take care of those boats." They really did! Every time a boat left the shore, they would wipe it out. My number-three and -four men made a pass on a gunboat, a big double-masted schooner with a motor in it. They let go with their 20-millimeter cannon, which fires 6,000 rounds a minute. One pass cut it in half and it sank like a rock.

They had already contacted the SA-16 flying boat—the "duck butt" we called it. It had just taken off from Danang and had flown about seventy-five or a hundred miles and was arriving on station near the DMZ when I was shot down. It was fully loaded with fuel for about a sixteen-hour flight with full drop tanks and everything.

Unfortunately, this was the crew's first combat pickup. The pilot must have been a little excited because he forgot to drop his tanks. He had a horrendous load of fuel. When he came near, I lit my smoke flare and held it up so he could see which way the wind was blowing. He came around and made his landing. What a sight it was!

I think they are supposed to reverse their throttles as soon as they touch down so they can minimize their landing roll as well as any possible damage from rough water. As he touched, he ballooned and went up in the air. While he was in the air, both throttles went full reverse and he backed into the water. He submerged like a submarine going down. Then he came straggling up with the water pouring off his windshield.

I thought, "Man! He's going to rescue me?" He taxied around and backed up to me. I paddled over in my life raft. The guy at the door was all excited. He had a gun ready to ward off any boarders. I was his first customer in combat.

He grabbed me and hauled me in. I said, "Hey! Be sure to get my helmet." I had a new Lombard helmet, molded for my lumpy head. I have funny head bones and it was a good expensive helmet. He was so excited that he let both the helmet and the life raft drift off. I said, "Well, sink it!" He started to shoot it but lost sight of it.

The pilot poured the coal to it and started to take off. We still had that full load of fuel and a strong cross wind, and we were going parallel with the swells. He had to reduce the throttle on one engine in order to keep it from turning into the wind. We made a takeoff roll for miles and miles, but we could not get airborne. It looked as if we were going to have to taxi home. He told me, "We can't get airborne. I'm going to have to turn into the wind." This meant he was going to have to go up and down into the swells.

We would get up to 60–70 knots and get to the top of the swell and be airborne. The plane would shudder, stall and we would impact the next swell. Before long the fuselage was buckled and part of the windshield was knocked out. We were taking on water like crazy, but most of it was rushing out through the holes in the back where the fuselage was ruptured. We kept getting airborne, then stalling, then flopping back into the next swell. This went on for a long time. That old airplane really took a beating. At last we really got airborne.

My rescuers admitted they had forgotten to drop the external gas tanks. Now that we were in the air I did not mind. They gave me a cup of coffee, wrapped me in a blanket and radioed in that I was okay. When we arrived in Danang, South Vietnam, somebody gave me a clean flight suit, T-shirt and shorts. I bought the crew drinks until I ran out of money.

Then I had dinner and sent a message to my operations officer at Korat saying: "Send an F-105-F first thing in the morning to pick me up." I received a cute message back from him that night: "Have assumed command and made some major changes. The next bus for Korat leaves in a week."

The next morning an F-105-F came in with a helmet and parachute and took me back to Korat. I started flying missions again the next day.

For some unknown reason, this mission was written up in *Time* magazine with my picture on the cover. At the time it was a great honor. But later, in prison, I would have much cause to regret that *Time* had ever heard of me.

In a few days I left Thailand for Okinawa and spent a night on the way in Bangkok. While there, I had a telephone call at the hotel from the deputy commander at Kadina, Buckshot White, saying, "Hey, when you coming home?" I answered, "I'm on my way." He replied, "Well, we're looking for you." I caught a KC-135 jet tanker and because of engine problems, we did not get in until daylight the next morning.

About seven-thirty some of the squadron brought up my foot-locker that had come off the KC-135. At the same time they brought a set of orders saying I was to go to PACAF headquarters in Hawaii the next day. That gave me one day and night at home.

From Kadina in Okinawa I flew to Hawaii and then to Washington, where I received the Air Force Cross. While in the States, I made several stops for press conferences to help explain to the American people why we were in Vietnam. Then it was back to Hawaii, on to Kadina and then to Korat. On September 16, 1965, I made my reservations for a seven-and-a-half-year stay in the Hanoi Hilton.

VIII

"How Do You Pray for a Broom in Latin?"

We were learning firsthand that the North Vietnamese were poorly equipped to handle the increasing number of American prisoners. The Hanoi Hilton was running at capacity with civilian convicts, and Heartbreak, which had been set aside initially as a cellblock for the American POWs, had only seven usable cells. One of the four cells in another cellblock, New Guy Village, was later to be used only for maximum isolation, torture or recuperation, although now it was used for recently shot down pilots.

About thirty-five miles west of Hanoi, near the mountains, another facility was in use which had been dubbed the Briarpatch. It was quite primitive, with no lights or running water. It held about twenty of the first POWs.

Now a new facility, the Zoo, was being opened up. It was near the center of Hanoi, about five miles from the Hanoi Hilton. It appeared to have been an old French rest area—a kind of motel. There was an empty theater with an inclined floor and stage. The buildings were constructed in a circle with a fifteen-to-twenty-foot wall around the outside with broken glass on top. In the very center of the camp was a pool the Vietnamese used both for swimming and for growing fish. Whatever its original purpose, Rest and Recreation was certainly not its use now. And, though structurally sound, it had literally not been cleaned in years.

Two weeks after I was shot down, the guard told me one

evening to get my stuff together. I was moving. I took down my mosquito net, folded up my blanket and grass mat, and emptied the water out of my teapot. These were my total possessions except for the clothes I had on, which consisted of my American underwear and the set of patched, ragged and threadbare peasant's clothes.

The guard returned shortly with handcuffs and a blindfold. I was taken outside to a jeep and herded into the back. I soon discovered that another American was also making the trip. Though we were not supposed to communicate, I learned it was one of my cellmates, Wendy Rivers.

It was a brief trip and soon I was escorted to my new home, which turned out to be the Zoo. Even with the blindfold removed, I was in total darkness. The cell was larger than at Heartbreak, but there was no bunk, and no place to hang a mosquito net. Dirt covered the cement floor. When I was ready to go to sleep, I had to put down my grass mat in the dirt and wrap myself in the mosquito net. The mosquitoes bit right through. It was one miserable night!

The next morning I was up early to check out the cell. It was solid, bare cement. There was a lot of chalk lying around, and some old film. A movie company may once have used it. There were no windows, and a solid door. A vent below the floor which went under the wall had a grate and screen over it which kept the rats out. The only air vents were three holes in front and back near the fifteen-foot ceiling. These vents were also the only source of light, so when it turned dark, it was totally dark. During the day it was dusky. (At least one meal was eaten in total darkness and I had to feel for everything.)

They gave me a small hand towel. The only way to wash was to pour a little water out of my pint-sized teapot, which was refilled twice a day. After pouring the water over my towel and wiping my face and hands with it, I would take a sponge bath if enough water was left. In three days' time the towel looked terrible, and it was never anything but dark gray after that.

One of the first things I did was to tap on the walls to see who, if anyone, was next door. On one side was Wendy Rivers. He and I were to become good friends. After I had bored a small hole through the wall with a steel rod pried from the grate I passed all my cigarettes through to him, and it was just a good feeling to be able to look through a hole and see a friendly face. We had made a pact that if anything happened to either of us, the other would visit his family and give them some words that we had for them.

On the other side of me were Paul Carey, an Air Force lieutenant, and B. J. McKamey, a Navy lieutenant (j.g.). They had been prisoners for quite a while. I began to talk to them, and they retaught me Morse code. I soon found out that Paul was a member of the same church denomination I had been raised in, and that his two sisters were going to the Bible school my brothers and one of my sisters had attended. That provided a tie between us.

While I was exploring my cell I heard a whisper coming through the grate. I stuck my head down in it and whispered back. It was my old friend Captain Bob Purcell! "Purcy" had been flying at about 200 feet when the North Vietnamese shot his wing off and he crashed in flames. His wing man was flying behind him in the flight; neither he nor any of the others saw a parachute. They had reported him killed in action. Now here he was. It really charged us up to talk to each other. When I told him our concern over the circumstances surrounding his shoot-down, he really got a bang out of it. He said he had parachuted with no problem and landed without injury.

He had been in captivity for several months but was blessed with a tremendous sense of humor and soon had me feeling a whole lot better.

He said, "Hey! You're the senior officer."

"Yeah, I know. What's my first course of action?"

"Well, you ought to talk to the camp commander and see if you can get some of the things we need."

"All I know we need right now are beds to sleep on, brooms to sweep the place with, some lights to see by, and we need to get outside of this stinking cell to exercise."

"Boy, you got it all!" Purcy said.

"How do I go about this? How do I get to see the camp commander?"

"Ask the guard for pencil and paper."

"But I can't speak Vietnamese," I protested.

"You just make the signs, and he'll know."

We had nothing to lose, that's for sure, so I decided to try it. To my surprise I managed to pantomime to the guard, and he brought pencil and paper. I wrote a note to the camp commander in which I, as the senior officer in camp, requested an opportunity to talk to him.

That afternoon they took me over and told me to sit on a low stool. This was a standard technique. They always put us below them. They would sit on a chair behind a desk, and we sat in the middle of the floor on a little stool. Normally we would have to wait for a while before they came, which was intended to create anxiety.

When an officer finally came, it was not the camp commander but his assistant, who also served as English-speaking interpreter (we dubbed him "Spot"). I told him I was the senior officer, and that it was my duty on behalf of the men to demand decent living conditions in accordance with the Geneva Convention. Then I prescribed what I considered the right sort of treatment, starting with a request for brooms. He sat dumfounded. When I complained that we were allowed to wash only every three or four days, he interrupted, "You're a liar."

"Why do you think I'm a liar? Ask the guard how often we are out. Ask all the other prisoners. And we're living like animals on the floor," I went on. "We have no lights. We're eating in the dark. Last night when I was eating the guard opened the door. His flashlight shone on my food, and I was sharing it with three big cockroaches. We don't even treat our animals like this."

Finally I told him we expected outside time to exercise for everyone. He was flabbergasted! He told me I was a criminal and to shut my mouth. After some political harangue, he sent me back to my cell.

When the opportunity presented itself, I called Purcy. "Well, I gave it to them. Now it's up to God."

"What do you mean?"

"I want you to pass the word to everybody to pray that we'll get brooms, beds, lights and outside time."

There was a stunned silence at the other end. Purcy is Catholic. Finally he asked, "How do you pray for a broom in Latin?"

Within days, they started letting some people out to exercise for about fifteen minutes; a wooden platform with sawhorses became my new bed; and I was given some string to hang my net. We still had neither brooms nor lights and were only getting to wash once every three or four days.

Five or six days later I heard Purcy say in a big, loud voice, "Let there be light, and there was light!" Sure enough, an hour later a lightbulb dropped through a little hole near my ceiling, and in another hour or two the light came on.

These were small gains that were soon to be erased by harsh reaction and repression. They were the prelude to a period of unmitigated torture and abuse. Most of us lived to tell about it. Others were obliquely referred to by the North Vietnamese as having "died in captivity." One of these was Ron Stortz, a "hero left behind."

IX

A Hero Left Behind

If I had not been moved from my first cellblock at the Zoo, I would never have met Ron Stortz. I had a pretty good communications system going in my building—the Barn. Then I was moved to the Garage. On one side of me was Lieutenant Commander Bob Schumaker. On the other was Lieutenant (j.g.) Ed Davis, and beyond him Wes Schierman, in the end cell. Ed had been kind of hard-nosed with the guards, and so had Wes. They were starting to lean on us, and for punishment had put us in "incorrigible row." It was nothing to be awakened at midnight or one o'clock and taken to interrogation and be kept there all night and into the morning. They would get angry, stomp around and threaten awhile, and then give us a bunch of political stuff. They would show us magazines from the United States, filled with stories like the Watts riot. They encouraged us to talk about anything. I always tried to be very careful.

The camp commander did most of the interrogation. He probably spoke English as well as anybody that I met all the time I was over there, with the exception of one or two. His wife was a physician at Vinh. He was a real handsome guy, taller than usual, with a straight, finely shaped nose and wavy hair. He was always well groomed in his fresh khaki pants and shirt, and was above average in every way. We called him the Dog. He would have me over at various times of the day and night, but he was not getting anything out of me.

When asked, "What do you like about the United States?" I would go on and on for hours, giving him the red, white and blue version of what I liked about America. Then he'd say, "Okay, now I've listened to you tell what you like about the United States. What do you not like?"

"I can't think of anything I don't like about the United States."

One day he pulled out a copy of the *Time* magazine with my picture on the cover. I was aware that they knew about it, but this was the first time they had shown it to me. When I saw it, I had a sick feeling. I wished I had not had any ID when I was captured and had come in as Major John Doe; life would have been so much easier. I have no doubt that they leaned on me heavily because they thought my name meant something. For instance, when Colonel Bud Day was captured, the interrogator asked, "You know Riner Robinson?"

"Who?"

"Riner Robinson!"

"No, I don't know any Riner Robinson."

He said, "Everybody knows Riner Robinson. I caught him and I interrogated him." Bud's interrogator had not been the one who caught me, but he thought that would impress Bud. The fact that I had received some publicity certainly didn't do me any good.

In addition to *Time*, the Vietnamese were regular subscribers to *Newsweek*, *U.S. News and World Report*, plus many others. They also received the *Air Force Times* and the *Stars and Stripes*. Their favorite seemed to be *The Christian Science Monitor*.

The Dog would use the latest issues to support his charges. He would tell me I was a hero in America for murdering the Vietnamese people and for blowing up their houses and factories. A standard threat was to turn me over to the people or to take me back to Thanh Hoa and give me to them. He did not really frighten any of us. We gave them nothing.

One time he said, "So you are an Indian."

"A little bit."

"I have heard how they have treated you. The Indians still live in the forest and hunt animals for food."

I almost fell off the stool, but I just let him think it. That really brightened my day.

He would get angry and say, "You have killed our women and children. Are you sorry?" I would not comment. "You will not return with honor or reputation. When you return, all your family will be living in the mountains."

"What do you mean by that?"

He said, "You will find out."

Later I learned that in North Vietnam when a family displeases the political commissar of a particular area or does not go along with the current doctrine, they move them to the mountains. It is so tough there that they can hardly survive. Not only will the soil not grow anything, but the family is in disgrace. In other words, the Dog was implying that he intended to disgrace my family and ruin them financially so they would have to live in exile.

When I found out what he meant, I did worry some about my family's welfare. The Vietnamese had also become quite interested in our financial situation. This worried us, too. We feared there was going to be extortion.

Between interrogations we would try to cheer up one another. My next-door neighbor, Bob Schumaker, and I could not get a hole through our wall, and to tap messages was slow. Finally we learned to talk to each other by putting our heads in the vents and throwing our voices. We carried on long conversations that way.

One day they replaced Schumaker with Air Force Captain Ron Stortz. I tapped on the wall to him, got his name, and so forth. He said that up until this move, he had been living with Captain Scotty Morgan. "I leaned on the door and broke the lock. Now I am over here alone being punished."

Ron told me he had been shot down in an L-19, one of those little planes called grasshoppers. Since he, as a forward air controller, normally worked with Vietnamese ground forces, he would carry a Vietnamese officer in the back seat. His mission was to circle and spot enemy positions or help the artillery batteries adjust for accuracy.

"One afternoon I decided to go up and buzz around by myself. I was just looking the area over, and I circled real close to the Ben Hi River. I knew that was the seventeenth parallel, but I didn't mean to get over the river. When I did a Vietnamese gun got me, and try as I might, I could not keep from crashing on the north side. I thought they were going to kill me when I got out of the airplane. They made me get down on my knees. One of the officers took my gun, cocked it and put it against my head. I figured I was a goner."

He had been in prison for some time and really wanted to talk. I could hear him moving around in the other cell. He hollered out the back vent as Bob before him had done, but I could never understand him. We tapped on the wall, but it was too slow and unsatisfactory. There were a lot of things we wanted to tell each other. Finally he asked, by tapping, "Have you tried boring a hole through the wall yet?"

I told him I had tried several places but could not get through. "Each time I try, I hit a brick after I've gone in maybe eight to twelve inches." I had several partial holes; in fact, the wall looked like a piece of Swiss cheese.

"Well, I'll try, too."

Pretty soon I heard some scraping and grinding. By that afternoon he was through. His hands were blistered, but he had made it. That gave me some incentive to try to go through the other wall. I really went to work, and I punched through there, too. We passed our tools through and let them work in the next room. In a few days, every room was connected up and down the hall.

Once we got the holes bored through, Ron said, "I'm really down in the mouth." I asked what the matter was. "Well, just the fact that I have nothing. They have taken everything away from me. They took my shoes, my flying suit, and everything I possessed. They even took my glasses. I don't have a single thing. They took everything."

Ron had indicated to me that he planned to become a minister when he got back to America. Consequently we talked about religion quite a bit, as all of us did. When he said he was depressed because they had taken everything, I told him, "Ron, I don't think we really have lost everything."

"What do you mean?"

"According to the Bible, we are sons of God. Everything out there in the courtyard, all the buildings and the whole shooting match belong to God. Since we are children of God, you might say that all belongs to us, too."

There was a long pause. "Let me think about it, and I'll call you back." After a while he called back, "I really feel a lot better. In fact, every time I get to thinking about it, I have to laugh."

"What do you mean?"

"I am just loaning it to them."

I will never forget the day he called me and told me, "They're trying to make me come to attention for the guards and I will not do it. What do you think I ought to do?

"What do they do?"

"They cut my legs with a bayonet, trying to make me put my feet together. I am just not going to do it."

I knew he meant it. He was an extremely strong man. I thought about it for a while, then I called back, "Ron, I'm afraid we don't have the power to combat them by physical force. I believe I would reconsider. Then, if we decide differently, we all should resist simultaneously. With only you resisting while everybody else is doing it means you are bound to lose."

He said, "Okay." I knew, though, that if I had said, "Ron, hang tough! Refuse to snap to," he would have done it without batting an eye. He was just that kind of man and he proved it a short time later.

It happened after we had begun to set up a covert communications system throughout the Zoo. By means of the holes in the walls, special hiding places in the latrine and other ways, we could pass a message through the entire camp within two days. I had put out directives establishing committees and worked out a staff. Certain people had been assigned specific jobs. One man was heading up our communications section. We had a committee working on escape. And we kept a current list of all the POWs and their shoot-down date.

I then decided to put out a bulletin. It was not too large, but it contained directives, policies and suggestions. Since Ron was next door to me, I dictated it to him, and he wrote it down. Despite the Vietnamese's denying us our dues as POWs, I still felt that we could outsmart them by using tactics such as these. We had only been at the Zoo around four weeks; given time, I reasoned, we could begin to effect some changes. I could not have been more wrong.

One day during this period a guard came in and made me stand at attention with my back to the wall. In a few minutes the Dog came in with another Vietnamese in a white shirt. The Dog did not say who the civilian was, but he paid him a lot of deference. Using the Dog as an interpreter, the civilian made a statement: "I understand you are also a Korean hero."

I was still standing braced against the wall. "That is military information and I cannot answer. I can give you only my name, rank, serial number and date of birth."

When he heard the translation, the cords in his neck swelled up and he turned red in the face. "We know how to handle your kind. We are preparing for you now." He turned and stomped out.

The Dog came back in a little while. He was either so scared or mad that he was still trembling. "You have made the gravest mistake in your life. You will really suffer for this." With that threat he left.

A few days later a guard caught the men two cells above me talking through the hole in the wall to Ron. He also found some written material. Then he went into Ron's room and caught him by surprise. He took two pieces of written work Ron had prepared; one was a list of all the POW names, the other was one of the bulletins I had put out. To make matters worse, Ron had put my real name on the newsheet instead of my code name, "Cochise." While still in the cell, one of the guards began reading the two sheets. Ron reached over, snatched one and ate it while holding them off with one hand. Unfortunately he had grabbed the wrong one. He ate the list of names which was not too important, but they kept the list of directives. They also found the hole in the wall. This so excited them that they stepped out in the hall yelling for reinforcements.

While they were out, Ron ran over to my wall and beat out an emergency signal to come to our hole in the wall. "They searched and found everything. I ate the list of names, but they got the policies. Get rid of anything you don't want them to find." I told him to deny everything, and I would do the same. He just had time enough to stuff the plug back in the hole when they came and took him away.

I passed the warning down to the other two rooms and they began to clean house. As fast as possible I began to try and dispose of anything incriminating. The steel rods that we had been using to bore the holes in the walls I put under the floor through the grate. I destroyed lots of paperwork, but the fat was in the fire. A big shakedown was on. One thing I had not destroyed was a sheet of toilet paper that had the Morse code on it. I didn't think it was any big deal, or I would have gotten rid of it. This was one of the pieces of evidence they would use to accuse me of running a communications system. The irony of it was that I actually was relearning the Morse code with the knowledge of my turnkey. He had even written his name on it for me.

They put Ron in another room for three days and nights without anything at all—no food, water, bedding, blankets or mosquito net. They just shoved him in and left him there. He not only got cold, but the mosquitoes chewed on him all night.

They took me before the camp commander for interrogation.

He had the piece of paper Ron had not been able to destroy and started reading the fourteen items it listed, such as: gather all string, nails and wire; save whatever soap or medicine you get; familiarize yourself with any possible escape routes; become acquainted with the guards, and in general follow the policy that "you can catch more flies with sugar than with vinegar." I denied the paper was mine. "Stortz has already admitted everything and said you were responsible." I knew that was a lie. They would have had to kill Ron before he did that. He might admit to his having done it, but he would never say that somebody else had. They, of course, told him the same thing and said that I had admitted everything, and all he had to do was confirm it.

After making the usual number of threats, they took me back to a different room at the end of the building. They left me a pencil and paper and told me to write out a confession that I had violated prison rules. "If you do not, you will be severely punished." The first thing I knew, I heard a tap. It was Ron Stortz in the next room. We exchanged what had happened in interrogation.

I said, "Remember, I'll never confess to anything."

"Roger, I won't either." He then tapped, "God bless you." I sent back a GBU.

I later heard that Ron was put in Alcatraz, a harsh punishment camp. Though he was an extremely strong man, the torture began to get through to him. The North Vietnamese hated him so that even when they moved out all the other POWs, they left Ron there alone.

I later saw one of the postage stamps put out by the North Vietnamese. It was typical North Vietnamese propaganda. On it is a picture of an American POW. He is big and tall. Behind him is a teen-age girl, very small, holding a rifle on him. The American was Ron Stortz.

When making their report on the POWs in 1973, the North Vietnamese said that Ron Stortz "died in captivity." Ron Stortz died as he lived—a brave American fighting man who considered his principles more valuable than his life.

X

The "Humane and Lenient Treatment" Begins

I had been left with writing materials and told to write a confession, which I refused to do. In a few minutes a guard came and took me to the interrogation room. There was a new intensity in the questioning now, a level of threats and hatred that I had not experienced before. "You were communicating and talking with others and you tried to take over the camp. Do you still refuse to confess your guilt?" The interrogators continued with this line for some time.

Finally, the one we called the Fox screamed, "What is the matter with you? Can't you understand?"

I lost my temper and retorted rather loudly, "Yes, I understand!"

"Oh," he said, "you understand it was against the regulations to talk, to make noise, to communicate?"

I was getting angrier by the second. "There are no regulations," I replied, "and you know it."

The Fox leaned over the desk and pointed his finger at me. "There are regulations, and one of the regulations is that you will be silent. After being here all this time have you not understood that? If all the other American officers are so stupid, then we Vietnamese have nothing to fear."

He was baiting me, and I knew it, but I could not keep from responding. I looked him right in the eye, and with as much intensity as I possessed, I told him, "I understand. You want us to live like dumb animals. You bet I understand perfectly. But let me tell you something. One day the whole world is going to know what you have done when we get an opportunity to tell them."

That was what the Fox was waiting for. He gave a signal to the two guards standing behind me. One of them grabbed my arms and handcuffed them while the other yanked my hair and pulled my head back. He said, "Open your mouth!" When I would not do it, he pressed his fingers into my jaws, forcing my mouth open. Now they began cramming it full of newspapers.

I had a cold along with my chronic sinus condition, so when they shoved the paper far back into my throat, I thought I wouldn't be able to breathe. In fact, I was a little bit frightened that I might choke to death. They tied a blindfold over my eyes, and with my wrists handcuffed behind me and my mouth full of newspapers, I was hustled out the door into a truck. Someone else had gone to my cell to get my gear, which they threw in the truck, and off we went. It was around eight o'clock in the evening on October 31, 1965, less than a month and a half after I had been captured.

During the half-hour ride my mind was racing as I tried to plan my strategy. At different times we all had talked about our conduct in front of the interrogators. I remembered saying, "You're an American fighting man. The war is not over just because we are in prison. When you come to attention, *snap* to attention. When you salute, give them the best you have. Let them see what the American military looks like and acts like under adverse conditions. Do not ever let them see you slump in what they figure is despair. Look proud and be proud. Show them how strong you are. And remember, give them nothing but name, rank, serial number and date of birth."

I began to wonder, though, whether I would ever need any such strategy unless we soon got to wherever we were going. My mouth and throat were so full of newspapers that I could hardly get my breath. Finally a horn honked, some iron doors screeched open, we drove in and they turned the motor off. They shoved me half stumbling through a series of doors and hallways.

After what seemed an eternity, they took off my handcuffs and blindfold and stood grinning as I feverishly yanked the newspapers out of my mouth and throat. When the last piece was out, I breathed deeply over and over. My jaw felt as if it were broken, but to be able to breathe was such a great feeling. One of the guards threw my gear on one of the bunks. Then he opened the leg stocks on the other bunk and motioned for me to put my legs in them. I could tell he and his buddy would enjoy my resisting. I got up on the bunk, lay down and put my legs in the slots. He slapped down the locks, tested them, and with a laugh they both left.

As I examined my plight, I saw immediately that this was not going to be any picnic; I had several uncomfortable hours ahead of me. Part of the discomfort was due to the design of the stocks. Instead of my legs resting on the bunk, the leg stocks were elevated about a couple of inches above the bunk. This raised both my feet and legs off the bunk so that in order to sit up at all I had to lean forward. That put all the weight and pressure on the lower pelvis bones which, in my case, had nothing covering them except skin. In less than an hour I felt exhausted. Too, the ligaments were still swollen in my right knee and the pressure was really giving me fits.

For the fun of it, I guess, they had left all my things in the corner of the cell. It took a while, but finally I was able to reach them. I worked my mat underneath me and tried to get my mosquito net up, but I could not reach the hooks. That meant a feast for the mosquitoes.

As soon as I got my bearings I realized that my new home was back at the Hanoi Hilton, only this time in cell #1 of New Guy Village instead of Heartbreak Hotel. That did not bode well, since the only time POWs were put in New Guy Village was for torture, extensive interrogation or recuperation from injury.

Dragon Doll, a woman guard, was now on duty. She was a

civilian and wore the pink uniform that some of the medics wore. While in Heartbreak some of the other guys had watched her through the window. They said she was so mean that she would harangue the women convicts until they cried. When the military guards brought me in, she opened the cell door and stood glaring all the time.

The next morning, right after five o'clock, the gong went off, and the music started playing. It was not long before Dragon Doll brought in a little boy about five years old. He was of course too short to reach up to the peephole in the door. She lifted him up and said something to him. He would go, "Shush! Shush!," as they do with an animal, and then she would take his fist and shake it at me. That hurt me so bad I could hardly stand it, for he was one of the first children I had seen in weeks. I thought how great it would be to take little Danny and bounce him on my knee or wrestle my other sons on the floor. They really loved to gang up on me and hold me down, and I usually let them win. It made me too lonely to think of them for very long, so I switched to the present.

They had cut my hair right down to the bone a couple of weeks before and had not given me a shave or haircut since. I was surprised the little boy was not scared to death when he saw me.

I kept waiting for that first day to drag by. They did not bring any food or water, nor did they let me out of the stocks to use the latrine or commode. I began to be extremely uncomfortable.

I had always been very active. Even on days off I could never lie down and take a nap. When I tried, I always felt I was losing something or the world was passing me by. I would wash and polish the car or go hit some golf balls—there were plenty of things to do. In the evenings I would run or go to the gym and play some handball. I guess it was nervous energy and I had never realized it.

Now I was tied tighter than a dog on a chain. I could not

stand up, walk or run. I was not sure how long I could take it; it was almost a phobia. When the pressure started to build up, I would pray. I would explain my problems and what was wrong and ask God for strength to make it. Minute by minute the hours began to pass.

I had no idea how long I would be there, so I decided to map out a schedule to help make the days pass. First, I decided to plan my oldest son's college education . . . where he would go, how many years it would take, how much money, what subjects, and so forth. I felt that would take a lot of time. Next, I chose to relive a trip that I had made from George Air Force Base in California to Hawaii, Guam, the Philippines, and over to Bangkok, where I then went on a "quick strike" exercise.

Planning this took quite a bit of time, and I felt it would really help in occupying the time. I designed some alternate exercises for the third and fourth days. But the following day when I started charting Rob's college education, I only made it halfway through and could not hack it any further. I had to give it up, for it was too much of an emotional strain to think so intensely about my family.

The second day ended, and still no food or water. And bugging me even more was that they would not give me any toilet privileges. I was living in my own filth. I could not get off the bunk and neither could I get anything up on the bunk. Just to urinate in the bucket beside my bunk sometimes left both my bunk and clothes soaked.

I felt sure things would change on the third day, but I was wrong. Periodically a guard would look in on me but that was all. I wondered if there had been a breakdown in communications or maybe I had been forgotten. Something had to give!

As that day began to roll by, I decided I did not care. I was amazed that I was not hungrier or thirstier. I thought, "I can starve to death and it is not going to bother me." No food, water, toilet privileges, exercise or sunlight—it probably would not take long. The thing that was bothering me most, though, had nothing to do with food or water.

It was the radio speaker right outside my window. It was driving me out of my mind with its loud singsong music over and over. I was already in a pretty sad mental state and the fact that I was locked down, could not move around or exercise was tough. But that radio playing was pure torture. It played all day Sunday.

In desperation I began to pray about it. I said, "Lord, you have just got to get that radio off the air or else I am going to be a screaming ninny in a little while." This was the third day, and I really prayed. I became ecstatic that evening when the speaker quit working. The guards came out and beat on it and rattled it around. Every time they hit it and it still did not work, I would say, "Thank you, Lord." It never did come back on as long as I was in stocks. I could hear the static but that was all. What a blessed relief.

On the fourth day I was given ten minutes out of the stocks for toilet privileges. I could hardly move. It seemed like only seconds; then the guard motioned me back into the stocks. That afternoon one of the guards brought a piece of bread and a cup of water, set the water on the floor and put my bread on the irons. As I started to pick it up, he hit me and I dropped the bread on the floor. He put the bread back on the irons. After a few minutes I reached for the bread and he let me have it again. Then I discovered that I could eat only on his command, like a dog. He would say, "Okay," I would pick it up, take a bite, and he would motion for me to put it back. Then I would have to wait at his whim before I could eat another bite. When I finally finished eating the bread, I asked for the water. He poured it out and took the cup with him. Periodically this same guard would decide to play this game again. I dreaded seeing him come even if he was bringing me bread and water.

As the days dragged by I kept a record of them by using a nail I had found with which I had made a one month's calendar on the wall. About nine-thirty each evening I would make a mark —another day down. How many to go I didn't know, but at least another one was passed. It was as if I had won one day's victory.

I was just existing. The only meaningful or significant thing I could do was pray. And as the weather started turning cold, I began praying to stay warm. It was a funny thing about the weather. This was not the coldest part of the Vietnamese winter, but no exercise and lack of food made it seem freezing cold. I was sleeping on a slab of cement with a thin mat under me, and for cover I had one blanket and the pajama-like prison clothes I had on.

I had hoped that they would not keep me in the stocks more than ten days, but by the eighth day I realized it might be a lot more—there was no way of knowing. I projected that they probably would keep me locked up for fifteen days—November 15. Over and over I kept telling myself, "You are going to be here another five days." By constantly repeating it to myself, it soon became old hat. When the tenth day rolled around and no one came to release me, it was not such a shock—I knew it would not be until the fifteenth. But as the fifteenth came closer, I had adjusted my expectations another five days.

Fortunately, my body was adapting to the confinement. And after the initial discomfort and pain were over, even my knee was beginning to heal.

With nothing over them, my feet and legs began to chap. I tried to sneak something around them, and when possible I would pull down my pants, although the guard would use that as a pretext to lean harder on me if he discovered it.

I was determined to maintain a sense of discipline, even though I could only sit. In the morning as soon as the gong went off at five, I would sit up. Whether drowsy, sleepy or tired, I did not lie down again until the gong sounded six hours later to announce the siesta, an Oriental custom. It was still hard for me to lie down three hours in the middle of the day. Sometimes I would sleep, but most of the time I lay there thinking. At two o'clock I would sit up and not lie down again until the bed gong at nine-thirty.

One day I was startled to hear, "Hey, Robbie, are you in there? Don't talk. Just cough if you hear me." It sounded like Bob Peel, so I coughed and kept listening. I was surprised that he was talking so loud, and noticed a funny intonation to his voice. But as he rattled away he explained that he was pretending to try to talk to his guard, who did not understand any English.

Bob was in the hall outside my cell where they kept a big water can. He was getting water for the wounded men he was taking care of. He said he had seen me go into the courtyard to the toilet area but had not known what building I had come from. He described a place he would leave a note the next time he was in the toilet, and he would try his best to stay in contact.

That really cheered me up. I had talked to Bob my very first day at Hoa Lo. Now here he was again like a bolt out of the blue. I had a piece of pencil lead stashed under my clothes. That night, while under my net, I very cautiously wrote a note on toilet paper. I told him I had been on bread, water or nothing for several days and was really hungry. "The stocks are not bothering me as much as they did at first. I am determined not to give them anything."

The next day when they took me out to fill my water pitcher, I acted as nonchalantly as ever. When the guard left me momentarily, I placed the note in the agreed-upon hiding place. Later I heard Peel getting his water and again as he "talked" to the guard he gave me a brief report on what was going on and said he had found my note.

The next day he left me some food—a piece of bread and a piece of orange. The injured men he was taking care of were getting fruit, because of their condition. Even though they needed it, they were sharing it with me.

It was too good an arrangement to last. The guard evidently caught on to what was happening and stopped letting Peel come in for water. Bob had to wait outside until the guard brought the water can to him.

Meanwhile the Dog, my old camp commander from the Zoo, was coming in every night to interrogate me. The only good thing about it was being taken out of the stocks and over to the meat-hook room. His basic line was, "Now, if you will answer some questions, we will take you back to the other camp, and you will have a good life, humane and lenient treatment, and be with your friends. Otherwise, you will stay here alone and never see another American again. Not only will you never go home, but you will die in the stocks."

He would promise great treatment one minute and threaten dire consequences the next. But I still would not give him anything. Each day I chalked up another victory: I had not given in.

As Thanksgiving Day began to approach, I kept thinking about spending it with my feet in stocks and on bread and water. Thanksgiving had always been a special day at home, not only because it was a holiday but also because it was the annual family reunion for the Risners. We would have a packed house—a lot of food, singing and horseplay, just good comradeship. We would get together a quartet and sing some of the old-time songs like "Here comes the man with a sack on his back; Got more crawdads than he can pack," or maybe "Salty Dog." Sometimes we would sing religious songs which Dad, who was a good bass, loved to join in on. Mother or one of my sisters would play the piano. There would be a lot of picture taking, pranks played, laughter, noise and confusion, plus plenty of good food, and visiting.

I thought about them more and more as Thanksgiving neared. Though it made me more lonesome, I somehow felt much closer to them. As I reminisced, one of the earliest recollections I had was when we lived on a farm in Arkansas.

It was cold and windy and the whole family had come down with the flu. Dad was on a trip to Flint, Michigan. Mother, though sick herself, was trying to keep us all in bed and warm. But we had an old potbellied stove for which the wood was almost gone.

Mother put newspapers on her feet and wrapped them in towsacks and went out in the snow to chop some more wood. While she was gone we kids began acting up. One of my brothers dropped a 12-gauge shotgun shell in the stove. When it exploded Mother came running, only to discover some scared little children with lead pellets in their bed!

During those early years Dad had a small stockyard and had just purchased several thousand hogs when the stock market crashed. Broke and poor as church mice, we moved to Pumpkin Center, Oklahoma, where we lived on oil-lease land while Dad traded horses and cattle. As I thought back I could remember looking out the window of the bedroom and watching the escaping gas burning and making eerie configurations in the night. Every night we went to sleep with the smell of gas and the sounds of oil-well engines and the shackle rods running back and forth.

It was then that I developed my great attachment to horses. My father told me I had a special knack with horses. I could ride some unbroken horses without them bucking. And I had a pet colt for a time that would follow me like a dog. Instead of barking he nickered.

We moved to Sapulpa, Oklahoma, when I was six. Then, after only six months, we moved to Tulsa, where Mother and Dad lived in the same house until his death in 1962 and where Mother remained until a couple of years before her passing. During most of those years Dad continued trading livestock, and even though we lived in town, I had a spotted horse that I kept in the backyard.

It was here that I came under the influence of the church. I began going regularly to the First Assembly of God in Tulsa. I formed lasting friendships in its youth group. We did everything together, from church activities to buying and riding cycles.

At age sixteen I got a part-time job as stock clerk for the Chamber of Commerce, and had an occasional job welding as a result of vocational training in school. Dad had also gone into the used-car business now. So on Saturdays I washed and waxed cars. Dad was a short Dutchman with a fiery temper. He had two forbidden topics: criticizing his children or President Franklin D. Roosevelt. One day my sister was teasing him about thinking too highly of FDR. He looked at her dead serious and said, "Mary, if you ever vote Republican, I hope to live to see the day that you go hungry!"

These and other memories flooded my mind and made me more lonesome than ever. Yet when no hint of release was forthcoming, I forced my mind to adjust to it. I repeated mentally several times, "Okay, I'm going to be here through Thanksgiving. I will just have to make the best of it."

When Thanksgiving morning came, it was like any other morning. But around two o'clock, at about the time Kathleen and the boys would be sitting down to Thanksgiving dinner, I began thinking about them eating with my place empty and not knowing if I was dead or alive. I was not even sure where they were, but I imagined they had returned to the States. I wondered which one of them would say grace. We were such a close family, I doubted that they would make it all the way through the blessing. The more I thought about it, the more choked-up I became.

That afternoon when they brought my meal, it was the same bread and a cup of water. I said a prayer of thanksgiving for the blessings that had been mine. And even though I was imprisoned and in stocks, I was glad to be from a country like America. Then I said a prayer for each of the boys and Kathleen, and closed by asking God to "Bless their food. Bless their lives. And protect them." It was a prayer I prayed thousands of times.

In fact, I was praying a lot, for it was one of the few ways I could occupy the day. I would pray not only for my family but also for each one of the prisoners that I knew of. Then I would go through all of my relatives and friends as well as our government leaders. Mentioning names in prayer gave me a feeling of closeness to them that was very meaningful.

Soon I would have been in stocks and on bread and water for over three weeks. Though I did not know how much weight I had lost, I could tell that my waistline had gone down around four inches. I was still unshaven, so my face did not look especially haggard when I peered at my reflection in the urine in my waste bucket.

Unexpectedly, though, I began having difficulty with the rest period during the middle of the day. The minute I lay down, my heart started to pump as if it were coming out. It beat as if I were frightened to death. When I sat up it would stop, but when I lay back down it would start pounding terrifically. My body was almost jerking, it was pounding so hard. It was impossible to sleep. Sometimes if I could lean over on my side for a little while, the hard beating would ease up. Since both feet were locked in so tight, I could not stay turned over very long. I could not understand what was happening.

Strangely enough, although I was getting weaker physically, I was feeling stronger emotionally and mentally. One day after I had lost control of my bowels, they gave me a little soup. I wrote "BOTTOM" in the base of the bowl. I was quite sure a POW was washing my dishes. Then I turned the bowl over and on the bottom I wrote:

> ROBBIE RISNER
> STOCKS 28 DAYS
> OKAY

The guard had never looked at my dishes before. This time, though, when he picked up my dish, the very first thing he did was turn it upside down. He did not know three words of English, but he knew it was some kind of message. He pointed his finger at me, went out and locked the door. For the next three days I did not get even bread or water.

That increased my miserableness, especially at night. I shivered like a dog. Sometimes I tried to shiver more, for I had read somewhere that when a dog shivers, he is warming himself and actually generating heat. I would lie there with my teeth chattering, goose bumps all over my skin, and let myself shiver. There was an old handleless broom in my room; I found that if I put it between my shoulder blades it would hold my back off of the bunk right at the base of my neck. I would do isometrics at night to generate enough heat to drop off to sleep, and wake up again shivering.

Many times I would be shivering or praying and look up and see someone staring at me through the peephole. I was like an animal in a zoo. People paraded by all day long. I never knew who they were. I imagine they got their money's worth, for I was looking pretty grotesque. My beard and hair were about an inch long. The more I thought about it, the more probable it seemed that I was going to be in stocks through Christmas. There had been absolutely no sign of them letting up.

Then, on the twenty-eighth of November, I lost control of my bowels again. It was one grand mess. They let me lie in it for a couple of days. The guard would come in with my bread and water and leave as quickly as possible. Eventually a medic came in and told them to let me out to wash up. He had them bring half a bowl of greens that looked almost like boiled alfalfa. They put me back in the stocks until the next day, when he again gave me the greens and let me clean up.

The next morning, December 2, I woke up before the gong went off. I was hungry, cold and miserable, my room still reeked, and I felt weak as a cat. As I had been doing every morning since my imprisonment, I started praying. Until this time I had not prayed for relief from what I was going through; all I had asked for was ability to stand it. But this morning when I started praying, I felt I should do it differently. I said, "Lord, I have been in long enough. I am half sick, miserable and cold and hungry. I am asking you to get me out of the stocks, to provide me more clothes, another blanket and some more food." An answer was not long in coming, though it was not like anything I had anticipated.

XI

"I Thought I Could Take Anything They Could Dish Out"

Though we were harassed and interrogated extensively, the closest thing to torture had been the stocks and the withholding of food. Most of us felt confident that was the extent of the punishment. We reached this conclusion during the time I was at the Zoo from information given us by a Thai prisoner of war. The Vietnamese normally had him washing dishes and doing odd jobs which put him in our area a lot. Fortunately, he could speak both Vietnamese and English.

Sometimes he would interpret for us. We would say something to the guard, and he would tell the guard what we said, or the guard would say something, and he would tell us in broken English what the guard had said. One day our guard volunteered that he couldn't lay a hand on us, for if he did he would be shot. I felt if a guard said they couldn't touch us, it was from the horse's mouth. So I spread the word. I said, "Don't rock the boat or take advantage. But understand that they can't torture us."

I was glad to learn this, but torture or not, I knew they would never be able to get me to a point where I would tell them anything against my will. They could torture me to death, and I would never say anything. They would not get a word out of me. I had believed this all my life. Much of it had been formed as the result of reading novels and fiction magazines where people had been tortured into unconsciousness and never uttered a peep. I believed without question that I was just as strong as they were, and that I could take it. And I certainly was motivated. I believed with all my heart in what I was doing and what the United States was doing. I had no thought or intention of ever giving a word to the enemies of democracy.

As I sat in the cell the afternoon of December 2, I felt pretty good. I knew God had heard my prayer that morning and that things were going to get better and I would soon be out of the stocks.

It was just beginning to turn dark when the cell door opened and several guards rushed in and swarmed over me. I didn't know what was happening! While I was still in the stocks they forced me over on my side cutting my legs. They had some rough rope with which they started tying my arms behind me. They yanked them as tight as two men can pull.

When they were about finished, Mickey Mouse, the camp officer, strutted in. In his broken English he charged, "You have broken the rules by trying to communicate. You have refused to cooperate with us. Now you will be severely punished." Then he read off the list of my supposed crimes.

He produced a couple of pads about an inch thick and as big as silver dollars. They were made of something like horsehair. The guards put them over my eyes, and by wrapping bandages around my head, forced the pads back into my eye sockets. It seemed as if they were driving my eyeballs right back into my head. I was sure they were ruining me and making me permanently blind. They took my legs out of the stocks. I was barefooted, with my wrists bound tight behind me. They were already tingling from the circulation being cut off.

They led me outside into the courtyard. I remembered that all around were great kapok trees with nuts about the size of hickory nuts which had dropped off and covered the yard. They marched me around on these for a while, and then we went through some of the open drainage ditches. It seemed as if half the time

I was getting up from falling. They followed this with climbing up and down stairs to the guards' quarters. I fell going up and coming down. I was getting banged up pretty good.

Each time I crawled out of a ditch or started back up the stairs, I would grit my teeth a little tighter. Horses had thrown, pawed and kicked me. I had had concussions and broken bones— I thought I could take anything they could dish out. The worse they treated me, the greater my determination not to talk.

I did feel pretty weak, though. Thirty-two days in the stocks without any walking to speak of had made me pretty unsteady. The lack of any food but bread and water, combined with diarrhea, had really sapped my strength.

Evidently this was just a primer, for when the novelty of seeing me fall into ditches and on stairs, plus running into a tree or two, wore off, they herded me back inside. They pushed me down on the floor and someone started working on my arms again. Only my wrists had been bound before; now, though, they had more rope and started working upward on each arm. After they had wrapped each one as tight as they could, they started tying them together, working upward again.

The pain began to be excruciating as they pulled them tighter and tighter. When they had wrapped them to a certain point, my right shoulder began to slip out of its socket. With a slight pop it felt as if it came out, I saw bright lights and my ears rang. The guards were oblivious to my pain. They kept wrapping and wrapping, pulling my arms together, tighter and tighter.

After they got all through, one of them slapped my arms real hard. Since they were tied so tight that they were like one solid member, it sounded like a smack on a solid piece of wood. I was really starting to hurt, but my tormentors had only begun.

Now they started on my legs. There are some sensitive nerves in the lower legs, and they knew where they all were. The best was saved for last. They pulled my ankles up behind me, wrapped the rope around my throat, and brought it back to my ankles and tied it. They were finally finished. My feet were pulled up behind me, I was blindfolded, bound hand and foot, and my chest was sticking out like a proud pigeon. If I relaxed my arched back, I would choke. I had never felt pain like that in my life.

When it got to be unbearable, I tried to stretch my legs and choke myself into unconsciousness. I had never done anything like it before, but I had to get rid of the pain. I was on the verge of unconsciousness when one of the guards came over to examine me. He hollered and someone came over, untied the knot and loosened my feet from my neck.

But that didn't stop the hurting. I began praying for oblivion: "Lord, let me faint." I almost succeeded, and then I would come to. I struggled up on my knees and almost managed to get to my feet. Then I threw myself forward on my head, hoping to knock myself out. It stunned me momentarily, but as I lay there with a bloody nose I knew I was still fully conscious. The guards evidently hadn't seen me, so I rolled over, and by using a post in the room, I almost stood again. This time I was determined to fall hard enough to pass out. When I hit the cement my head almost cracked open. The pain shot through my temples. I thought I might have broken my skull, but I was still not unconscious. One of the guards must have caught on to what I was doing, for he came over and tied me to a post. Now they were hurting me and there was absolutely nothing I could do about it.

When the pain started really ripping me, I began desperately to pray. I kept quoting a scripture verse from the Bible over and over: "My grace is sufficient." I thought this meant God would give me grace to bear whatever I had to bear without giving in. But nothing was happening. I cried, "Lord, you promised grace to bear anything. But this pain . . . I can't stand it . . . God! Help me, please help me!"

I don't know how long I endured it—several hours. I was hollering now. Really, it was a scream out of my guts that I couldn't stifle. I was in such pain that it was involuntary. I knew

I couldn't last much longer. My will was ebbing away. My guts and determination were shattered. I was no longer a man with a mind and body and soul. I had been reduced to a mass of rope and sheer pain. I kept praying. When I saw I wasn't going to be able to hold out any longer, I prayed, "God, you've got to help me. I can't afford to give in. I'd be a traitor." I believed that with all my heart. It was unthinkable that I could be brought to a point where I would have to give in. I couldn't even destroy myself.

Finally I hollered, "Okay, I'll talk." The minute it came out I felt miserable. I had never been so disappointed or had a lower opinion of myself. It was utter contempt. I despised myself for giving in. All my bravado and resolve were gone. I was shouting, "I'll talk, I'll talk."

Mickey Mouse came in and said, "Be silent."

I said, "I can't. I'm in too much pain."

"Be silent!"

I kept hollering and the guards began to beat me. They knocked me down from the post, then set me up again. I could feel the thuds but it wasn't hurting. I was in too much pain. There wasn't anything else that they could do to hurt me.

This went on all night. They wouldn't turn me loose. Mickey Mouse would come in and say something. The guards would then chop on me.

Sometimes I could hear someone screaming in the distance. I would wonder who it was and where they were. Then I realized it was I. I would be so close to passing out that the sound of my voice appeared to be coming from somewhere else. But I couldn't fall into unconsciousness.

I had done what I thought I would never do—agree to talk. But they ignored me. I had agreed to go against all I believed in, but it was not enough. They simply let me continue screaming.

Just before daylight Mickey Mouse came in. Again I told him I was ready to talk. He said, "Okay. Answer my questions." "Not until you untie me." I was only willing to talk to get rid of the pain.

So he said, "All right. Loosen the ropes on his arms." They loosened them enough to ease the pain. That felt a little better.

I had the impression my trial was being held. There was quite a bit of talk and stirring around. Finally they must have determined their course of action. Mickey Mouse asked, "Where did you fly from?" They knew this already from some other people and they had confronted me with it more than once. Each time, though, I would neither confirm nor deny it. Now when they asked I told them. When they wanted to know what type of aircraft I was flying, I told them.

They asked, "Will you write a statement?"

"What kind of statement?"

They explained that they wanted a statement of apology to the Vietnamese people. I was in no condition to refuse. I told them, "I think my arms are dead. I don't think I can write, but I'll try."

A couple of guards took the ropes completely off of my hands and arms. I was quite sure they were damaged but I did begin to get some feeling back. They took the blindfold off and removed the pads. It took the longest time before I could focus.

They left the ropes on my legs; my shoulder was still killing me, although when the ropes were released, it felt as if it had slipped back in place. I had an intense pain right below the breastbone. There was a big knot where they had pulled my ribs loose which was to stay for several years. I could move my hands, but I didn't have much feeling in them and no feeling whatever in my outer fingers.

Someone gave me a pencil. Mickey Mouse said, "Write now!" He dictated what he wanted me to say. It was in broken English, which was great, for I certainly didn't want it sounding like me. He had me write that I was forced by the United States to bomb. I apologized to the Vietnamese people for violating their sovereign air space and also for committing grave and heinous crimes against the Vietnamese people.

I wrote it as he gave it. When I finished you could hardly read it. It looked like the beginning penmanship of a first grader. But Mickey Mouse seemed satisfied.

He nodded to one of the guards, who came over and took the ropes off my legs. I sat on the floor in shock. I didn't know where they had me except that I was somewhere in the Hanoi Hilton prison complex. It was very cold. One of the guards had on some sort of a jacket, but even his teeth were chattering.

It was a few minutes before five in the morning when they took me back to the cell. I automatically put my feet on the stocks, but the guard was already closing the door. I rolled over, and for the first time in thirty-two days I lay on my stomach. It was ecstasy, sheer ecstasy. I pulled the blanket over me and immediately dropped off to sleep.

In less than ten minutes the gong went off. Though I had not slept all night, I was so terribly glad to be out of the stocks that I jumped out of the bunk and almost fell on my face. I was weak, aching and numb, but I was so glad not to be tied down any longer that I began walking and exercising—up and down, back and forth. It was glorious.

Around eight the guard came in with a heavy shirt, another suit of clothes and a blanket, and at nine-thirty I got the regular morning meal. That day I received the normal food ration, which was about half a bowl of soup made out of something like spinach, and then, in a little side dish, maybe three spoonfuls of either cabbage, turnips or squash, and a small loaf of bread.

Interrogation was an everyday thing now. I had already told them where I had flown from, my mission and the aircraft I was flying. Evidently they had a fairly active research department, for they had all kinds of information from newspaper clippings and magazines and two articles in *Time,* my cover story and the later one when I was captured. They had a lot of information on my family as well. When they started putting the questions to me wanting confirmation of their information, I admitted to a lot of it, but deception seemed easy. I had never before experienced pain such as they dished out—I wasn't ready yet to buck them head-on again.

They didn't seem to be particularly interested in propaganda material right then. Instead, they wanted to know what kind of formation we had flown in Korea to shoot down the MIGs, and the kind of fighter tactics we had used. When they wanted to know which of our planes could whip their MIGs, I was extremely optimistic in my assessment of our aircrafts' capabilities, and Charlie was initially quite gullible.

Now that I was out of the stocks, I began to develop a regular routine; an important part of it was exercising. How wonderful it felt each morning to run in place, do push-ups and set-ups. I felt stronger each day.

It was getting colder all the time. The wind really whipped in under my door. Apparently the only time the wind blew in Vietnam was in the winter; in the summertime it seemed deadly calm twenty-four hours a day. Since I had no shoes, I would walk up and down to keep my feet warm, otherwise the concrete floor kept them constantly cold. Because of the height of the bunk, the next-best alternative was to sit on the bunk so my feet wouldn't touch the floor.

My fears that I would be in the stocks at Christmas time had not materialized. The torture was over for now. I was no longer on bread and water, and I had better clothes and an extra blanket.

XII

Christmas in Hanoi

Being on bread and water for a month had left me with a voracious appetite. The thought of food became a twenty-four-hour obsession. Though I was getting regular rations, I was hungry one hundred percent of the time. I dreamed of food every single night, all night long. It was maddening: I would be in a cafeteria line with a big tray of marvelous food, especially pastries. Before I could eat it somebody would carry my tray off, or I would drop it or not have the money to pay for the goodies.

Dream or not, I needed more food and there was no way to get it. One day a rat jumped up and grabbed a piece of bread lying on my bunk and was dragging it off before I saw him. I grabbed the bread and chased away the rat. He was probably covered with every disease germ imaginable. I had watched rats come right out of the sewer where we emptied our body waste, garbage and everything else. I knew he had been wallowing around the bread with his front feet, but I was so hungry that it just didn't make any difference. I removed a little tiny bit where his teeth marks were and ate the rest.

In mid-December one of the new pilots shot down brought some news that cheered me for a while. Captain John Reynolds said that he had read in the *Air Force Times* shortly before his shoot-down that I had made full colonel.

At about the same time the Vietnamese moved me to Heartbreak Hotel and gave me what they thought was a demotion—dishwasher! They knew too about my promotion, since they received the *Air Force Times*. Because of my being the senior ranking officer, they were sure dishwashing would be demeaning and embarrassing. What they didn't know, though, was that I was glad to get it, because there was always the chance someone would leave some food in his dish. Usually the new POWs were in such a state of shock and so repulsed by the food that they would leave most of it the first days. I was tickled to get it! Too, dishwashing meant a chance to get out of the cell, which was always a pleasure.

My next-door neighbor was Navy Commander Jim Stockdale, who had been there awhile, too. How I longed to see that kindly face again, weathered by years of sun and salt water spray, with crow's-feet around the eyes from squinting through the windscreen of a jet fighter. He had a shock of iron-gray hair falling down over one eye, which gave him a remarkable likeness to the writer Carl Sandburg. He loved philosophy and intrigue and was an outstanding leader—one of my dearest friends.

Since Heartbreak was the processing center for the incoming pilots, Jim and I would brief them and try to orient them to what to expect. One of the first things we would tell them was, "If you have any bread left, don't throw it away. Save it; we'd like to have it." To get it we would take down our transom covers, put out our hands and throw our clothesline strings across to them. They would tie on the bread and we would pull it in to our cells. We were so hungry, every piece was like chocolate candy.

Another big part of the day was the twice-a-day food report, at nine-thirty and three-thirty. First, a guard would bring in the food and set it on a little stool by the wall. Then he would go after the water. While he was gone, it was a real big deal to report to everyone what the food was. The color of the soup. What kind of vegetable, if any? How big were the loaves of bread?

After we ate, a guard would take me down to wash the dishes.

He watched constantly while I was washing the dishes to make sure I didn't get any extra food. If I caught him not looking, I would eat every scrap available, including that which had been partially eaten. If they caught me, I would have to pour everything out on the floor, which was filthy. It was virtually the habitat of the rats. This was the room where for forty years guards had relieved themselves in a pit and where we emptied our waste buckets.

But despite the filth, as soon as the guards turned away or left, I'd pick up the scraps and devour them. There were times when I found banana peels that had turned black. They would be thrown in a corner, where I knew the rats had nosed over them. If the guard wasn't looking, I would put them under my shirt, take them back to my room and eat them. I was so starved that anything with any substance or bulk was a blessing.

I decided that the Vietnamese did not want me to get extra food even when it was available because hunger was another form of punishment. The more tractable I was, the more chance they had of getting the information they wanted. The weaker and hungrier I was, the less chance I had to gain my strength or courage to resist them.

My hunger was even tougher to take, since this was the Christmas season back home. I thought I heard a turkey gobbler on several occasions. But I decided it was somehow related to my food dreams. Without a doubt, that Christmas was one of the most dismal times of my whole life—as well as every other POW's. It's hard to describe how depressing Christmas time was in a North Vietnam prison. It was December and the weather was miserable —misty rain, low clouds and kind of a steel-gray atmosphere outside. In the daytime the lights were off. The room stayed drab the whole time—gray walls, gray ceiling and floor, gray bunk and a dirty green door. Over the window in each cell, a wide long overhang covered the view of the sky and blocked the light that would otherwise have come in. The hall running between the cells was totally dark.

And when Christmas Day came, it was even more depressing. Everyone was quiet with his thoughts turned inward and homeward. Even when we had an opportunity, there wasn't much to be said. For most of us, Christmas was annually one of the most memorable occasions in our lives. It was a time of closeness to our families, a time of giving, of gaiety and joy, of forgiving, and even a time of closeness to God.

But that kind of Christmas seemed far removed from our dim cells—except for the closeness to God—living in a cement box with filthy floors, infested with rats, cockroaches and spiders. We had nothing of our own. I had on the underwear I was shot down in and two pair of North Vietnamese peasant shirts and pants. I also had a water jug, a tin cup, a mat, my blankets and my net and a dirty gray hand towel. That was it.

We tried to cheer up one another by sharing past Christmases at home. As we communicated in code and whisper, the one thing we thought about most was our families. I tried to relive decorating the Christmas tree and all the children wanting to help. Sometimes we would break as many ornaments as we put on. The thought of the tinsel, the snow and the cotton, and finally climbing up the ladder and putting on the star—those things were so vivid that they hurt like physical pain.

I closed my eyes and imagined the smiling faces of Kathleen and our five sons. I tried to picture what they were doing that day. I breathed a prayer for Kathleen and I wondered if she had managed to get gifts for the children. I hoped they had remembered to buy her a Christmas present for me. Kathleen always wanted to shake all the packages, just like the children, and try to find out what was in them. She always wanted to slip in and open just one of them on Christmas Eve.

I thought about my mother, almost eighty years old, whom I might never see again. I knew she was praying for me. I could see her white head and her smile. How I wanted to be there with my arm around her and ask her questions that I had never taken time to ask before.

In the midst of my reverie, I said to myself, "My reason for being here must be awfully important to be worth all of this." I wasn't really asking if it was worth it all, because that never entered my mind. But it was Christmas and everything was sad and dismal. It was almost the essence of despair. If you could have squeezed the feeling out of the word "despair," it would have come out gray, dull and lead-colored, dingy and dirty—just the way everything was that morning.

The guard brought our morning meal, and then we waited impatiently for him to go to lunch. Normally, the guards ate around eleven or eleven-thirty, which meant we were left alone for a period of time. We would have someone be on the lookout through a nail hole into the courtyard. That way we would know when the guards returned. Someone would lie on the floor and look under the door to watch the corners. We had an agreed upon signal when everyone had checked their area—our normal danger signal was one cough, and another was to clear our throat. We used these intermittently along with others. When the guards caught on to the cough and the clearing of our throats, they started putting the heat on, then we began using the bucket lid. If there was danger, we would drop it on the floor or hit it with the hand. The same thing applied to our cups. The Vietnamese learned all of these tricks after a while, but there was very little they could do about them.

That morning after we had had our morning meal and the guard left for his, we had a talk session to try to cheer up one another. We quoted some scripture and talked about the birth of Christ. Naturally, everyone mentioned his family. We all agreed that the war couldn't last too much longer. "We'll probably be out of here by June."

We tried to count our blessings. We mentioned the families

of those men we knew had been killed. We whispered a prayer for them. When we finished talking, we lay back on the bunks. It was going to be a long, long day.

Then about two-thirty, too early for the second meal, a guard began making a lot of noise—he was bringing in food! It was unbelievable, but he just kept bringing it in. It looked like a special meal, something we had never had nor expected from the Vietnamese. He brought in turkey, a big piece of pork fat, some potato soup, a salad with fresh lettuce leaves and something like watercress with little pieces of carrot, and a whole red pepper, plus some cookies. It was like a gift from heaven. It's impossible to describe how it looked and tasted. We ate every bite. It was the most we had had to eat since being imprisoned. Without exception, I think we all cried a little as we bowed our heads in thanksgiving to God. We were so terribly grateful and surprised.

After dinner the guard took me out to wash the dishes. A lot of new men had been shot down and were being kept in New Guy Village. That meant fifteen or more sets of dishes. Several of the new men had left food on their plates—big hunks of pork and turkey drumsticks. When I saw it, I was like a blind dog in a meat house.

The guard stood in the door and watched as I set down all the dishes with their leftover food. He knew how hungry I was because I told him at every opportunity that I was *doi*, meaning hungry. I was really anticipating filling up; then he told me to pour it all out. I almost cried. I began pouring out the soup which I had intended to drink. Some of the meat I had already put up in a little cubbyhole on a piece of paper. With him watching, I squatted over the drain hole. I was sleight-of-handing some of the meat and shoving it either down my sleeves or the front of my pajamas, as we called our peasant clothes, which I had tied at the bottom with string. I was really stashing it away.

As soon as he left, I got the other stuff out of the cubbyhole and put it down my shirt. Unfortunately, most of the meat was covered with grease, which began to soak through. As luck would have it, he noticed it when I went back to my cell. He shook me down and had me take my clothes off. He found the food and made me throw every bit of it into my bucket.

I had hardly settled down on my bunk, berating my bad fortune, when they came for me. I thought Christmas Day was a strange time for interrogation. They took me to a big office I had never seen before, with marble floors and overstuffed leather chairs. It was the warden's office for the civilian camp, but on this occasion the Cat, a Vietnamese major who was in charge of all of the American POWs, was occupying it. With him was a civilian and his interpreter—the Rabbit. On the tables were what looked like peach blossoms, mixed with lilies and other flowers. There was a small mock orange tree, and on the table were some glasses and cups, a teapot, a thermos bottle, some cookies and assorted types of homemade candy. (Candy was made by taking little shreds of carrot and cooking them in sugar. They came out crisp and tasty.)

When I came in, the Cat introduced me to the civilian who was the Reverend-Minister-somebody. I later saw a picture of him sitting beside Ho Chi Minh. In my opinion, he was a Communist first and a minister second, if a minister at all. Anyway, I met him and he was very congenial and wanted to be friendly. He said they knew about the American Christmas customs, and then he told me about the Vietnamese ones. I just sat there amazed. All during this they had me help myself to the goodies.

I was all agog and so naïve. Actually I thought, "This confirms that they have decided to treat us as POWs, and I am finally getting the appropriate treatment from the camp commander." I even wondered whether maybe someone had found out that we were being tortured and mistreated, and whether now they were trying to make amends.

A photographer slipped in and snapped a picture. The Communist minister even stood up and said a prayer. He tried to reach over and put his hand on my head. I could just imagine the propaganda mileage they would get out of that—"Colonel Robinson Risner prayed for by North Vietnamese minister at Christmas brunch"—only a month after they had bent me out of shape and starved me. I backed away so fast that my neck cracked.

After a half-hour or so the guard took me back to the cellblock, and as soon as he had locked me in he took out someone else. This procedure continued until everyone in Heartbreak had been over. When we had a chance for debriefing, we discovered that each one had been through the same routine. We were all equally amazed. We knew that the Vietnamese did nothing without a purpose; regardless, a day that had begun in dreariness and depression had completely reversed. It was a welcome respite from torture, interrogation and mistreatment. But it did not signal a new policy or end the old one, as the next few months would show.

XIII

What Do You Tell Your Buddies When You Spill Your Guts?

One day, without warning, we heard someone scream from the meat-hook room at the other end of the courtyard, about seventy-five to a hundred feet from us. We could hear him groan and holler each time the pressure was applied.

Torture was such a frequent occurrence that it didn't surprise us, although it always upset us. There was nothing we could do but pray for the guy being tortured, and some would cuss the tormentors.

I knew both of the torturers well. When the decision was made to let me have it, they had imported a guard who most of us thought had flipped his lid. He would sit around talking to himself, laughing and giggling. He was continually fixing his bayonet, then sneaking up behind somebody. He would stick the bayonet right up close to the back of their neck and then he would holler something. He was not only dangerous but a real nut! I passed the word to the fellows to be careful around him, never to turn their back on him or make any sudden moves when he had his bayonet fixed. His helper in torture was the cook, who was actually an imbecile. They were a pair! Whatever they lacked in science they made up for in zest.

After a guy had been tortured the guards would put him in a cell, and as soon as all was clear, we would try to communicate with him. On one side of the cellblock, the cells had no transom covers. On the other side we would take them down when the guards were out. Then, by standing on the end of the bunks or the stocks, you could look through the bars to the other side and see one another. There was something important about looking across and seeing an American and putting a face to the voice you were communicating with.

On this particular day they were making someone scream pretty loud. Later they brought him over to Heartbreak, threw him in a cell, locked the door and went away. As soon as we were sure it was safe, we began to try to talk to whoever it was they had been working on. When we asked him if he had been injured, he told us that he had broken his thigh when he bailed out.

I asked, "Was that you we heard scream a while ago?"

There was a pause, and then kind of quietly he said, "Yes."

Someone said, "What did they do to you? Were they torturing you?"

He replied, "No, they were just twisting my broken leg when I wouldn't talk!"

He felt crushed because he had talked; he figured now he was a traitor. We all knew the mental anguish he was going through because most of us had been there ourselves. One survival technique we developed, though, was to try to be absolutely honest about what we had "confessed." After we were tortured, we would tell the others every bit of information we had given. If we had said something, for example, about the communications system, it was absolutely imperative that the word was put out so we could be prepared for whatever might come.

Sometimes it really hurt to be honest, but the longer we were there, the more we appreciated it because it helped everybody. I've heard men come back saying, "Boy, I spilled my guts." But I don't believe anyone ever gave any national or strategic secrets. I'm absolutely convinced of that. The men would reveal the airspeed of an aircraft on attack or something like that. Many times they would lie to their interrogators or spin some fairy tales. At other times they'd give actual information which they knew had already been given. The Vietnamese wouldn't know the actual from the false.

We worked now to raise this kid's spirits. We said, "Don't sweat it. Most of the rest of us have been through the same thing. Let us brief you and tell you how things are going to go. You'll get your guts back in no time." By telling him what had happened to us, we knew he could put the information he gave in perspective and balance. That way he didn't figure he was the sole one giving information or that he had become a traitor because he was not strong enough to take torture to death.

One day they brought in a young Navy lieutenant and put him across the hall from me. I started talking to him and asked him to take down his transom cover so we could see each other. I warned him, though, to be ready to put it back up if the guards came in. It took him some time to remove it, and while we were talking he dropped it. It made a lot of racket. I told him to hurry and get it back up again before the guards came running.

He dropped out of sight and stayed away for a long time. Then he came back up and worked to put it back in place. He struggled and struggled. I couldn't believe it when he dropped it again. By now I was worried by what the guards would do to him. I asked him, "Is there something wrong with your arms? Why can't you get it up?"

Then he told me. Both of his arms were broken. He had taken down the cover and had been trying to put it back with broken arms!

When the guards came, he told them that it fell off. Since both his arms were broken, they believed him and didn't put him in the stocks. They did move him to another cell, and after a few days they put casts on both arms. The guard fed him the first meal or two, and then wouldn't feed him any more. He had to slide his soup bowl over to the edge of the bunk, get down on his knees, get the bowl in his teeth, and tip it up to drink the soup. To eat the vegetable, he had to stick his face down in the little bowl and eat like a dog.

At this time there was a cease-fire, which we were not aware of. All we knew was that the prisoners stopped coming. We suspected the cause but were not sure. We also thought that perhaps our captors had switched camps and were now processing people somewhere else. Most of the men who were in Heartbreak were moved during the next month or so to the Zoo. Jim Stockdale was put over in New Guy Village for punishment.

The last guy left was the Navy lieutenant who had the broken leg. Naturally, we became very good friends. He was a very young man. I talked to him about his fiancée, his home and his brother. We grew quite close and prayed for each other regularly.

When they finally moved him out, he said, "God bless you." It was as if I had lost a member of my family. It was deadly quiet, with no sounds of any kind.

For a month or more, I was totally alone except for my turnkey. I talked to God a lot and told him about my problems and my loneliness. I prayed an awful lot for my family. I really received a great deal of satisfaction from praying because I knew that God heard me. Praying was like talking on the telephone.

I guess if there was any one thing that happened to many of us in prison, it was that we were no longer embarrassed talking about God or religion. We gained a lot of strength not only from our private prayers but also from sharing our feelings about God with each other.

This was true both for men who had been fairly active in their church as well as for those who had been virtually irreligious. A good example of that was a young pilot who was put in the cell next to me early in 1966 when the air war picked up and the prisoners were starting to filter through again. Most of them were wounded in some way. Jim Stockdale was brought back for a short time from punishment in New Guy Village. We were able to help the new POWs get started by telling them the things we thought important as well as teaching them the tap code. Without the code, to communicate would have been almost impossible for them.

When they brought in this young pilot, I gave him the tap code by whispering, and soon we were communicating through the wall. With him, as with most others, one of my first topics of conversation was "Are you a Christian?" He replied, "Yes, I am a reconstructed Episcopalian." So we talked and he told me that he was really going to be a different sort of a guy now. Evidently he and his buddy has been real rounders. They were known as the Gold Dust Twins.

"Incidentally," he said, "would you help me pray for my buddy?"

I told him I would, and asked, "What's the matter with him?"

"He was shot down and killed a couple of months ago."

I thought maybe I had misunderstood. "Did you mean you wanted me to pray for his folks?"

He tapped back, "No, I want you to pray for his soul in purgatory."

I had never done that before. I thought about it awhile. The tapping through the wall was fairly slow. I finally told him I didn't know Episcopalians believed in purgatory.

"That's right," he replied, "but I don't want to take any chances."

I laughed and agreed to help him pray for his buddy's soul in purgatory—a first for me. Later that day I asked, "By the way, what's your buddy's name?" When he told me, I realized it was the Navy lieutenant who had been across the hall a couple of months before, very much alive and with only a broken leg. When he heard this news he was one happy fella.

With new prisoners passing through, Jim and I were sending out information and sometimes directives to the Zoo to Commander Jerry Denton, who was running that camp. Jerry was really tough, smart and motivated. Jim Stockdale and I would gather information through various sources and send it forward. As best we could, we kept Jerry apprised of what was happening, the torture being used, and how interrogations were being conducted.

I was beginning to feel strong again. In the interrogation sessions, I was able to give them tit for tat. I didn't know it, but that was not going to last very long.

The pressure was increasing. Every time I left my cell to empty my bucket or go to a quiz, they would comb my room for any irregularity. They were digging for excuses to lean on me. Even such minor things as string would be taken. They knew I was tying it around my pants legs to keep the cold air out. I had made them believe that I smoked so that I could pass my cigarettes on to the other men. My turnkey would always find my hiding places. Or if I had saved some of my bread to eat later and had it hidden under my bunk tied to a string, he would find it.

On about the first of May, a guard came in and said, "Fold up!" I started to take down my net, but he shook his head no. He also had me leave my water pot, and my waste bucket. So I carried my other stuff, which consisted of a grass· mat, a hand towel, the toothbrush I had gotten at the Zoo, and soap we were getting every ninety days now.

For a moment I hoped I might be going back to the Zoo, where most of the prisoners were; instead it was to New Guy Village, which meant total isolation, and very possibly torture again. They moved me right into Jim Stockdale's cell, and (I learned later) they gave him mine. It wasn't long before the purpose for the move was explained.

XIV

Tryouts for Radio Hanoi

"We have decided to move you to a quieter place where you can concentrate." It was the Rabbit talking.

I asked, "What do you want me to concentrate on?"

He answered, "On your crimes."

I responded by saying I had not committed any crimes. He smiled and said, "We think you will be able to understand better in solitude."

Soon I was quizzed by the Cat, with the Rabbit interpreting. Besides being in charge of all POWs, the Cat was a member of the Joint Staff. He was a smart cookie and pretty intelligent. He always paved the way for his interrogations by starting off with something like this: "Even though we are enemies, there can be a bridge between us—not of friendship, but a bridge of understanding and respect between two officers of enemy camps." After he had peddled that garbage, he started getting specific. "We are going to permit you to atone for some of the crimes you have committed."

I said nothing because I had heard it several times before. Continuing, the Cat said, "Would you and your comrades like to hear the news of what is happening?"

Of course I answered yes.

"Good," he said. "I will take your suggestion." (This was always his ploy. He would ask me a question, and if I answered in the affirmative, he would call it my "suggestion.") Then he added, "I can tell you already that this will be approved. If I recommend something, they always approve it at higher headquarters because I am a member of the Joint Staff."

Now came the catch I had been waiting for. "I'm going to let you help your comrades by permitting you to read the news personally on the camp radio. That way you will know it is all accurate, and since your comrades know and trust you, they will know it is accurate."

I immediately told him, "I can't do that."

Then he started his harangue. He said, "You have no choice."

I responded by saying "You're right. I have no choice. I can't do it."

Now he started his usual threats. "Remember, you're in my hands. You are an enemy, an American and a criminal. I have full power of life and death over you, and you will do as I say. That is a direct order. You are a military man and you must take an order."

I said, "I can't take that order. That is an illegal order from my enemy. It is certainly not binding, and I refuse."

"You refuse to take my order?" With that he jumped up, knocked his chair over, grabbed his briefcase and stomped out. The Rabbit stayed behind for a moment. He said, "You have made a very grave mistake. You must know that you cannot win. For you to win is for him to lose. For him to lose to a criminal is unthinkable. But for him to lose to an American is intolerable. It will never happen, as you will soon see. You cannot refuse him and live." With that he, too, left.

Back in the cell, as I thought about these events, I was not totally convinced that what the Rabbit had said was true. I knew that if the Cat made up his mind, he was going to get something from me and that he had seemingly absolute power to try.

But I was over my torture now. Although they had hurt me pretty good, I felt ready to buck them again, ready to go to the mat. Then I pulled a real dumb stunt. I had been standing on my bunk looking through the window. In the alleyway between the buildings and the wall a Vietnamese prisoner, probably a trusty, was sweeping. He did this every other day. Next door to me were some South Vietnamese prisoners, probably pilots or commandos. Periodically they would say something to the prisoner below the window. He would look furtively around and say something back. They would then toss him some cigarettes and matches, and something else which I couldn't make out. He would look all around and pretty soon he would reach down, grab the things and put them in his shirt. I thought about this for a while and pulled a wild one out of the air. I decided that maybe he was an agent.

I had a pencil stashed away. I ran and grabbed it, took a piece of toilet paper and wrote in great big letters about two inches high: "Do you understand English?" I jumped up on the bunk, and as he came abreast I coughed. When he looked up, I held my sign up to him. He suddenly had the most frightened look on his face. He shook his head no, swept about two more strokes, and then took off at a dogtrot.

I knew then I had made a mistake, so I tore my sign in four or five pieces and dropped it in my waste bucket. I knew it was safe in those buckets, for the guards shied away from them like the plague. In a couple of minutes I heard them coming from all over the place. A civilian guard was leading the way. Evidently my new "friend" had reported immediately that I had held a sign up at the window. The civilian had brought the turnkey and some other guards around and immediately wanted to know where the piece of paper was that I had made a sign on. It had never happened before, but the first thing he did was to take the lid off my bucket. When he and the others looked down, there was the paper still visible in the waste. "Ah ha," they said, and began fishing it out with some sticks. They laid the pieces on the floor, and using their sticks began to put them together.

Meanwhile one of them ran to call Mickey Mouse, the camp officer. While their attention was elsewhere, I grabbed the pieces and shredded them before anyone else knew what was happening. When they saw it, they threw me up against the wall and held me until the camp officer came. They had evidently briefed him on the way, for when he walked in, he immediately leveled the charges at me: "We know what you did. You tried to communicate with another prisoner." When I denied it he said, "There is the evidence which you were trying to destroy. If you were not trying to communicate, why did you tear that up?" I told him I did not want them to read anything I wrote. He replied, "I do not believe that. Let me assure you that you will be punished."

The news circulated quickly. In a few minutes I was called out for an official quiz. The interrogator began citing the charges. "You have insulted the staff officer"—the Cat. "Unless you are willing to do what the staff officer ordered and to apologize for your insult, you will be punished. Also, you have now tried to communicate with another prisoner, which will be double punishment."

They were serious this time. When I refused, they told me to get on my knees and to remain there at attention. For someone with bony knees, that did not take long to start smarting. As a change of pace, they would have me stand with my hands over my head. They also withheld food and water. The next morning they began asking, "Are you ready to apologize? Are you ready to do what the staff officer has requested?" Each time I refused. This went on for almost two full days without respite. They were getting more disgusted and angry by the minute. They intended for me to apologize and to read on the radio without harsh torture, but it was not working.

Now the Rabbit came in and ran through the whole repertoire of what was going to happen if I kept refusing to cooperate. I said, "It is not going to make any difference because I'm not going to do that ever." Then I cited my reasons. "I am a prisoner of war, and according to the articles of the Geneva Convention, I am only required to give my name, rank and serial number. The order of an enemy officer is not valid. The order to read on the radio is contrary to every principle of appropriate and humane treatment of prisoners of war. I will not do it."

He asked, "Is that your final answer?"

I answered, "Yes."

He left, and pretty soon Mickey Mouse came in. He went through his standard insults: "Despite our efforts to be lenient with you, you have not given up your aggressive attitude. You are still carrying on the war; therefore, you must be treated as an active combatant." Then he warned, "This is your last chance. If you do not do as the staff officer says, I will punish you immediately." He apparently meant business. He had already brought a guard in with him. "What is your final answer?" I said, "No."

He motioned to the guard, who pushed me to the floor, turned me face down and started tying the ropes. In a matter of minutes one arm was completely wrapped and the same incredible pain had begun. When he started on the other arm, it triggered all the agony of that night in the past. The memories of those hours in torment flooded my mind. I could see the handwriting on the wall. I was on a dead-end street.

I decided to change my tactics. Instead of trying to withstand pain, I would outsmart them. Before the guard was through, I told Mickey Mouse I would do what they wanted. I was afraid they would go ahead and leave on the ropes to reinforce my decision, but this time they were in a hurry. They took them off, brought me some food and sent me back to my cell.

I spent the weekend wondering what I was going to have to do. On Monday they told me, "You will practice reading on the camp radio in three days." I asked them what they meant. Mickey Mouse replied, "You will make a tape." My heart sank.

Back in my bunk I sat down and prayed about it. How in the world could I deny them this? If I had not realized it before, I did now: they would keep trying to use me. They had a distorted view of my importance in America. Instead of looking on me as only one of many pilots and officers, they felt the *Time* article made me unique. They knew something about the stops I had made across America for the Air Force to meet the press (at the time when I received the Air Force Cross), to help the American public better understand what we were doing in Southeast Asia. The Vietnamese also attached some importance to my making "ace" in Korea. To top it all off, my promotion to bird colonel came along while I was in prison. And since I was still the senior ranking officer, other POWs would unquestionably be influenced by what I said or did.

I began a desperate assessment of the situation. I decided that first of all they wanted my voice. The others in the camp would recognize it, and if it was played outside, I knew it would be identified both before and after. Second, I concluded they wanted the use of my hand to write a statement. It boiled down to the use of my hand and my voice.

Now I began to look at my options. The surest one was to kill myself. That would certainly deny them any propaganda value they were planning to get out of me. But I was not sure I should really do that. I had always had strong religious feelings against suicide. Also, I believed suicide was either a coward's way out or the act of someone deranged. I did not like to think I was either. Then I thought of my family. If I killed myself, I would have denied my children a father, as well as my wife a husband.

Nobody likes to think of killing himself, and I wanted to live very much. Before I was shot down, I felt that I had had a wonderful life. I had already had as much enjoyment as most people during their total lifetime. But a year in prison had given me a different perspective. There were so many things I wanted to rectify, plus new things that needed to be done. Part of it was rationalizing, I am sure, but the greater part I felt very deeply. I knew I could not kill myself. I decided to fight it out, to do the best that I possibly could.

What would that be? They had just proved that I could not

take enough pain to deny them what they wanted. Yet, if I did give in, I would be going against the best interests of the United States government, dishonoring the Air Force, violating the code of conduct, and doing a disservice of unknown scope to my fellow POWs. Killing myself was one answer, and I had just decided that I was not going to do that.

Did I have any other alternatives? I had a razor blade, and I felt I had enough guts to cut the tendons in my hands. I began searching my arm to find the tendons and see which ones worked what fingers. I realized I actually did not know if one tendon did it all, nor whether in cutting the tendons, I would also be cutting the arteries. Somehow or other I could do it and I was willing.

But it was my voice they wanted most. How could I render it ineffective?' I tried to remember what I had heard about people losing their voice. As I recalled, drinking acid had done it for some. I had also heard of people who had lost their voice through being struck in the throat.

Suddenly the foolishness of thinking this way dawned on me. Or was it foolish? I wondered. Really, I did not have any choice. Before I tried, I knelt and prayed. There was no one else to talk to. I said, "Lord, is this the right way to go? Should I cut my wrists? Should I try to destroy my voice?"

When I finished praying, I still felt I had to go through with it. I decided that I would try to ruin my voice by hitting my larynx. I began pounding my throat as hard as I could. My eyes watered and sometimes I saw stars. I gave frequent judo chops to the throat that were very effective as far as judo goes. I choked and struggled to get my breath. My neck swelled up, but it did not affect my voice. I did not know if I was hitting the right spot, but anyway, it did not work. I could still talk.

Then I thought about the acid that I had heard about. I knew I could not get hold of pure acid, but my bar of soap had a tremendous amount of lye in it; so much that it would almost eat up the skin. I took my cup and filled it with a third cup of water, and part of a bar of lye soap. I crumbled, mashed and stirred it into a mushy, mucky substance. Then I began gargling with it.

It burned the inside of my mouth like fire, almost cooking it, and I accidentally swallowed some. The taste was enough to make me vomit. To increase the effect of the acid, I decided also to try to damage my vocal cords. I held a rag or towel over my mouth and screamed as loud as I could but at the same time compressing the air I was expelling so there would not be much noise. I continued this for three days and nights, staying awake as much as possible. By the third day I could not whisper. I tried all ranges. I tried to talk, then tried to sing. I could not do either. It had worked! I was now a mute—a mixed accomplishment.

I went to bed in the middle of the night, figuring I had really solved my problem. They were not going to get my voice. The next thing I would have to work on would be my hand. I dropped off to sleep, confident that I had won this battle with my captors. I would not be reading on the radio!

The next morning the gong went off. I woke up and tried to talk. I still could not make a sound. All I could do was whisper. Then I coughed—just one big cough—and it cleared the whole thing up. I could talk without any trouble. The whole effort had been a gigantic waste of time. I had gargled that terrible, nauseating stuff, my mouth was a raw mess, I had diarrhea like crazy, and my throat was sore as a boil. Three days down the drain!

On Thursday afternoon, Mickey Mouse sent for me. He had the tape recorder ready. He was fairly congenial and asked me to be seated. When he was ready, I stood up. "I have to go to the bathroom."

I had never pulled this before. He said, rather incredulous, "What?"

I answered, "I have diarrhea."

I pulled this twice. When I tried it the third time, he was boiling. "Read!"

I kept stalling. He stood up, red-faced. "Do you want to read with the ropes on?" I had pushed as far as I could.

He turned on the recorder and I started stumbling through the material. It was so bad that he could not understand me. I would not put the right inflections in, I slid through the periods and stopped at every comma. I mispronounced half of the words, and to top it off, I tried to effect a German accent. I was hamming it up so that it would have been obvious to a child.

Mickey Mouse knew what I was doing. He was so furious that he looked ready to explode any minute. He knew also that I was not going to read unless he tortured me. For some reason he was not ready to do that again. He turned off the recorder and said with venom in his voice, "You will read. You are not going to get by with this." With that threat he left and I was hustled back to my cell.

The weeks passed, though, and nothing happened. The first of June he had me in for a quiz. "We are moving you to a new camp. There you will read on the radio." I knew better than to provoke him needlessly. I did not say a word. "You had better improve your attitude, otherwise you will be back here to renew your acquaintance with the rats and cockroaches." The rats had given me a terrible time. I despised them. They were all over everything, on top of me, running around me, filthy, dirty and a menace. Mickey Mouse knew the conditions. He warned, "If you do not obey all of the camp regulations, you will be back." I had won a battle, but he was going to make sure I did not win the war.

XV

The Hanoi March

Conditions had improved at the Zoo since my brief stay in the fall. There were brooms, beds, and a rope strung across for the mosquito net. It was a great improvement over the Hilton, which was such an old, old prison. Everything was so dingy-gray and morbid there that I was tickled pink to get away. When I saw there was more than one bed in my new cell, I thought perhaps I would get a roommate. It seemed like months since I had conversed with anyone.

When I first checked in at the Zoo, I tapped on the wall but found the adjoining cell empty. In a couple of days they moved in Lieutenant Colonel James Lamar, whose arm was broken and in a cast.

The guard took me over to the camp commander who had replaced the Dog. It was none other than the Fox, the same guy who had had my mouth stuffed with newspapers. Spot was now the interpreter. He asked me if I remembered the commander. I said no. He couldn't believe it. He asked again. "You do not know him? He is the camp commander." The Fox was somewhat annoyed that I did not recognize him, but I refused to give them any little satisfaction I could withhold.

They gave me the rules and regulations on how I was to act. They informed me that I would be given a few minutes a day to exercise. "You will empty your bucket in the morning and get another bucket of fresh water to bathe your body." This was certainly an improvement.

I went back to my cell and started the new routine. I emptied my bucket in a ditch behind the building, rinsed it out, went in and took a shower from the hydrant. Then the guard gave me a two-gallon bucket, and I filled it full of fresh water. I followed him twenty-five or thirty yards to something like a bullpen made out of woven bamboo. He put me inside, closed the gates and waited for fifteen minutes while I exercised in the sun. It was a great feeling.

In my cell there was a little speaker in my room high against the ceiling which we called the Liar's Box. It was such a cheap model that the broadcasts were unbelievably garbled. Coupled with the poor quality of the equipment was the terrible English and pronunciation of the readers.

They had two or three junior Vietnamese officers who had just completed their English training. We had to sit in a certain place on the bunk and listen to each broadcast. The guards would check every few minutes to make sure we were listening. Failure to do so brought punishment.

Naturally, these young officers were concerned that we should understand the garbage they were pushing, which was the same thing over and over: "The Vietnamese cause is just. We will win certain victory. The Yankee imperialists are being defeated on every hand. The puppet South Vietnamese government is toppling by big chunks and pieces." Then they went on giving us a history of their "glorious heritage of four thousand years of successful struggle."

After such a broadcast one of the young officers would run over and ask, "How do you understand?" I would tell him, "Fine. Understand it all." The next day a different one would read. He, too, would come for an evaluation. I would tell him there must be bad acoustics, or else whoever was reading was not speaking plainly. It would wipe them out. We gave them such a hard time that they tried to make some Americans read, but that did not work either.

I did not realize it, but I had been moved to the Zoo in time to participate in one of the biggest propaganda flops the Vietnamese would try during my seven and a half years—the Hanoi March.

I had only been there a few days when they came in for my clothes. They had been stamped "TU-31," which was the camp number. Now they marked them "570" in great big numbers on both the shirt and pants in about four different places. I think they put such high numbers for propaganda purposes, to make people think there were a lot of prisoners. In 1966 there couldn't have been a hundred prisoners.

A couple of days later when I heard some activity outside, I pried the molding off my vent to look out. They were taking guys one at a time over toward the office. The guard would be inside for a short time, and then he would go and pick up another POW. Each man was blindfolded and then—something I could not figure—his sandals were tied on with gauze. Everyone had the new stamped shirts and pants on with numbers like "230," "420," etc. That meant they would be coming for me shortly.

I tried to guess what was happening. I thought it might be related to an incident that had happened at the Hilton shortly before they moved me. There had been a mob directly outside of the prison wall in New Guy Village. Some man would chant something, and then the crowd would repeat it. I did not know what it was, but the longer it went on the more ominous it sounded. Every time the leader said something, the mob would get more agitated. This went on for about ten or fifteen minutes. That day I had a quiz with Mickey Mouse, the camp officer of the Hilton. "Did you hear the people demonstrating outside your cell?" I answered no. He said, "You did not?" I replied, "No, I sure didn't. When was it?" It infuriated him when I played dumb, for he could never tell for certain whether I knew or was putting him on.

He ignored me and stated, "The people came crying out for your blood. They were demanding you be released to them. They were demanding you be brought to trial, and that your blood pay for the blood you have shed of the Vietnamese. You will be brought to trial."

I did not know what to make of it. Then, when they moved me to the Zoo, in the interrogations and over the Liar's Box they kept saying we were criminals and would be tried for war crimes.

Something was about to happen. Sure enough, they came after me, tied on my sandals and made me put on the newly marked set of clothes. They blindfolded me with my hand towel and took me over to the same place I had seen the others disappear, where I sat on the floor handcuffed to another prisoner. The guard told me, "If you talk, you will be shot on the spot. No communication." What they had not learned was that having a handcuff between us was just like a telephone. All either of us had to do was move the handcuff or put pressure on it, and we could communicate.

We could tell there were a lot of Vietnamese around still bringing in other prisoners. While they were standing talking. I began communicating with the man handcuffed to me. It was Air Force Lieutenant Jerry Driscoll. Jerry had been brought to Heartbreak Hotel and put in the end cell about two or three days before they moved me into New Guy Village. Several of us had tried regularly to contact him, but with no luck. What we did not know was that he had gotten a blow on the head when he bailed out of his plane and had not regained full consciousness for several days.

Neither of us knew now what was happening. After a while they uncuffed us and had us crawl into a couple of two-ton trucks covered with tarpaulin. Then they handcuffed us again. But our blindfolds were put on in such a way that we could see a little bit by moving the blinds.

An officer came out after the trucks were loaded and told us, "You are being taken to a new place. If you communicate, the guards have instructions to shoot you on the spot. There will be no investigation or questions; you will be shot immediately."

We traveled for what seemed thirty minutes. The tarps over the trailer bed were completely enclosing us. Was it ever hot! Finally we stopped and they took off the blindfolds.

Instead of arriving in a new place, we were in downtown Hanoi on a blocked-off street. There were forty to fifty POWs lined up in a double column down the street with maybe fifteen feet between each pair.

As Jerry and I got out of the truck they uncuffed us and marched me over to another POW and handcuffed me to him. It was Ev Alvarez, the first American pilot shot down in the Vietnam war, on August 4, 1964.

I was tickled to death to see him. Old Alvarez was hanging right in there. Because he had been there longer than anybody, it gave us all a lot of strength. If he did not complain and get bitter, nobody else had the right to, for there was always one guy who had been there longer than anybody else.

He was a strong guy. I later read a statement by one of the early releasees who chose not to wait on the rest of us. He told the newspaper reporters that the Vietnamese had said, "Quote: Alvarez is an unreconstructed hawk. Unquote." It made everyone of us so stinking proud.

When I was in the Zoo for the first time, in October 1965, Ev exercised one day in front of my cell. I could see him and we could communicate, although he never saw me. So, when we were handcuffed and in line, he whispered out of the corner of his mouth. "I'm Ev Alvarez." I told him who I was and I asked him what camp he was in. It was Briarpatch, and he told me there were forty-six others there and who the senior officer was.

I asked, "How are spirits?"

"Sky-high," he answered.

There were two trucks from our camp. In the truck I was in, there were eight people. That would make sixteen people from the

Zoo. If they brought that same number from the Briarpatch and the Hanoi Hilton, it would mean we had forty-eight POWs in the march.

Ev and I were the second pair in line. In front of us were two young fellows. Both of them were tall and one had a shock of bushy blond hair that stood up. Against the Vietnamese they looked seven feet tall.

The Vietnamese townspeople were lined up on both sides of us, from the curb to the buildings. A huge crane truck had been rigged up with platforms built on both sides and cameras and loudspeakers. The crowd in the street was very quiet and serious, but underneath there was a soft murmur.

The people were getting a little restless when we finally started to march. About a foot immediately behind each one of us was a guard carrying a rifle and an open bayonet. He was holding it as though he were charging. We were handcuffed and weaponless but supposedly so dangerous and capable of such terrible crimes that he had to be ready to plunge the bayonet in us.

As the speakers started agitating the crowd, the flash bulbs began popping and movies rolling. We were told to lower our heads, but nobody was doing it. Every once in a while our guard would take a free judo chop because we would not bow. The further we went, the more agitated the crowd became, until they started pressing in on us from all sides. Finally they got in so close that they could hit us. They began to pummel us with shoes and hit us with bottles. The two guys in front of us were walking proud and tall and would not lower their heads. Some of the political types were jumping up, grabbing their hair and yanking them down. But as soon as they turned it loose, their heads would pop right back up. There was a bunch of young hoodlums wearing caps who looked to be eighteen or twenty years old. The two guys in front were getting the hoodlums' special attention. Now and then they would drift back and catch Ev and me.

A man on the crane truck was taking pictures from an elevated platform about fifteen feet in the air. Even though we did not bow our heads, he could make it appear that way from above. The Vietnamese wanted us to show submission in front of the Vietnamese people and to the cameras. We were not about to.

The two boys in front were practically out on their feet. Each of them was holding the other one up. Alvarez was getting hit really hard, and I helped support him. There were times when I would have gone down had it not been for him holding me up. We knew that once we went down they would really work us over.

The guards were not doing anything to help keep the crowd off. That began to make the political types anxious. They started now to try to hold the people back. But the crowd had already become so agitated by the speakers that they were almost out of control. I have not forgotten the sound of that mob to this day. It was ominous.

The men and women began running in, hitting us on the fly. After one of them hit me a judo chop, I almost went out. I could not see. Fortunately Ev was able to hold me up. While I was staggering, somebody gave me an uppercut, and it nearly tore my nose off.

There were times when we could not even move. We would stop, and they would have at us. Some of the political types were trying to keep them away from us by forcing their way in front and moving the two lead POWs off again. We went for about two miles like this and ended up in the stadium in Hanoi. The crowd was really bad by the time we started in the gate. The rocks began flying. They partially closed the gate and left it open only wide enough to let us in.

Finally, when we were in, they sat us down two by two on the track. We were a pretty beat-up looking group. Some were bleeding and swollen and others sagging, semiconscious. We had really taken the punishment.

We stayed seated on the track for maybe an hour while they waited for the crowd to dissipate. It took a while, for they remained at the gates hollering, screaming and beating, trying to get in.

When the crowd finally disappeared, they handcuffed us to the person we had started out with and put us back in the trucks. This time, because it was so hot, the guards stayed at the back of the truck and pushed the tarp forward so they could stand with their heads out. I was sitting up front with my back to the cab.

We immediately began to whisper. Jerry Denton, who had been running the Zoo, reported to me what he had done and the directives he had put out. If anything, he had made them even more explicit, and tightened them up some. He had done a magnificent job, as he did the whole way through. He was an Annapolis graduate and tough as whang leather—perhaps tougher on himself than on anyone else. He had a nice build—he was five-ten and weighed a hundred and fifty-five pounds—and had heavy dark hair and eyebrows. His flashing eyes reflected tremendous energy, and he had a sharp imaginative mind. He was uncompromising in his principles—with a tender heart as big as a house.

I asked Jerry about Ray Merritt, one of my flight commanders. He said Ray had been next to him and was doing a great job. I asked him about some other people. Then he reached under the legs of Air Force Captain Bob Peel, to whom he was locked. I reached under and we shook hands. It was a wonderful feeling, a bonding of friendship that strengthened us both.

My hand-towel blindfold was up enough so that I could see quite a bit. I saw one of the guards at the other end get down on his hands and knees and creep toward us. I pressed my foot against Jerry, giving him a signal to hush, but he did not get it. I shoved him again, but he kept right on talking. When the guard got to him, he really whacked him. Somebody else was talking on the other side, and he went over and slugged him too. Then he crept over right against me. I could see his face, probably six to eight inches from me, but he was not aware I could see him through the blindfold. He stayed there for perhaps five minutes, hoping to catch me talking. I didn't say a word.

When we got back to the camp, they unloaded us and started working us over. I heard them hit Jerry Denton, and he yelled, "Ow!" so we would know they were working on him. I heard the officer say, "You were told to be silent, and you were talking," and then hit him again.

A lot of the rest of us were getting similar treatment. They handcuffed my hands behind my back. Then a couple of guards took me by the arm and started dragging me at a very fast pace. Wham! They ran me right into the back of a truck or something. Then they pulled the same stunt and ran me toward my cell. With no warning, I hit the steps full tilt with my hands behind my back. It really battered me up. I was so stiff and sore the next day that I could hardly talk. When I told Jim Lamar what happened, he said he was glad his broken arm had kept him from going.

Later, on the Liar's Box and in the quizzes, they gave us the reason for the Hanoi March. They said, "You have seen with your own eyes the hatred of the Vietnamese people. They are demanding your blood. Our law is blood for blood. You have shed the blood of our compatriots, our women, our children. Now the people are demanding your blood in payment. If you will confess your crimes and cooperate, then you will receive humane and lenient treatment. Then we will know you have laid down your arms and no longer are fighting us. But if you do not, then it will be treatment reserved for the very blackest criminal and eventually trial and probably death."

They would not admit it, but I think the whole thing was a bust. They had counted on showing the Vietnamese people that we were as cowed as their own convicts—brainwashed, or "reconstructed" as they called them. But the people did not see that in us, which is the reason our captors were so angry. We were supposed to walk with heads bowed and a hang-dog look of repentance; instead they saw some proud American airmen who had done nothing to be ashamed of.

But even more, they had hoped to release these films to the

world and to show the American people how we were being paraded through the streets of Hanoi in total subjugation. They had hoped the result would be a stampede to the White House to demand an end to the war. All it did was arouse the righteous anger on the part of the Administration and the American people themselves, so the whole thing backfired.

A few days after I was back at the Zoo, Jim Lamar interrupted me while I was tapping a message to him on the wall. Somebody was in the room next to him. When he checked it out, it was a young officer who had been captured only a short time before. He told Jim that the cell next to him had been turned into a "library." They had the *Vietnam Courier, Vietnamese Studies, The Life of Ho Chi Minh* and other material of this ilk. It was pure propaganda. For an hour or two once a week they brought each man in there.

When Jim reported back, he asked me, "Is there anything you want me to tell him?"

I said, "Yes. Pass the word around, 'Resist all attempts of the Vietnamese to get anything from you.' "

The question came back: "What if you're tortured?"

I sent back a reply: "Resist until you are tortured. But do not take torture to the point where you lose your capability to think and do not take torture to the point where you lose the permanent use of your limbs."

It was important to resist, but the propaganda value they would get out of our statements was not worth the permanent loss of a limb or of sanity. This young pilot went back and spread the word through his building.

The next day some young aggressive type, in the bullpen for his exercise period, wrote in great big six-inch-high letters: "RESIST." When the Vietnamese found it, they came running and took me over to interrogation, saying, "You are still preaching resistance and opposition. You continue to refuse our humane and lenient treatment. You will confess to this latest aggressive act."

I told them I had not written anything or ordered it to be done, and I would not confess to something I had not committed. They said, "Okay, you will be punished."

They put me in what I called the hot box, a room in which all the ventilation holes had been covered, leaving only a small crack under the door. The month of June is unbelievably hot anywhere in Vietnam twenty-four hours a day, and perspiration always poured off us. This room was as hot as a firecracker. They put me in fully dressed with my hands cuffed behind my back. I still had diarrhea at the time, with sores and boils. I was completely covered with heat rash. Diarrhea or not, with my hands cuffed behind me I could not untie the drawstring to get my pants down. I was dressed in long "pajamas"—pants and shirt. It was a mess. They did bring me food and water twice a day. One of the cuffs would be removed while I ate and I could clean myself a bit.

On the third day the guards came for me. They tightened the handcuffs down another notch and moved me outside. I had to walk in front of all the guards and the officers. One of them had a small dog, which they would sic on me. They thought that was great fun.

They took me back to my old room. My gear was still in there. They told me to sit on the bunk and listen to the radio program.

This procedure continued for five or six days. The hot box, the walk to my old cell with the dog nipping at my heels. Then I would sit on the bunk and listen to the radio program. After it was over, back to the hot box and an additional notch tightened on my handcuffs.

While this was going on, I learned how important little things can be for encouragement. There were two prisoners from Thailand. One of them had been there before I came and another had been captured in 1966. The Vietnamese were using them as slave labor. Sometimes the Thais would bring me my food. The larger one of them would open a little vent and shove my food in to me. The guards would already have opened my handcuff to allow me to eat. When I would reach out for the food, this Thai would look up and catch my eye and give me a wink. It was as though he were saying, "Hang in there, buddy. I'm with you."

On about the seventh day they took me over as usual for the radio program. I really felt I needed to talk to someone. They put me inside, sat me on my bunk and left the door open. There was a guard who walked patrol back and forth in front of my door. He would check on me each pass to make sure I was seated and listening.

When he passed, I slipped to the wall and signaled Jim Lamar. I told him what had happened to me and that I would not confess. He had just started to respond when the guard caught me. He hollered real loud, and another guard came in and began to give me judo chops and used his fists on me. He almost went out of his mind. When an officer came, he inquired what it was all about. I told him that I had been walking around for exercise and the guard had come in and started beating me. They took me back, tightened my handcuffs another notch and pushed me into the cell.

The next day when they took me over for the broadcast, they handcuffed me to a ring on the wall opposite Lamar's cell. The same guard that beat me was acting strangely this time. After the broadcast, he unlocked my handcuffs, braced me against the front wall and made me face it. I watched out of the corner of my eye as he walked behind me. He climbed up on the bunk and reached up on the wall. There was a nail sticking out which he wiggled until he finally pulled it out. He placed it on the bunk where I had been sitting. Then he came back to the wall, turned me around, and said, "Sit down."

When I sat down, I saw the nail and picked it up. He came over, took it from me and pointed at me. He locked me to the ring again and then disappeared. Pretty soon he came back and marched me to the interrogation room. I had just been framed!

Now I had three counts against me: writing "RESIST," communicating and hiding a nail. Of course I denied all of them. I was especially peeved that they were trying to lay the nail charge on me. The camp commander charged, "You hid a nail, to communicate with, and this is in violation of camp regulations."

"The guard did it," I replied.

"The guard said he found it on you."

"The guard is a liar."

"Are you calling the guard a liar?"

"Yes, I saw him pull it out of the wall and place it on my bunk. Either the guard or you are framing me."

He sent me back to the hot box and the guard pressed the cuffs to the last possible notch. Later that evening, after he had dinner and rested, the guard came over and used me as a punching bag for his judo chops. I had big welts across my face, knots on my neck, and bumps. He really worked me over.

After he left I found a position that I figured I could maintain through the night. The pain from my wrists got worse and worse. I wanted to scream, but I decided I would not give them the satisfaction. Two or three of the guards would come and look in. If they caught me groaning, they would have had a big laugh.

It was a long stinking night. The next morning my guard came in with rice. After I had finished it, they took my cuffs off and led me to the interrogation room. The interrogator said, "I understand you are ready to confess."

I was boiling. "I'm going to write what you tell me to write because of the pain—not because it is true. You know all three of these charges are lies."

"I am not interested in any of that," he said. "We will investigate later." With that he gave me a piece of paper and told me, "This is what you will say, 'I wrote "RESIST" to get the men to oppose the camp commander and his policies. Second, I communicated with other criminals. Third, I secreted a nail to use in communication with others. And fourth, I have committed crimes

135

against the Vietnamese people and am a criminal.' "

"I won't write that," I replied.

"Do you want more punishment?"

I said, "If it is necessary, but I'm not going to say that. I'll confess that I wrote 'RESIST' to the propaganda we are getting on the radio." (I was not about to admit to organizing a prison revolt.) "And I'll confess to attempting to communicate with the other officers, but that I was unsuccessful." (I knew they would lean on the other officers if they had the least excuse. We were having a rough enough time as it was.) "You know I did not hide that nail, but I'll confess to it anyway. However, the fourth is totally wrong. I have not committed crimes against the Vietnamese people, and I am certainly not a criminal. I am an officer in the Air Force of the United States of America captured in the line of duty. And I should be getting appropriate treatment as a prisoner of war according to the articles of the Geneva Convention."

With that he blew his stack, and they rushed me to the hot box. The guard took both hands and forced the cuffs to the last possible notch. It was excruciating, for my wrists and arms were already swollen.

It was not long before I agreed to write paragraph four. That was the beginning of the torture programs at the Zoo to get confessions to being a criminal. To my knowledge they got one from everyone in the camp. They printed them in the *Vietnam Courier*, and they forced some guys to read them on the radio.

That night they came for me and made me sit in the driveway outside the courtyard, and then they dumped all my gear beside me. I was not making a sound, but I could hear some other people being moved. After a short wait, a truck came and loaded me. I was blindfolded and handcuffed as usual. Somebody was sitting beside me, and we communicated by tapping our elbows. He told me he was Navy Lieutenant Paul Galanti. I had just told him who I was when the guards saw us sitting together and separated us. I was headed back to New Guy Village at the Hanoi Hilton, cell #5.

For the second time I had lasted only a month at the Zoo. The last time they had brought me back to the Hilton to bread and water and a month of stocks followed by a night of pain and torture. This time, in July 1966, I did not know what was in store, but in retrospect I would gladly have traded my first two tortures for what was to be the longest six weeks of my entire life.

XVI

The Longest Six Weeks
of My Life

Mickey Mouse, the Hilton camp officer, was on hand to welcome me back when the truck rolled in that night. He said, "Aha! You have come back to renew your acquaintance with the rats and the roaches. You should have listened to my advice to obey the camp regulations and not start trouble. Now you will be punished, but we will wait until tomorrow to start."

They took me to the cell in New Guy Village where I had been before and removed the handcuffs. The next morning when they brought me into the interrogation room, there were two men present. One of them was the Rabbit, the Cat's interpreter, who not only spoke fairly good English but also knew idioms and slang. The man sitting beside him was a rather large Vietnamese who looked part Chinese. He was about five feet ten inches tall, weighed around 180 pounds, and had a large moon-type face with the most mobile features I have ever seen. He could move his face around like the skin on a cow switching flies. He began by telling me that I had taken advantage of their humane and lenient treatment. "We have been far too easy on you."

Even though he was using an interpreter, I looked him straight in the eyes. I had always used the eyes as a weapon, and most of the enemy I would look in the eyes until they finally dropped theirs. I had never lowered mine. The quiz had been in progress for only five or ten minutes when I realized that my interrogator was from a different league than any I had confronted before. His eyes bored into mine like a drill. After only thirty minutes or so, I had to drop mine. I could not match the intensity of his gaze.

Somehow or other, even though he spoke a strange language, his eyes, the features accompanying his words and the way he said them, produced a strange effect. He would ask me a question, which I would answer with a lie. The crazy thing was, he would then tell me I had lied and proceed to relate what I really meant and thought. No matter how I tried, I could hardly ever deceive him. That really threw me.

When he asked me what I thought about the war, I would give him a half-truth, though sometimes different from what I believed. He would immediately tell me what I really thought.

"What do you think about the Vietnamese people?" For some reason I did not want to anger him. Also, I was rolling with the punches and certainly wanted to avoid any more immediate torture. I answered, "Well, they seem to be very highly motivated and industrious—and very determined fighters." When I finished he said, "You do not believe that. You think they are ignorant, duped by their government, and not far removed from savages." That was exactly what I thought, but how did he know?

I had never experienced anything to compare with this. How could he pick my brain with such ease? True, I felt pretty weak physically. The diarrhea, the confinement, the pain and harassment had really worn me down. But not this much, surely!

When they took me back to the cell for the morning meal, I could hardly eat. My mind was racing with questions. Who was this man? I had never heard any of the prisoners speak of him before. He must have been trained somewhere else. The Vietnamese did not have the capabilities to give a man this kind of training. I knew I had never met anyone of any nationality that could do what he was doing to me. Perhaps no one else had really tried, or maybe I had never been exposed to it. But I had the feeling that he was a unique person, in a league all by himself. If he had been simply a run-of-the-mill psychologist or psychiatrist, I felt I could have handled that, but this was something else.

By the time the day was over, I felt dirty and soiled as though he had been in my mind walking around with filthy old boots on. From the time they took me back to my cell I dreaded meeting him again worse than physical torture. That thought consumed every waking moment.

The next morning the guard took me out to wash, brought me back to my cell and did not even lock me in. He waited until I pulled out my shirttail. (One of the quirks of the camp was that in the presence of a Vietnamese we could not wear our shirttails inside. They wore theirs in, and we had to wear ours out as a sign of subservience.) When I had my shirttail out, he took me to the interrogation room and stood me in a corner facing a wall. No one else was in the room.

After a while I heard the door open and someone coming in. I could hear the chairs being fixed as they adjusted their seating. The Rabbit called, "Come here and sit down."

There was a little stool in front of the desk which I sat down on. I looked up at the man behind the desk and almost immediately I had to avert my eyes. The events of the day before started again, only with more intensity. Over and over again he walked into the chambers of my mind against my will, seeking to break me. After the final session that night I lay on the bunk in my cell trying to get a handle on what was happening.

The next day was the same, only worse. On Sunday, the only day we took off, I could not relax, not only because of the anguish of the day before but also because of the prospect of starting again the next day.

This thing continued for weeks. I cannot explain the apprehension and mental torture each session produced. I dreaded them as much as being thrown into a barrel of snakes. I dreaded them as a person dreads the thing that he fears most. He was not making me do anything. There were no ropes, no judo chops, no uncomfortable positions. And yet, it was as if he had a tourniquet around my head and was turning it ever tighter.

I was unable to look him in the eyes except for brief moments. The best I could do was look at the bridge of his nose or his upper lip. The expressions on his face and the tone of his voice when he snarled made each word drip with acid. Occasionally he would make me jot down his question on a piece of paper and then write an answer. He would read my answer and tell me that I was lying and misrepresenting things. For instance, one day he asked, "Do you think the Vietnamese people are right in wanting to reunite their country?"

I was so apprehensive about his catching me in another lie that I wrote something like "I believe all people have the right to freedom." I was trying to circumvent a confrontation. With venom in his voice he said, "You do not believe that. You are still opposing us in your mind. You are a Yankee who has not laid down his weapons."

That was a common tactic. Every time I did not answer a question the way he wanted it, I was opposing the Vietnamese people and still carrying arms. He hammered on this day after day and week after week.

The thought of having to face this guy the next day made every waking moment pure torture. I kept trying to recall what I had said each session because I was doing my best to defend myself. I could not tolerate the thought of joining his line and acquiescing to his thoughts. It was as though he were absorbing my will.

At times when he asked me a question, the first thing that popped into my mind was to search for an answer that would please him. It terrified me to realize that he had pushed me so far that I would give an answer to please him instead of sticking to my guns by telling him the truth or lying.

What made it doubly difficult was the realization that none of the information or propaganda he spewed was new. I had listened to the Liar's Box the entire month I had been at the Zoo. They were peddling the same old garbage that he was putting out. I had read a lot of it, too. We were so hungry for written material that we normally would read whatever our captors gave to us. They knew this and tried to capitalize on it by inundating us with their propaganda.

Luckily he never used me for propaganda. I only wrote one formal statement. He dictated it, and I wrote it on a yellow piece of paper. I thought at the time that he would probably correct it and then make me write it over and sign it. But I never saw it again, nor did I sign it.

It was their regular old line that we heard day after day, which simply was not true. They kept preaching to us that North Vietnam had been tricked. To hear them tell it, the Vietnamese people had been guaranteed that they would be reunited, and that all they really wanted were free elections. We knew that was a lie. The story of the Communist takeover in North Vietnam was a three-day blood bath in which they murdered five hundred of the top men in the country to pave the way for Communism. Their "freedom-loving people" jazz did not pull the wool over our eyes.

But despite the fact that his material was not new, he had me mentally reeling. I did not seem to have the capability to recover as fast as I needed to combat him. From the time he dismissed me in the afternoon or evening—sometimes we would have three sessions a day, morning, afternoon and night—I would spend the rest of the time in absolute misery thinking about my previous performance. Why hadn't I been able to lie to him? Why hadn't I been able to beat his eyes down? Why hadn't I been able to convince him that my way was correct and not his? It was all going his way.

Finally he got me to a certain place and seemed unable to take me any further. His intent had evidently been to force complete submission of my mind so that not only would I answer his questions as he wanted them answered, but also I would believe them. He could not take me to that place. I did not believe what he was saying, and no amount of threats or intimidation changed that. He did get me to where a good many of my answers were shaped out of the desire to please him—but that was my only defense to minimize the agony and anguish he was causing me. People who have been drugged have described similar symptoms to mine, but I never felt I was drugged—maybe hypnotized but not drugged. They did give me tea and at times I wondered if there was something in it, but I really do not think so.

He had brought me to a point where he could tell me when I was lying and when I did not believe what I was telling him. But he knew that my mind was not submitting, and that it never would as long as I had any conscious will left.

When I reached that line, I felt reassured and it steeled my will. It was apparent for a week or so, and after he ascertained it, he disappeared and I never saw him again. One morning the door of the interrogation room opened and for the first time in six weeks he was not present. It was Mickey Mouse, the Hilton camp officer. I had made it through the longest six weeks of my life.

XVII

Burning My Bridges

Now began weeks of solitary confinement. One day around the middle of October 1966, I asked the Cat, "How long are you going to keep me by myself like a caged animal?"

He waited awhile and then answered, "You have made that decision yourself. Every time we sent you to the other camp, you stirred up trouble and caused the others to resist and oppose us. You are a troublemaker, a reactionary leader and the core of resistance. Everywhere you are there is resistance, which is why you are being kept isolated.

"How long before you can rejoin the other prisoners? You will never get to be with the other prisoners again." With that he stood up and left.

Back in the cell I tried to consider the implications of his statement. It was a pretty stinking situation if I had, in fact, sealed myself off permanently from the other men. I had no doubts about the rightness of what I had been trying to do. Given the same situation, I would do it again and hopefully more effectively.

Beyond that I wanted so desperately for them to quit trying to change me. I figured if I could convince them I was incorrigible, they would leave me alone. No more torturing and harassing. No more trying to use me for propaganda. And if they really believed I was incorrigible, why wouldn't they let up trying to change me and use me?

After the devastating six weeks of intensive interrogation, I was now trying to rebuild my psyche. That guy had delivered a one-two punch that nearly put me on the ropes. To restore my sense of emotional well-being, I was burning my bridges behind me at every opportunity. I wanted them to know that regardless of what they had ever done or would do to me, I would never change.

They had tortured me into signing statements and confessing that I was a criminal. They had bent me out of shape so that I would make a tape saying I had violated the air space of North Vietnam and committed crimes against their people. Everything I had given them had followed periods of either intense punishment or excruciating torture. Every chance now I tried to underscore that everything they had been given was obtained under duress. "You know what you made me do, but you will never make a Vietnamese out of me. You will never change my heart or mind, if I am here until I die."

Telling them this was really important to me. I had a deep need to cleanse myself. My mind and soul felt dirty and I wanted to purge them clean. My chance came the next time they tried forcing me to write a statement condemning U.S. action in North and South Vietnam. When they brought me paper and pencil to my cell the instructions were: "Write or be tortured." I felt strong as a lion and really gave the old red, white and blue treatment. In three pages I spelled out my position as unqualifiedly as if I were sitting in the front room at home before I was shot down. I told them why we were in Southeast Asia, what I felt and what the other men felt. I told them our cause was just and correct. And then I described how wrong the North Vietnamese were. After I had finished and read it over, I really felt good about it. When the guard came to get it I thought, "Boy, this is going to cost me, but it's worth it."

I expected torture to begin immediately, but they did exactly the opposite. They left me alone. They even stopped interrogating me and giving me propaganda. Now it was isolation—nothing!

Then one day they moved Commander Jerry Denton into cell #4 of New Guy Village. They had brought him in from the Zoo to torture him. He was handcuffed over some sort of an iron bar so that he could neither sit nor lie down. He was just there and getting more tired all the time.

Even though we were at opposite ends of the building, we could communicate by whispering out our back windows which bordered on the wall. Our whispers would bounce off of it.

Jerry said they were trying to force him to see a visiting delegation from abroad and had really been working him over. They had used the ropes several times trying to break him, and they had bent him badly. As we talked about what was happening, we both agreed to keep going, and giving it the old college try, bucking them right down to the wire.

He told me they had forced him to say he would appear before the delegation, but he had said to them, "You can force me to go, but you can't force me to say what you want me to say. I'll blow it."

Jerry was hoping to make them fearful of trusting him. They kept telling him, "If you say anything other than what we tell you to say, we will punish you from now on."

After a while he told me, "Robbie, I have been praying, and I think what I am going to do when I get up there is appear to have a nervous breakdown. I'm just going to blubber and cry." We talked about it for a while and agreed that it just might work. I told him I would be praying for him all the time he was gone.

When they came for him that afternoon I started praying, and I prayed for him until after midnight and still he had not come back. The guards checked several times and made me go to bed. I finally went to sleep in the middle of the night, and Jerry still had not come back.

The next morning I got a signal from him quite early. He said he had blown the whole thing, and the Vietnamese were furious. After it was over they had brought him back to the torture room to write down what he had said and why he had said it. They promised extended torture for disgracing them in the eyes of the world.

The following afternoon they took him out again, and he did not come back until sometime after midnight. We talked briefly for a minute and he said, "Everything is okay." The next morning, just about daybreak, he was starting to describe in detail what had happened, when the guards came in. As they went out the door he began to sing, "Moving, moving, moving." I hollered back, "God bless you." I was alone again, but his short visit had really lifted me.

One night several weeks later they marched me over to Heartbreak Hotel. The guard turned on a special radio program and told me to sit on the bunk and not move. Immediately I began to tap on the wall. Next to me was my buddy from the Zoo, Lieutenant Colonel Jim Lamar. In the other cells were Commander Jim Stockdale, Commander Jerry Denton and Lieutenant Colonel Sam Johnson. We talked up a storm. And as an unintentional bonus, the guard left me for thirty minutes after the program was over.

Somehow Lamar had gotten word of my wife and family. It was the very first I had had since I was captured over a year before. That made the day. Then one of them said, "Robbie, why don't you get them to put you in here with us?" I asked, "What will I do?" The thought of being with them was something I would have given my eyeteeth for. They were in solo cells, but at least when the guard was out they could talk by whispering. In a little while the guard came to get me. I went back to my cell high as a kite.

Thanksgiving and Christmas 1966 I was alone and miserable. The only break in the tedium was gritting my teeth and praying as they tortured someone in the meat-hook room or the acoustic room. Occasionally the guards would leave me for a short time when they took me to the latrine to empty my bucket. There was a rathole at the bottom of the door through which I could see the door to the acoustic room. Sometimes I would see them take a guy out or bring a new one in. If the guard left us alone, I would holler out the window to whomever they had been leaning on. The acoustics were such that the noise would bounce off the walls, go in through his transom and bounce off his wall. It was just as though I were talking from the ceiling. (Before we were released, I had guys come up to me who knew I was in New Guy Village for a long time. They would ask, "Did you ever sing out the window?" I said, "Yeah." They would say, "You know what? I was standing in the room in there after my capture, and heard a voice come out of the ceiling singing, 'Have faith. Don't give up. Keep your chin up.' I would look all around and it was just like a voice right out of the sky!")

In January of 1967, I had a long quiz with the Rabbit. He said, "I want your ideas."

"Ideas on what? What do you want to know about? You didn't come here to get my ideas on everything." I could talk to the Rabbit pretty straight. Since he had worked for the Cat as interpreter, I knew him quite well.

He said, "I just want to see how you feel about things, to see if your attitude has changed."

"I still feel the same as I did when I first was brought here," I replied, "only more so. You have forced me to say things I know are wrong, to prevent harsher treatment. But you know I haven't changed and never will. You can change my words and even my actions, but you will never change my heart."

He shook his head and asked, "What are your ideas on the war?"

I gave him the red, white and blue, with no punches pulled. "We're going to win, and South Vietnam will be free of Communism when we leave." I gave him the whole works, just the way I felt.

This went on for some time. When I stopped, he would ask, "And what else?" I would answer, "Nothing else." Then he would ask me another question. I was just in the frame of mind to give it to him with both barrels. After an hour and a half or so, he said,

149

"Well, I disagree with you on all but one point."

"What point was that?"

He just shook his head and said, "You have no need to know," and I never did find out. I now had burned my bridges.

We were approaching Tet, which to the Vietnamese is Christmas, New Year's, Thanksgiving and Easter all wrapped into one. It was a traditional time of amnesty for convicts and political prisoners. We could expect a special meal and better treatment for a few days.

The Cat had me over for a special quiz, as he did on most holidays. During these times, as well as the entire length of my imprisonment, he tried to establish a rapport with me. He was so vain that he wanted me to think he was someone very important. He greatly enjoyed talking about himself and his theories, all the while trying to "build bridges between us," as he called it. "The gap between us has been formed by hate, but we should have the respect between us that normally accrues between two officers in the service of different countries. There is a special understanding between you and me." And yet, he was the one who ordered the stuffings tortured out of me. In fact, he controlled and initiated the whole torture program.

In February, during Tet, he was in a good frame of mind, helped by drinking several glasses of wine. He could turn it on and off like a faucet, but now he was quite jovial and friendly. "How would you like to go home?"

I answered, "We all would like to go home."

He said, "No. I mean before the war is over." I knew what that meant and told him no thanks.

"You do not want to be released?"

I said, "Only when everyone can go."

"You would not like to go home now?"

"No," I said, "not unless the rest are released, too."

"You know you are in our power," he threatened, "and that we can get from you anything we want."

"That may be," I conceded.

"If you would only behave and change your attitude, things would be so much better for you. If you would not continue to be reactionary, your treatment would greatly improve."

I responded, "You know there are principles worth dying for."

At that he held up his finger and said, "Wait. Let me tell you a story. There once was a woodcutter, a very old man who worked very hard for a living. He was bent and tired by many years of hard labor. Each morning, very early, he would go into the forest and toil all day long. At the end of the day he stacked his wood outside the forest, bundled it up, put it on his back and carried it to the village, where he tried to sell it to make enough money to buy food to live on.

"One day he finished nearly exhausted. He was so tired that he decided it was not worth it any longer. His daily life was one continual hardship of merely existing.

"He sat down on the pile of wood that he had cut that day and said, 'Death, come and take me. I am tired of living.'

"Death heard him. He was dressed in a long black robe with a hood. You could hardly see his face, and in his hand he held a long dagger. He walked up to the old woodcutter and said, 'I am Death. I have heard you call and I have come to grant your request.' As he drew back his dagger, the woodcutter threw up both hands and said, 'Oh no, Mr. Death, I was only kidding.' "

The Cat said, "You remind me of the woodcutter." Then he got up from his chair as though he were restless. He asked, "Would you like to have a roommate?"

Naturally I answered, "Yes, I would like to have a roommate. We all would like a roommate. It is the only humane way to treat us"—they were always impressing us with the fact that their treatment was *humane* and *lenient*—"so let us live together like ordinary prisoners of war."

He walked around the table and stopped beside me. "So you

want a roommate," he said. "I tell you what I am going to do. I am going to honor your request." I said nothing. "I am going to give you a roommate," he went on. Then he walked back around the table and stood there looking at me. "What do you think of that?"

I thought he was lying. They would dangle a carrot and then take it away to coerce us. "I think that's fine," I answered.

"What is your feeling?"

I replied, "I haven't had time to think about it."

He wanted me to show great gratification so he could get something to bargain with me. I let it show that having a roommate was of no particular significance. He was very disappointed. That ended the session, and I was returned to my cell. I was sure he was lying and never thought for a second I would get a roommate.

On the sixth of March, 1967, at about eight-thirty in the evening, I heard footsteps. Some keys rattled and the lock was opened. The door swung wide open and an American walked in.

XVIII

My First Roommate

Air Force Lieutenant Ron Mastin had only been in the Air Force a short time. He was an ROTC graduate from Kansas University, where he had been on the track team and a business major.

It is hard to describe the feelings I had when he walked in. I jumped down in front of him, grabbed him by the hand and said, "Welcome, man, welcome." The guards and Mickey Mouse stood in the door grinning.

When I realized that they were there watching to report what response I showed, I quieted down and told him where to put his bundle. We began to talk in quiet voices so the guards could not hear. I helped him put his stuff out and to arrange things. Finally the guards and Mickey Mouse, who had said nothing but only watched us, closed the door and left.

Then I was able to really tell Ron how glad I was to see him. We stopped fixing his bed, went over and sat down on my bunk and started talking. What a wonderful time that was!

I really began to pump him for information. He was from Kansas City, well educated, intelligent and very capable. He was really a bright light in a time of darkness to me.

By design of the Vietnamese he did not have much military information. I suspected all senior officers were given junior officer roommates for that reason. But Ron had a lot of information that I was interested in. My eldest son was then eighteen and just entering college. There was so much that I did not know about college—the curriculum, fraternities, the social life. I was interested in everything, besides being starved for someone to speak to. I just talked his leg off. He answered questions for a long time.

The Code of Conduct says: "The senior officer will take command, and if you are junior to him, you will take his orders." I told him right off there would be no rank differences in the cell. I insisted that we call each other by first names, and that we do everything equally. We took turns doing sweeping and emptying the bucket. There was the normal amount of banter, joking, and sometimes even a heated discussion.

One day I was throwing some pebbles out of our window. I tried several times to hit a bar and it was amazing how often I did. They were only an inch in diameter, and there was much more space than there were bars. "You know, the chances of hitting a bar are pretty remote," I said, "and yet I am doing it rather consistently."

This started a discussion that ran for days. Whatever his final conclusion, I disagreed with it. He reached it mathematically, and I could not understand it. It kept us going for a lengthy period. Anything that would cause an animated discussion was great because it broke the everyday humdrum.

I taught Ron the different communications systems we had. We would practice these every single day. Ron taught me some math. This was to be a lifesaver to me when he was moved out.

He had come from the Vegas compound, which was on the other side of the prison complex in the Hilton. It had only opened in January of 1967. He knew the names of some of the people there and had started on the tap code, so we practiced this, as well as the Morse code and some of our other systems.

I told him my feeling about things, the directives I had put out and my policies. He got to know me quite well, but I knew he would not be staying very long. When I became accustomed to having him, I believed they would threaten to take him away and try to force something out of me.

Before this happened the Bug, who was to become infamous among us, arrived to replace Mickey Mouse. The Bug was about five foot three inches, with a round face. (By the time we left he was so fat that he looked like a small Buddha.) His right eye had more white than his left, and it was also kind of cocked. When he became excited, it would veer off at an angle. Sometimes it looked like a false eye, but it was not. He would always emphasize everything by holding his finger about a 45-degree angle above and in front of his head. He would get angry and start shouting. The bad eye would look off at a tangent, and then look out! Something bad was coming.

Ron had not been there very long before they started putting the pressure on us. They began to throw a lot of propaganda material into the cell. A lot of it was atrocity stories, burned babies, maimed women and children. These were things they felt would really tug on our heartstrings. They played the children up a lot, knowing that our children were so important to us. We would give the propaganda back to them in an hour or two, or as soon as the guards would take it.

The Bug became quite angry about this, since he suspected that we were not even looking at it. Consequently he began taking me out of the cell once or twice a day to make me read the material out loud to him. After a day or two of this, I discovered that he was not listening and did not know what I was reading. Sometimes I would skip a paragraph or even a page and read it any way I wanted to; he was not listening.

One morning about the middle of April, they took me to a quiz with the Dude, another interrogator, who was something like a political commissar for the Cat. The preparation and groundwork for meeting delegations and all of the big propaganda extravaganzas were his special task. And he had even interpreted for the minister when they had the propaganda church services.

At my meeting with him he was angry, very angry. When I first walked in, he was white around the mouth. I did not know why, for he normally was much smoother than this. He started right off by haranguing me. "You have now to make a choice. You can choose life or death. You either will cooperate with us and do what we tell you or you will die. Make your decision now."

He was so angry that he was shaking. I still did not know specifically what he wanted me to do. He asked, "What is your decision?"

"I can't cooperate with you," I answered.

"I will give you one day to think, then you must make it known; otherwise your fate is sealed."

"How do I make this known?"

"You will find a way."

I went back and told Ron what had happened. I felt they were just trying to intimidate us, but I did not want Ron to feel I was making his decisions for him. After I reported what I had told them, I asked, "Do you buy it?" "One hundred percent," he answered. "Whatever you say is good enough for me. Any time you want to speak for me, feel free." (Although we shared in everything, Ron always followed my lead.)

The following day the Bug had me to a quiz. He asked, "What is your answer?"

I replied, "What is the choice?," as though I had not even talked to the Dude. He repeated what the Dude had said, "Either cooperate with us and enjoy a humane and lenient treatment, or death."

"How is the death to come about?"

"Very slow"—he emphasized it with his finger raised above his head—"and very painful."

I replied, "Well, I'll have to try it."

He shouted something to the guard, who hustled in. "If you do not cooperate, your punishment will start tomorrow."

I retorted, "I am already being punished."

He shouted, "Out!"

The next morning Ron and I went about our normal procedures. The guard opened the door when it was time to eat. I picked up the food and Ron was supposed to get the water (there was always a water can sitting there from which Ron would fill the water jug while I took the food in). As I was carrying the food Ron called out, "Where is the water can?"

"It's sitting right there."

He said, "No, it's not, it's gone."

The guard meanwhile had gone down the hall and was watching us. I called out, "Where is the *nook*"? He did not say anything and only smiled. I said, "*Nook?*" He shook his head. I began to get a little bit aggravated and made sort of a fuss about it. He stood up, came and pushed us into the cell and locked the door. That afternoon they let us have one small pot of water of a pint or less. I said, "Ron, I guess they've started." For ten weeks we had no toilet paper, no soap, no toothpaste, one bath a week, and the daily pint of water between us.

When it started we were exercising pretty hard from seven-thirty until eleven. Then we would start at two in the afternoon and go until about five or five-thirty. Since we were getting hardly any water, we decided to knock off one of the exercise periods.

Fortunately we were also washing the other prisoners' dishes. If they had not eaten all their soup, we would drink it, plus our own soup, since the hydrant water wasn't potable. But the lack of water took its toll on me in an expected way.

Early in the evening of May 24, 1967, I started having pains in my back, stomach and groin. As the evening progressed, the pain worsened. I hoped it would pass, so both of us went to bed and slept. A short while later I woke Ron up groaning.

He came over to my bunk to find out what the matter was. I told him it was probably kidney stones. Once in 1960, while stationed at Maxwell Air Force Base, I had passed out from a comparable pain. When they took me to the base hospital, it was diagnosed as kidney stones.

By two o'clock I was almost incoherent with pain. Ron finally persuaded the guard that it was serious enough to check with his duty officer. Eventually they brought a stretcher and let Ron help carry me to a truck that had been brought around. Then they drove me to a small building attached to a local hospital. In a little while a physician came out. He crawled up in the truck and started to examine me.

I was lying on my stomach groaning with pain. The Vietnamese officer told the doctor he thought I had kidney stones. The doctor raised his fist and hit me a sharp blow right over the kidney.

The last thing I remembered was pain so intense that I passed out. When I came to, I was vomiting and choking. No one would help me from the truck. They refused to use the stretcher to carry me in. I began inching my way out. On my hands, knees and stomach, I crawled to the door of the hospital.

When I got inside, I could not straighten up enough to get on the treatment table. They brusquely lifted me up and again we waited for a medic or doctor. Finally someone dressed in white came, either a medic or an intern, thumped my back and decided on the treatment.

It was a long needle into my kidney through my back, and then a couple of injections through the needle. I lay there for a while, until my guard told me it was time to go. Again, no stretcher. I hobbled out unassisted. Only if I went down (my knees buckled) would they grab hold of my arms and drag me along. I finally made it to the truck.

I was told later that the shot in my kidneys was to dilate them so that the stone would pass. This may have happened. All I know is I was in pain for days and days. They gave me medicine orally to ease that.

When I returned from the hospital, an old doctor who could

speak French came by the next day. We had seen him before, and he actually was not a bad guy. A lot of the men thought he was a horse doctor or a foot doctor. He was not very good, but neither was he unkind, vindictive or harsh. He seemed genuinely interested in alleviating the pain. His explanation to the Bug was that I had not been getting enough water. There was nothing to flush my system and that was what had caused the stones to form.

The Bug bought his explanation, for now they flooded us with water. We were even getting extra pots of water. It was coming out of our ears. They never short-changed us again. My sickness caused them more trouble than it was worth.

I started getting weaker and weaker and my nerves started to go. I had torn my clothes wallowing and crawling on the ground. Ron was trying to help as much as possible. It was so hot that he put a shirt over our broom and used it as a fan. My back was turned to him, facing the wall on my side. He started fanning me, but I was so nervous that I could not stand it when the air hit my back. Although I was burning up, hot and sweating, I begged him to stop. The pain and fatigue plus the pressure we had been under were really getting to me.

After I don't know how many days, I finally passed the stone. At least the pain ended. I had not been able to take any fluid or food for days. Now I started to recover, though I was still weak. They put the pressure back on. The Bug insisted that I read the propaganda trash to him again. Spliced in between were his threats and harangues. I started eating again; then in June I had another attack. This seemed worse than the other. Since they knew what it was, they did not take me to the hospital.

The pain literally blew my mind. Ron would hold my hand while I thrashed about. For a ten-day period I was too sick and in too much pain to eat or drink. They started bringing me bananas, sugar and canned cream, trying to get me to eat, but I couldn't. After about ten or twelve days, I must have passed the stone.

Now I began to eat some of the bananas and cream. They

brought a whole pound of sugar, encouraging me to eat it. It seemed that I was a valuable piece of property for propaganda purposes.

About the last of June, the Bug came in and inquired about my health. I had started to move around and was on the road to recuperation. He asked, "How are you?"

"I'm okay," I said.

"Is your health all right?" he wanted to know. I nodded. He said, "The staff officer [the Cat] has been intending to come and see you while you were sick, but he has been away. He will see you soon." That foretold no good.

XIX

Meeting the Delegations

Of all the indignities we were forced to undergo, I guess I resented meeting the foreign delegations more than any other. The North Vietnamese were intent on presenting a humane and beneficent appearance to the world. They did it at the cost of the blood, sweat and tears of the POWs.

There was something so basically inhuman about appearing before delegations and being asked how your food was and having to say it was excellent when it was not. Or to questions of your treatment, to lie in front of cameras and say it was great, when they had literally tortured the stuffings out of you to make you appear.

But even more than this, to make statements critical of our country and the cause for which we were in prison really tore my guts out. One of the few things that kept us going and helped us bear the humiliation was the absolute conviction that we were fighting for a just and worthwhile cause.

While I was writing this book, my hometown newspaper, the *Daily Oklahoman,* ran a 1969 picture of me smiling. The picture was supposedly taken of me appearing before a delegation. When I saw it, I cried inside. The pain and tears that finally brought me to a condition where I would appear could not be shown. Now to see it printed in my hometown paper as though it were all fun and games really crushed me.

The Dude felt I should have a special affinity for the first delegation I appeared before because they were to be Caucasians.

I said, "I won't do that." He told me what was going to happen if I did not. When I told him I still could not do it, he said, "It is not going to be very bad." Again I explained that I could not do it. He told me I had no choice. I agreed with him and said, "I have no choice, I cannot." This went on and on. When he told me there would not be any recording, I let him know that made no difference. He said, "These are Caucasians from the Western world," although he did not know from which country.

We had several sessions a day for almost a week. I was adamant. Since I was just getting back on my feet and they wanted me to look good, they started easy at first on the torture. They put me in the corner with my hands held straight above my head. If my hands came down, they would whop me one.

After a day of this, the Cat came in. He was snarling, his clothes were rumpled, and he did not have a tie on. He said he was tired of coddling me, and went through his standard routine that he did not make threats—he carried out his word.

Then he repeated a little story he had told me when he was in a more congenial frame of mind. "We have many poisonous snakes in Vietnam and we have an antidote for them. We carry a little medicine bottle attached to a string around our neck. If we get bitten, we just drink this and it saves us. But there is one snake for which we have no antidote. If he bites you, you die immediately. That is the wood snake. He is only a little short snake, about as round as your little finger or smaller and perhaps a foot long. He is quite harmless as he lies on the dry wood—unless you disturb him! Once you disturb him, he is deadly."

The Cat looked at me with venom in his eyes. "You can just think of me as the wood snake. Do not disturb me.

"I do not have time to bargain with you. Furthermore, I have no intention of bargaining with you. I have been polite to you because of our relationship. But you will not have that, so I must treat you now as captor and captive. You will do what I tell you, and you will say what I tell you to say. Is that clear?"

I answered, "I understand your words."

"Do you want me to use force on you right now?"

"No," I replied.

"I am through toying with you," he continued. "I am through bargaining with you. I will have your answer. You will do what I tell you, and you will appear before this delegation."

I said, "I cannot do it."

With that he left and they brought in the ropes and started to put them on. He had always done what he said he would, and he meant business now. I said, "Okay. I will appear." My only hope was to bargain with them on what I would say.

The Cat came back. I was standing in the corner. He snarled something, and I sat on the stool in front of the desk. I was to meet an East German delegation. "These are the questions they will ask you. Here are the answers you will give them." He read them off one by one. One of them was, "How do you think the war should be settled?" My answer was to be, "The United States should withdraw all troops from South Vietnam, dismantle all bases, and cease all aid to the puppet government of Thieu."

I agreed to the others, but I said, "I can't say that."

The Cat exploded. "This is not a request. It is a direct order!"

I said nothing else. They made me record my answers. They would ask the questions, and I would answer them. Then we would listen to them.

He appeared satisfied, and as a reward he gave me two pictures that Kathleen had sent of the kids and her. I could not believe it was they. When I got back to my cell, I was lost for hours staring at each of them. It had been two years since I had last seen them. It was an unbelievable feeling to hold them in my hand, if only in a couple of pictures. That night I placed them to my lips, said a prayer for each one of them, and told them good night.

I was taken before the East German film crew on July 3, 1967, the day before Independence Day. My nerves were so bad, they were jumping like frog's legs in a salt barrel. I felt as if I were suppressing a deep scream. Before I went in, the Bug sat me down and made his usual threats as to what they were going to do if I did not come through for them.

Since I had been sick, I did not look very good. My ankles were swollen and discolored. There were dark circles under my eyes, and I was more haggard than usual. To make me look relaxed they gave me some hors d'oeuvres, a bottle of soda pop, and offered me chewing gum. Before the cameras started rolling, the German film crew came around. One of the guys started talking to me. When the Bug saw I was alone with him, he ran right over beside me for fear I would tell them something that had not been programmed.

When the questions started, I tried to vary my answers from what I had been briefed. I desperately tried to show that this was not a voluntary appearance. I dangled my scarred ankles in front of the cameras. The Cat, who was standing off to the side, was furious with me during the whole appearance. During an intermission for fifteen minutes or more, the Cat, the Bug and the Dude told me what I had said wrong. The Bug said, "I will throw you out of the truck on the way back to camp, and let the townspeople have you. They will tear you to bits." When we went back in for the final session, they made me ask for the questions to be rephrased and to answer them exactly as rehearsed. I guess I didn't come through for them.

After it was over, I signed a statement for the German film crew. They filmed me while I was signing it. Since I had no glasses, I could not even read what I was signing. The Cat made it clear I had no choice.

I was angry, and yet my nerves were so bad that I was coming unglued. The mental anguish caused by what I was doing, coupled with the knowledge that I could not do anything about it, was unbearable. When we finished, one of the film-crew members said, "Wipe the sweat off. You've looked terrified the whole time." I was glad to hear it.

Then he said, "I understand you have two pictures of your family. We would like to use them, and then we'll give them back to you." They were going to use the pictures of my smiling family for their lousy propaganda show! I muttered, "Ask the Vietnamese." That made the Cat more furious. They said, "We will." As they took me back to the truck, they knocked me around a bit.

They had me reeling. I hoped I had thrown a hitch into things, but I was not sure it was enough. I was really down when I got back to the cell and when I told Ron about it, I broke down and cried like a baby. I couldn't help it.

The Bug had told me he would be coming for the pictures. "They'll never get to use those pictures," I told Ron. "They won't use my family for propaganda. I'll die before they do that."

So I tore up the pictures in little bitty pieces. It was like tearing my heart out. Then I put them with a rock in a piece of paper and sunk them in my waste bucket, which was almost full to the top with Ron's and my refuse.

The Bug came in after a while and said, "I have come for your pictures."

"I've torn them up," I told him.

He blanched. "You are lying! You would not tear up the pictures of your wife and family."

I had had two cellophane covers to keep them in, so I said, "Here are the empty containers."

He exploded and hollered for the guard. After posting him in the cell to watch me, he ran to report to the Cat, and soon I was taken to interrogation. The Dude was running it. The guards put me on my knees and the Dude began to harangue me about disgracing them in front of foreign dignitaries. They demanded the pictures. I told them they were gone . . . destroyed.

They did not believe me. They were almost white with anger.

Also, they were scared of what the Cat was going to do to them, I guess. (They could have gotten the pictures while I was meeting the Germans; then they had left me alone in the cell and now I would not produce them.) They were really under the gun.

They said, "We will get the truth from you." They called Big Ugh, a mean torturer who, as his nickname indicated, was big and ugly. He was one of the largest Vietnamese around and he enjoyed his work.

He threw me down on my side. The ropes were no longer being used, for they left permanent scars. Instead, he was using a nylon strap, about one inch wide, that had come off one of the survival kits connected to a parachute. It was heavy, slick and tough. He started pulling my arms together and forcing my shoulders behind me by pressing them with his knees and pulling. Then he sat me up and ran a strap over my right shoulder and around my crossed feet in front of me. He pulled it back up across the left side of my neck, over my shoulder, down through my arms and around the rope that had been used to tie my arms. Bending me forward and bouncing with his knees on my back, he began pulling up the slack. When he had me good and solid with my feet under my throat in one solid piece, he tied it.

I began to groan and strain to get my breath. When I hollered, they filled my mouth with rags. I was having difficulty making a sound, but I could still scream in my guts. Big Ugh drew up a chair, sat down and put his feet on the table. He enjoyed it. I don't know how long they let me scream. It probably seemed longer than it was.

Later Big Ugh left and the Dude, the Bug and the Rabbit came back in. The Dude pulled the rags out of my mouth and said, "Be silent." By that time I had no way of controlling my screaming. He said something to Big Ugh, who loosened the straps. The Dude ordered me, "Stand up." All I could do was groan. "Get up. Immediately!" he shouted. I could hardly move; there was no way I could stand.

After a while I managed to crawl toward their table. They began interrogating me. They kept saying, "Wipe your face." Big Ugh had mashed my nose and cut my head. I did not bother. They wanted to know where the pictures were. "I told you. I destroyed them." The Dude said, "All right. We punish you again."

Big Ugh started toward me. I had had about all I could take. "I tore them up, I said!" They still did not believe me. I assured them that I had. But I did not want them to get the pieces, so I would not tell where they were. Back in the ropes again.

Big Ugh did a better job on me this time than before. He worked on me quite a while before getting everything snug and tight. He was really brutal tearing the skin off my shoulders and neck and cutting them deep. The same procedure on my ankles. Everything was bleeding, but I didn't even notice that. I was in too much pain. When they bend you up like that, everything protests. Your hip joints pull and are almost dislocated. As I well knew, they can pull your shoulders out of joint if they want to work on it. You are already sticking out in front like a ship's prow and then they bend you forward and put your feet up against your throat and mouth. You are forced forward and compressed so that you can hardly get your breath.

Another thing that works for them is that you don't know how long you are going to be in this position. The first time around when they are seeking information, they normally let you up once you say "Okay, I'll talk," because they are eager to get the information. But when they are punishing you to get propaganda, they want to hurt you bad enough not only to teach you a lesson but also to convince you that it is worthless to resist. They want to make you into an animal that will react like Pavlov's dog.

They left me longer this time. It is hard to explain your feelings after you have been in pain like that for a long time. It sucks your will in a hurry. You start balancing the pain against the value of what they want. I wanted desperately to protect my family, by not letting the Cat and the others get their dirty hands on those pictures. Those pictures were sacred. I could not bear the thought of letting them have them. It was almost a question of the principle of right and wrong.

After a substantial length of time in the straps the second time, they came in and ordered Big Ugh to release me. Then they told me to sit on the stool in front of the desk, which I could no more do than I could fly.

They had really hurt my back. It seemed paralyzed. I thought maybe they had seriously injured me, for I could not move my legs either. I finally started coming around, and I was able to get up on my hands and knees. The harangue lasted a long while this time; while it was in progress I finally made it up on the stool.

The Dude really wanted the pictures. I still refused, but when they started to put me back into the ropes a third time, I said I would get the pieces.

Two guards dragged me back to my cell. They had Ron stand braced, face against the wall, with his hands above his head. I was groaning with pain the whole time.

I had to put my hand in the waste bucket and search around until I found the pictures. When I retrieved them, they threw water over them out of our water jug and took me back to the quiz.

Both the Dude and the Bug were furious. I had disgraced them and caused them to lose face in front of a foreign delegation. Big Ugh started working on me again. He pulled both hands up behind me to the base of my neck and put bracelets with tightening screws on them. They were about an inch wide, and you could tighten them right to the bone. Somehow he twisted my arms in such a way that I could not bring them down.

Then he put the jumbo iron on my left leg. This was a bar twelve to fifteen feet long and about an inch and a half in diameter. It had a U device that fitted snugly around the ankle with the bar running through the eyes of the U-shaped device and resting against the lower shinbone. The device would also pull down on the tendon in back. Every time there was motion it would slide down a little more, putting more pressure on the ankle.

They tied one end of the bar to the right side of the stool so it was balanced, and then tied both of my legs to the stool so I could not move, and left me. The entire weight of the jumbo iron rested on my left ankle.

I was so glad to be out of those ropes that for a while the bar and bracelets did not bother me too much. Then the pain set in. My arms began cramping and my right shoulder was really giving me fits. My left leg and thigh began to feel as if they were on fire.

Sometime during the night I heard Ron go past. I did not see him again until shortly before our release. I could hear his bucket rattle, and I knew his walk. He was trying to tell me he was leaving. During the night, Pigeye (whom I did not consider especially vindictive, just an efficient torturer) came in and took off my handcuffs and the bar from my leg. He gave me some soup and rice to eat. After I ate, he put the bar and cuffs back on. Shortly before daylight they took them off and returned me to my cell. After putting my feet in the leg stocks, they twisted my hands into an unnatural position, and handcuffed them that way. If I relaxed, it was even more painful. I was sitting up, of course, and could not lie down. When I accidentally fell backward on the handcuffs, one of them would sometimes close another notch, which was excruciating.

My stomach muscles were quite strong and so were my back muscles. Fortunately I could hold myself forward for long hours. But in doing so, I sat right on the lower pelvic bones. I haven't very much covering there and it was not long before the skin was worn right through to the bone—raw.

There was no reason to yell calf rope. They were furious at what I had done and were determined to punish me. I was not going to give them the satisfaction of hollering, if at all possible.

When they brought in the food, they would unlock one of my handcuffs so I could eat. It was terribly hot. I was dressed in shirt and pants, and covered with heat rash and boils. The handcuff on my right wrist was biting into the bone, and my wrist was becoming infected. Four or five infections developed on my right wrist and began erupting and running. The arm was swelling from the elbow down to my fingertips. It was most unusual-looking. I did not think an arm could swell that much and keep from bursting. Then I started getting red streaks up my arm and shoulder. The guard would look at them and I suspected he was reporting it. But nothing was being done. Then my wrist got so big that he could not close the handcuff. Evidently, though, he had his orders, so he would use both his hands and force it into the flesh, and the bloody pus would run down my fingers.

To make it, I prayed by the hour. It was automatic, almost subconscious. I did not ask God to take me out of it. I prayed he would give me strength to endure it. When it would get so bad that I did not think I could stand it, I would ask God to ease it and somehow I would make it. He kept me.

Finally, though, the pain and aching increased to where I did not think I could stand it any longer. One day I prayed, "Lord, I have to have some relief from this pain." I quoted the Biblical verse that He would hear us and that we would never be called upon to take more than we could bear.

While praying, I fell backward out of fatigue and my handcuff hit the bed. This time when it did not close and lock another notch, it started me thinking. I fell sideways over the edge of the bed where there was a sharp edge. I reached over and hooked the ratchet of the cuffs on the bed. Then I pulled with all my might and the right handcuff came completely undone.

They had left me in the stocks for so long that I hadn't been able to relieve myself. I was already fouled up enough, and I did not want to urinate in my clothes again. I was bursting. I had gone so long without relieving myself that I had a bladder lock. So I prayed, "Lord, you got me out of the handcuffs. Now I have to get out of these stocks." There was a big lock on the end of my leg stocks that secured the two pieces of iron together. I reached over with my right hand, which was all swollen out of shape, and pulled back and jerked the lock one time, and it unlocked. I opened the stocks, got up and hobbled to my waste bucket, which was about one step away.

After I relieved myself I climbed back into the stocks, locked the lock and put my hand back in the cuffs. I felt ever so much better, because I was no longer in pain from inside. I only locked my right cuff one notch, and I did not push it the rest of the way until I heard the guard unlocking the door. On one other occasion when I had just reached my limit, I was able to unlock the handcuffs. But I was never able to do it again.

When I had been in the stocks and cuffs for ten days, I reached the stage when my mind was no longer working. The pain and fatigue were such that I could not even remember the names of my children or my wife. Praying for the Lord to help me bear the pain was not enough now. On the tenth morning I prayed, "Lord, I have had all I can take. I am asking you to take me out."

After a little while I lost track of things. I awoke with a start to discover Pigeye standing by my bunk. I did not know what was happening now as he stood looking at me. I must have looked a sight in my filth and with my swollen arm. He actually looked compassionate. Finally he said, "*Bao cao*," with an insistent tone in his voice. Then he pointed to the office. Normally, if we wanted to talk to an English speaker or to an officer, we would tell the guard "*Bao cao*," which meant "report." That is all we were supposed to say—nothing else. Now here was Pigeye asking me to "*bao cao*."

"This must be the answer to my prayers," I thought. I said, "Okay. *Bao cao*." He unlocked my right handcuff, left and came back with pen and paper. Then he took off both handcuffs, my feet out of the stocks, and helped me over to the other bunk so I could write.

My hand was so swollen that I could not get my fingers to close. They were like huge balloons, and the skin around my wrists was black, with big red streaks running up my arms to my shoulders. The only way I could hold the pen was to wrap my towel around it.

I wrote a letter to the camp authorities apologizing for causing them trouble—that was a word they always liked to use—and promised to try to do better in the future. It was about two paragraphs. I signed it, Pigeye took it and left me there.

In about five minutes another guard was back just as mad as could be. He motioned for me to get on the bunk. He opened the stocks, stuck both my legs in and then slammed the stocks closed as hard as he could. If my legs hadn't been exactly in place, he would have broken both shin bones. He grabbed my hands, twisted them and ran the handcuffs up until they went tight against the bone. All the time he was muttering, "*Bao cao! Bao cao!*" I didn't know what the matter was, but after he left I concluded they were not satisfied with my letter. It hadn't been very apologetic.

Several hours later another guard came in. I said "*Bao cao.*" I couldn't take any more. He brought a pen and paper immediately, released the cuffs and let me out of the stocks. I wrote another, more abject apology, which evidently sufficed because they let me stay out of the stocks and handcuffs.

I lay down on the bunk where I had been in torture and put a folded pair of shorts up on the stocks. I put my head on them, stretched out on the bunk and slept the night through. I don't think I moved until dawn of the next morning.

During the day a medic came in and pulled the core out of one of the worst boils. I could see the exposed tendons working in my wrist. Then he gave me some shots for the blood poisoning.

Their first test to see if I were deserving of their "humane and lenient" treatment was to appear before a North Korean delegation. I was given explicit instructions by the Cat: "I remind you of the wood snake. Do not anger me again! If you make a mistake—even one—I will not be lenient this time."

When the time came I walked in, and according to prior

instructions, stood with bowed head awaiting an order to straighten. For five minutes I had to stand at a 60-degree angle in front of the North Koreans. Finally the order came to stand up.

There were two interpreters. The questions would be asked in Korean to a Vietnamese, who translated it to Vietnamese. Then another Vietnamese would ask me in English. I answered him in English, and he gave it back to the Vietnamese, who would retranslate it into Korean.

One of the first questions was, "How many crimes have you committed against the Democratic People's Republic of Korea?" They knew my background and that I was a Korean ace. I answered, "I have never committed a crime against your country." They asked, "How many Korean villages have you bombed?" I replied, "I have never bombed your country. The only thing I have done in your country is to shoot down eight of your aircraft in air-to-air combat." They kept asking this same line of questions, and I kept answering the same. I was trying very hard not to offend them.

After a while I was taken out and the Cat appeared to be quite angry. He said, "You will write a letter of apology to our comrades in the struggle against the American imperialists!" Then he dictated a letter that said something like "I apologize for my insolent attitude to the distinguished representatives of the Democratic People's Republic of Korea. I apologize for lying because I have committed many grave crimes against your people and country for which I am sincerely sorry." I signed it.

Evidently they thought I was doing better, for not too long after that the Dude informed me that I was to meet another delegation. This time, of all things, it was an American—an American woman.

They briefed me on what to say and what trend the conversation should follow. They said, "Maintain control of the conversation."

I asked, "What do you mean?"

"We do not know her too well and do not want her asking leading questions. Do not say anything—regardless of what she asks you—do not say anything to disgrace or slander our country. If you do, you will suffer for the rest of the time you are here"—as though I hadn't been!

They showed me a magazine that had articles written by Mary McCarthy on her visit to South Vietnam and also some about the bombing. To meet her, they took me over to another camp, about three miles from the Hanoi Hilton, which was called the Plantation. It was a nice-looking prison, where the staff was headquartered. I sat at the end of a coffee table, for this was supposed to be very informal. Mrs. McCarthy was on my right. She was a rather large woman and looked as though she might have been a sports enthusiast in her earlier years. Next to her was the president of a Vietnamese friendship committee between the Americans and the North Vietnamese. Naturally, the Dude and the Rabbit were present. Immediately on my left was the Cat.

I was in my regular prison garb. They had brought me needle and thread to sew my buttons back on and repair it. It looked more decent now.

The interview was in fact much more informal than any of the others. She said her husband was a diplomat in Paris. She asked me about myself, and told me she had requested the interview to be with me. She also talked quite a bit about Senator Eugene McCarthy and his chances for the presidential nomination, about which she was optimistic.

Then she wanted to know what I missed the most. I told her a Bible. She asked, "Don't they give you Bibles?" I said no. She was a rather forceful woman. When she turned to the Cat and said, "Can I send him a Bible?" it caused a big flap. While they were talking, she said, "How about if I sent Bibles for everyone? Can't they have them?" The Cat said that would cause problems and they put her off.

Then she asked, "What else do you miss?" I said, "Sweets."

She said, "I'll send you a cake." Then she turned and asked the Cat, "Can I send him a cake?" The Cat replied, "He does not need that. We give him plenty of wholesome foods." Then he looked at me. "Isn't that right?" I answered yes. He explained further, "We provide these things for all the prisoners. And besides, cake would spoil."

Then she asked them a different kind of question. They began to circumvent it. Finally she looked at me and said, "You know, I don't think they understand me." I raised my eyebrows and said, "I think they do." Another time she mentioned hopes for an early end to the war. "We had better knock on wood," and she knocked three times on the table.

I was in interrogation for three hours trying to convince the Dude that raising eyebrows and knocking on wood were not secret signals.

I sometimes wondered if Mrs. McCarthy was playing a dual role. I know I suffered because of her request to see me, and to my knowledge she did absolutely nothing to help our cause. This was true of all the appearances. The Vietnamese were not about to show anyone who would throw a monkey wrench in the façade they had created for the world.

XX

The Passing of the Night

It was the middle of the morning in early August when I heard a clatter outside my window. The guard had brought my meal to me a few minutes earlier, and I was sitting on the end of the bunk eating. At first I didn't know what was happening, then I realized that my only source of light was being closed off. Despite the fact they had really hurt me bad, they evidently did not feel I was coming through for them enough.

A Vietnamese convict appeared and then another, and they began boarding up my window. It started getting darker and darker. Soon I could hardly see the opposite wall, nor my hand in front of my face. As I watched, all of a sudden the base of my neck started turning hot. It was almost as though a blow torch were directed against it. It became so uncomfortable that I wet my hand towel and put it on the back of my neck.

I was becoming so agitated and nervous that I could not sit still. I stood up and began to walk while eating my food. For nearly a year after that, I never sat down to eat my food.

It was not fear of the dark, for I had been in the dark before. But something strange was happening to me. I began trying to calm myself, saying, "Now you're acting foolish. Just go over and take a nap. Prove to yourself that being in a dark room is not going to bother you."

I walked over to the bunk, folded my shorts, put them on the leg stocks and laid down my head on them. The agitation continued to build and build. At the end of five minutes, I thought I was going crazy. I jumped up and began to run up and down the room. I ran and ran and ran. Sometimes I switched to push-ups and then sit-ups. It was a couple of hours past the nine-thirty gong when I finally stopped that night after hundreds of push-ups and as many as a thousand sit-ups.

It was as if I had an animal on my back. Absolute panic had set in. The fact that I could not control this thing driving me or get rid of it caused me to be even more panic-stricken. I could not understand it, and I could not get rid of it.

Sheer desolation permeated the miserable dark cell I lived in twenty-four hours a day. I was absolutely convinced I would never get to leave that cell until the war was over. And I had no idea when that would be. What I was going through would continue for as long as I could think. I was not scared of anything they would put me through because I felt they had already done their worst. But I was terrified because I could not get rid of the panic. I would go to sleep only after I was completely exhausted, then awaken during the night—at twelve, two, three—and immediately jump up and start running. The instant I awakened, the shock of it would hit me—there I was, in the same place where I had gone to sleep. It was always going to be that way—until the end of the war.

One of the worst times was when the sirens went off for an air alert. The guard would make me get under the bunk, which almost drove me out of my mind. I did push-ups and leg lifts under the bunk—anything to keep moving.

Because of having exercised methodically most of the time of imprisonment, I automatically kept track of how much I was doing. I knew approximately how long or how many steps it took me to run a mile. To combat my panic, I would run as much as twenty-five miles a day. My only salvation was exhaustion—the only time I could stop running.

A couple of months later, around October, I began to get a

little relief for an hour or two at noon by thinking of math problems that Ron and I had worked on. I had never liked mathematics before, perhaps because I did not understand it. But now it furnished me a welcome respite.

Ron had helped me review things like square root and fractions. And what was especially helpful, he had taught me to solve for unknowns. Because of the darkness I couldn't see well enough most of the time to write anything down, so I had to use relatively simple equations. But even then I could make up simple problems with as many as three unknowns and solve them in my mind.

For about a two-hour period during the day, there would be a reflection of the sun that was just right. A small rathole at the base of the brick wall let the sun shine on the end of my bunk. I would work a math problem on the end of my bunk with a piece of brick if the guard was not around. When I had made mistakes and could not find the solution, before the sun went away I would write down the problem under my bunk and set my waste can on top of it to save it for the following day. I was careful not to have anything written on days I felt we were going to have inspection, for they searched with a flashlight. Math became something like a personal friend because it was one of the few things to provide a break in my twenty-four-hour routine of terror, which went on for month after month after month.

Sometimes it would give me great relief to scream. When I thought I was going to die if there was not a change, I would hold something in my mouth and another rag over my face and just let myself holler.

Other times it seemed to help to cry. I remembered having read that women live longer than men because they are able to get rid of suppressed emotions by crying. I needed any outlet possible. I cried a lot. Much of it was out of concern for the other guys in prison.

To keep the guards from seeing me or hearing me, I buried my head in the blankets. At night under the net, after I had sufficiently exhausted myself so I could go to bed, I would cry; and if that did not help, scream.

When it seemed as if I could not go another minute, that I had to get out of that dark room to see somebody and talk to them, I would say, "Robbie, you can make it one more minute." Over and over I would tell myself that anybody could take anything for one more minute. "Regardless of what happens, I can take it one more minute." I literally lived one minute at a time.

There were times when I thought I would have to *"bao cao"* and tell them, "I'll do whatever you want me to. Just take me out of this black room and give me someone to talk to." I prayed. I ran. I exercised. I hollered and I cried, but I did not capitulate. I was hanging on like a man hanging on to a cliff by his fingernails.

I did my best to hide what was going on from the camp command. They knew, though, what they were doing. If they tried something and it didn't work, then they would try something else. They had all the time they needed with people doing nothing except trying to break us. This was their total job, twenty-four hours a day.

Then one evening in June 1968, after almost ten months of darkness and solitary confinement, the Bug came in. He said, "Fold up. You are going to move." I had had no indication I was going to move at all. He was snarling and angry. I asked, "Am I going to leave this room?" He answered yes. I was really surprised and wondered if he wanted me to take the clothes and all. He said, "Take everything! Take the strings, the clothesline, everything!"

He was very curt and like his old self. Evidently the civilians had routed the military out of this particular cell. I was the only American POW in that section of the Hilton which held around 850 Vietnamese civilian prisoners. By his attitude, I concluded that he was angry about my moving for he knew it meant that I could communicate with the others now.

It was after dark but they blindfolded me anyway and then led me by the arm through some places I felt sure I had never been. I suspected they were taking me to Vegas, where Ron, my old room-mate, had come from. When they took off the blindfold I immediately looked to see if there were any windows. There, as beautiful as anything could be, were two small windows with shutters on them, and both of them were open. I could not believe it!

Big Ugh was there to meet me. Although he was not my turn-key, I guess they felt he had hurt me bad enough so that I would be intimidated by him. He gave me my instructions. I was not to belch, nor pass wind. In other words, I was not to make any sounds at all, not even with the bucket lid. If I did—he pantomimed the ropes.

The next morning I could hardly wait for the sun to rise. By going back against the wall, I could see outside. There was a run-way or an alleyway between my building and the shower stalls. Prisoners were going back and forth between me and the showers. I could see everyone who lived in the building next to me. I could wave at them and get their attention.

I had made it. The night had passed and the sun had risen. Here were friends. Whatever was ahead, I felt that now I could take it. Fortunately there was someone on the other side of me, although he did not yet know the tap code. Soon I had taught him, and effective communications began.

I began to devise ways of communicating with the rest of the men. Because of the explosive political scene in America in 1968, we were getting a heavy barrage of propaganda. What was especially difficult for us was that some outstanding Americans had begun to say the same things that we had been *tortured* into saying.

All of us knew of the great majority with which President Johnson had been elected in 1964. Now to have such opposition, with riots, demonstrations and protest marches was difficult to understand. What had changed to warrant this kind of reaction?

We were seeing Communism as it really was—harsh, repressive and cruel. Anyone who envisioned North Vietnam as anything other than a totalitarian dictatorship was totally confused. From the birdseye perspective we had, North Vietnam was not worth one riot, demonstration or protest march.

One thing the demonstrations did was to help us focus on what was really important. In our controlled living situation, we had to reduce everything to sets of easily understandable and communicable positions. We did not have the resources, nor were we permitted the opportunity, for discussion and debate. There were no subtleties or nuances. To present a unified stance required some very basic, clear positions. These positions were determined by the effective senior ranking officer at the particular POW camp. Sometimes the actual senior ranking officer was so isolated that he had no channels of communication. But whoever was the effective senior ranking officer devised the stance and policies which should be followed.

When I was in charge, I tied it into a pretty simple package for myself. Maybe it was not always totally accurate, but when I was under terrible duress or alone for long periods of time in a dark room, or being tortured or harassed, I needed something simple. It could not be complicated or intricate. It must always be there, it must be strong and it must never change—that is what I had to have.

That is one of the reasons we all spoke so similarly when we came out. We had to home in on something that would give us strength on a minute-by-minute basis. We could not afford the luxury of changing horses in midstream. Our stance had to remain static and strong. It was reduced to four essentials:

First, when shot down, we were American fighting men, fighting the enemy of freedom and of our way of life—international Communism. We were fighting not only the North Vietnamese but also to maintain the freedom of all Southeast Asia. Many of us had been to Senior Service Schools; several had master's degrees in political science and international relations. We were not in a vacuum. We knew what we were fighting for and we believed in it.

As prisoners of war, we did not stop fighting. Our job was not done; it was just beginning—only now we had to fight without guns, airplanes or bombs. All we had was our minds, our faith, our pride, our determination—and our "Yankee ingenuity."

The longer we stayed, the more we realized the importance of not providing the Vietnamese with any propaganda resources, for we were their prime war weapon. They did not have the power of military retaliation against the American forces, but they could use us as a propaganda tool in an area in which they were really very good—influencing world opinion. This was where they hoped to win the war, not on the battlefield. The real battlefronts for the Vietnamese were the capitals of the world and the streets of America.

The second essential way was duty to our country. That may sound like flag waving. But that misses the point. Duty to our country was something to focus on in prison. For "country" is an all-encompassing term. It includes the Administration, the state governments; it includes our freedoms and rights.

The most visible and obvious symbol of our country was the President of the United States, for not only was he our Commander in Chief as military men, he was also elected by the people. His viewpoints and philosophy had the backing of the majority of the nation. At first President Johnson and then President Nixon stood for the goals and aspirations of our nation. We were proud of them as they led our nation through a terribly difficult period.

Another aspect of duty to our country that we realized had been overlooked by too many of us was patriotism. We had permitted the nuts and the kooks to make honest-to-goodness patriotism a dirty word. Many of us had not been as forthright as we should have in claiming the heritage that was ours as citizens of a great nation. In prison we had a reappraisal of values. The flag, our President and what this country represents are things to stand up and be proud of.

The Vietnamese kept getting this line from us, and in turn

they started to pick the country apart. "Your country stands for equality, and yet look at the way America is treating the minority groups." They would pull in every news item and every bit of propaganda to show that the minority groups in the United States were being mistreated or receiving unequal treatment. They purported to show that the majority of the men being killed in the Vietnam conflict were black.

If America was founded on "justice and liberty for all, what are you doing over here in South Vietnam? Are you promoting liberty in South Vietnam?"

All the time we were imprisoned, they tried to convince us that we were not doing what was best for our country. They wanted us to believe that we had been misled. Our cause was an unjust one; consequently, we were guilty of committing criminal acts. Against that onslaught, it required some pretty basic convictions.

Third, we believed the American people were behind us. We were fed an unceasing stream of propaganda on the pouring of blood in the files at the induction centers, the burning of flags and draft cards, and protest marches. We were told continuously that demonstrators were representative of the true Americans. We knew this was an out-and-out lie. We knew the American people to be honest, stable, and in general supporting the Administration in time of need.

Everything bad in our society was pointed out on a day-to-day basis—the inequities, the crime, the inflation, dirty politics, any dirt under the rug. We knew America was not perfect, but we knew it was not anything like what they wanted us to believe. We knew it to be the best place on earth.

And we knew the American people had not changed. We were only doing what any other American fighting man would have done. We were American citizens in uniform, trained to fight in an area of need. We were not a select group. We represented America and the American people.

All of us hated to hear of the Watts riot, or the assassinations of Martin Luther King, Jr., and Senator Robert F. Kennedy. But that did not make us believe, as the Vietnamese tried to convince us in 1968, that those were political assassinations planned and executed by high administrative circles. That was how their government operated, not how America operated.

But as important as all of these were, none was more important than the fourth—faith in God. Before imprisonment many of us had been too busy to put God first in our lives. A North Vietnamese prison cell changed that. We learned to feel at ease in talking about God, and we shared our doubts and faith. We prayed for one another and spent time praying together for all kinds of things. Our faith in God was an essential without which I for one could not have made it.

I often ran these four essentials over in my mind: 1) We were fighting the common enemy of freedom—international Communism. 2) We were fulfilling our duty to our country. 3) I was sure the American people were behind us. 4) I believed God would bring me out of prison—better for my stay.

XXI

Tortured As a Spy

One of the big hurdles, once in the Hilton's Vegas cellblock, was to establish methods of communication. The one which was to be my downfall was the passing of notes through my leftover food. I established contact with the POWs who washed the dishes, and I told them to watch my dishes. They knew that if there was any leftover food, they should check it for notes. I had been communicating several other ways, but the circumstance required the more risky note.

I never attempted to pass notes when Big Ugh was on duty, for he was watching me very closely and was cunning and suspicious. One day—it was November 2—he was off duty and I wrote down some instructions on toilet paper (with some lead I had hidden), and also asked for some information. When I had it all set, the guard unlocked my door and it was Big Ugh! It was too late to change. As I set my bowls out, I noticed him eying the pieces of bread I had left.

I received an acknowledgment that my message had been received, but immediately after that I saw Big Ugh in the courtyard hollering. He laid something down on the ground and all the guards gathered around looking at it. I had a sick feeling that it was my note.

Before long the guards descended on me. They made me write some things and then tried to compare my handwriting. The

Bug then had me in for a quiz. I denied writing the note, of course. For beginning punishment and to keep me from communicating, he made me sit at attention on the other bunk in my cell that night and all the next day and night. The vent was left open so the guard could check me frequently.

Two days later they moved me again. I was blindfolded and taken to the meat-hook room. The Bug put me on a stool and started interrogating me. When I denied everything he became furious. His eye popped to one side, and his right index finger pointed in the air. He began working on me with his fists, cutting and bruising me.

I sat at attention for about three days in the meat-hook room with no facilities of any kind, but they gave me a cup of water twice a day and a bowl of food. Every five minutes they were checking to make sure I was not moving.

About three days after that the Bug resumed his interrogation. He went out of control again, working on me with his fists. He was hitting away when I dodged, and he hit the side of my head and hurt his fists. That really made him angry!

After a while the Dude came to take over. He accused me of spying for the United States, charging that I had been planted by the United States to organize the prisoners to oppose the Vietnamese. I thought that was a weird one, although I had heard that a North Korean colonel allowed himself to be captured during that war in order to be in the American prison camp.

They threatened now to hang me to the hook. That would be bad, but the thought I hated most was being put back into that black room. I really did not know if I could take that.

It seemed as if the Bug were waiting for something. For several days he would keep me on my knees, then standing at attention or standing with my hands over my head. But he kept holding off from the really tough torture of the past.

Finally, after about four days, he must have gotten the permission he needed from the Cat, because he seemed quite happy when he started. When a guard came in and whispered something, the Bug sent him away and then turned to me. "He has come to ask if the guards can beat you for spying." I said nothing.

Then he sent for Big Ugh. "You know him well." That I did! He came in with his nylon straps and started working me over. The only difference in his treatment this time was that he would put my sleeves or clothing underneath the strap to prevent scarring so badly.

It did not take long. I said, "Okay, I'll confess—I wrote the note."

The Bug said, "Write down what you did and the punishment you deserve."

I wrote that I had communicated with others and set up a new communications procedure. That was not enough. I had to add that I had also given several people directives. Then he ordered me to write that I had been spying for the United States and that I had been sent by the United States to organize the prisoners.

I told him I would not do that. He yelled for Big Ugh, who brought the straps with him again. With him standing there, he said, "Write." So I wrote that I had been gathering information for the U.S. government, but I would not write that I had been sent as a spy. I did not want to be tried as a spy.

When it came to what punishment was appropriate for so grave a crime, I wrote I had already received all the punishment I deserved. He would not accept that. "You have to write some other punishment." That really made me angry; I had already been hurt pretty good, and here he was camping on me again. I retorted, "I think I should be stripped to the waist, tied to a tree, and whipped in front of all the American prisoners." He thought that was great at first, but he evidently took it to somebody smarter than he was, for he came back threatening to punish me for being insolent. (Such an incident would have made the other POWs so mad that the Vietnamese would have had bad trouble.)

They kept shuttling me back and forth between the meat-hook

room and room #5 in the main courtyard, another room used for torture. I found out later that Jim Stockdale was on the same shuttle. Since there were no cells with bunks, it meant sleeping on the floor. I also had to meet a delegation, a French woman. This was normal procedure after being tortured. And if it was not meeting someone, it was writing a statement or making a tape.

However, they were getting smarter about letting us appear before the delegations. They steered us clear of most political questions and tried now to impress upon the delegates how well we were being treated—plenty of food and clothing, a toothbrush and toothpaste, etc. And they made a big deal about the special meals at Christmas and Tet.

Their standard harassment now was to put me on the stool for days at a time. When the Bug came by and beat on my door with keys, I would almost come undone. Every time he came in he hit me with whatever he happened to have in his hands. It did not make any difference what that was—stick, scissors, keys—he let me have it as his way of greeting. Each day was a twenty-four-hour nightmare, whether asleep or awake. In my dreams I would holler for someone to awaken me. While awake, I longed for oblivion. The Bug used my nightmare noises as an excuse to punish me for attempting to communicate with the other prisoners.

Then, about the sixth of March, 1969, they moved me to the Riviera, a six-cell building in the Vegas compound. My cell had a louvered window and front door, all of which had been covered up except the top two louvers of the door. It was so terribly hot that I ate and slept on the floor, where it was cooler. When I was not exercising, I sat on the floor and fanned myself with the woven bamboo fans we had been given the year before.

They did not really catch me, but while in the Riviera, they accused me of communicating, which I was actually doing. As punishment they sealed all of the louvers so that no air was coming in except under the door. In Vietnam at that time of the year, we perspired around the clock whether there were windows open or not. But to close everything off made it an oven. When I complained to the camp commander, he had them open two louvers at the top of the door and two at the top of the window. The guard could look in on me from the back as well as from the front. When he caught me communicating again, they moved me to the Mint, another part of Vegas, where the rooms were very, very small, seven feet long but with only fourteen inches between the bed and the wall. (I could not stand or walk straight but had to lean to one side, or my shoulder would be rubbing against the wall.) There was only room to exercise on the bunk, but they would not permit that; their excuse was that I was trying to look out the window and communicate.

Early in December they moved me back to the meat-hook room. On the day before Christmas Eve, the Bug had me in for a quiz. "Do you want a roommate?" I knew this was a ruse of some kind, but still I answered yes. "Then you will have, but do what I tell you and do not give me any trouble. Understand?"

I did not believe a word he was saying. They had something they wanted me to do and were dangling a carrot. I went back to the cell and the guard opened the door. When I looked in, I don't believe I have ever seen a more beautiful sight—another American. It was Lieutenant Colonel "Swede" Larson. We greeted each other like lost brothers as the guard stood there grinning. Swede had been in solitary confinement in a dark room for eighteen months. We talked for two days and nights until we were so hoarse that we could hardly whisper. We did not even go to sleep the first night, and the second night we were up until four or five o'clock in the morning.

That Christmas dinner was probably the finest I ever had in my life. For the first time since 1964, I had someone with me to eat Christmas dinner. What a glorious Christmas it was! We said the blessing with more gusto and sincerity than ever before in our lives.

XXII

Passing the Time

I had passed many long, uneventful, boring months when there was absolutely nothing to do for hours, especially after exercising until I was exhausted but still not able to sleep. Sometimes in the summer, the sweat would run off my body around the clock and form a pool on the bunk. During those unbearably hot hours I often lay with my head on the stocks looking at the ceiling and watching the play of the insects and animals.

One animal that furnished hours of entertainment was the gecko, which is something like a lizard. There were normally a male and a female in each cell, hanging from the ceiling. They would come out at night to catch mosquitoes and other insects that flew into the 25-watt light bulb suspended in the ceiling. It was very unusual for more than two geckos to be seen in one room. They would stake out their territory and others seldom bothered.

The geckos would go after almost anything that moved if it was not too large; however, they were discriminating. I had one insect that crawled in a small circle on the wall, around and around and around. I saw it there night after night. The geckos would see it and run for it. When they were within tongue distance, they would stop abruptly, sit there and watch it. After a while they would leave and sometime later they would see it again and make another dash for it, get right to it and leave it alone. It was plenty small enough to eat, but for some reason they would not eat it.

I saw a cockroach with a body larger than the gecko fly off the wall with the gecko holding on. They fell with a crash. Once the geckos caught hold—some of the flying cockroaches were two inches long—they would hang on. Sometimes they would catch a cockroach headfirst and would only get it down their throats maybe a quarter of an inch. There would be a noise like someone beating on the door or the wall at a very fast tempo. It would be a gecko with one of these great big insects partially down his stomach. He would be slamming the cockroach up and down.

The geckos make a sound that can be heard about half a block or more. Many times they will call one another and you can hear them answer. They also make sort of a chattering noise when the male is around the female. He chatters at her, and she will switch her tail, much like a female lion. The geckos fought, played and mated up on the ceiling while we watched them by the hours.

There was a little black spider, furry like a very small tarantula, only more compact and friendly. It too, would eat the ants and other insects around the light bulb. A most peculiar thing was that it would hang upside down on the ceiling; when an insect drew near the spider would jump from the ceiling onto the ceiling again as though it were reversing gravity. The only thing we could ever figure out is that it might have attached a web somewhere in front of it and was following this thing. But the jump was sometimes a half inch or an inch across the ceiling. It was as though the spider were flying upside down.

A game was played frequently between one of the geckos and this spider. I often saw a gecko make a run toward the little black spider. It would jump, and if the gecko pressed the issue, the spider would leap off the ceiling and climb down a web clear to the floor. The old gecko would sit there puzzled and then go about his business. I wouldn't see the little spider for a few hours and then soon it would be back up there. Later that night or the next night the same game would be played. The gecko would make a dash for the little black spider, and off the ceiling it would come down the silken strand to the floor.

Some of the guys had these black spiders trained so that they could feed them insects. Others tried to train geckos also, but they found the geckos would only eat live insects. The geckos were a real asset: the more geckos, the fewer mosquitoes. Sometimes the geckos would run up and down the bunk, where there seemed to be thousands of mosquitoes. The noise from the mosquitoes was often such a loud hum that it sounded as if you were in a hornet's nest.

When I first arrived in the Hilton and as long as I stayed in Heartbreak, there was a little mouse that everyone claimed for their own. This same little mouse went around to all the cells begging crumbs. It was as fat as a forty-pound robin and had two white paws. One of the paws was white about halfway up its foreleg, and the other was just a white slash across its paw. If you sat still, the mouse would run across your feet. Everyone, even though we were sometimes terribly, terribly hungry, would share a few crumbs with the mouse.

Some of the guys even became friendly with the rats. A litter of rats would hatch in the walls and some of the guys wouldn't even kill them. They watched them play, chase one another and wrestle, just like cats and dogs. If you didn't despise them because of their filth and the germs they carried, they were actually rather cute.

We learned that nothing was safe from the rats and the mice. A rat could jump onto the tallest bunk. He could also climb up the corner of a wall, cement or brick, and go almost anywhere he wanted to go. I have seen them walk wires to get to places, just like tightrope walkers.

When I was in New Guy Village, I used to watch through the top of the window as the rats came across the prison wall, across the broken glass embedded in the cement, and then across an intermediate wall, down some wires and up onto a rafter that ran under the five- or six-foot overhang which all of these buildings had because of the torrential downpours. The overhangs provided a dry path around the buildings. Underneath the overhangs the rats would have a regular causeway, coming over the wall, down the wire and up over the rafter where you could watch them run back and forth. There would be fifty or sixty of them in an evening, and you could hear them quarreling and fighting.

There was one male, an old gray-headed rat, which was as big and maybe weighed more than a squirrel. He was heavy in his forequarters and haunches, had a bull neck on him and was scarred all over from his fights; his neck was just a mass of scar tissue. He looked like an old pit bulldog, muzzle-gray from age. Most of the other rats would give way when he came along.

The birds provided us with a great deal of entertainment. I remember through the years hearing the birds, even when I could not see outside. They would start singing and chirping about dawn or just before. Although we had no clocks and couldn't hear the bells downtown, the birds would tell us by their chirping when it was time to get up. I lay by the hour listening to the birds.

I had been told that at the nap gong, about eleven o'clock, everyone had to lie on the bunks until about a quarter of two. During this period there was a quietness that was remarkable, especially in the camps outside the center of town. At the Zoo around eleven-thirty or twelve o'clock there seemed to be a silence that settled on the camp like a veil. Evn the birds seemed to take a siesta. I remembered one of the lines of the song "In the Garden": "He speaks and the sound of His voice is so sweet that the birds stop their singing. . . ."

There was a bird nest in a hole in the wall outside of the window of the toilet in New Guy Village. Sometimes when they took me to dump my waste bucket, they locked me in the toilet for an hour or two if they were busy. I watched day by day as the birds laid their eggs, the eggs hatched, the little ones grew, finally left, rebuilt their nest, remated and came back. It seemed as if the same birds were there several years in a row.

There were millions upon millions of ants. Sometimes I would have fish or fish meal, and if any little portion of it dropped on the floor, it would be only minutes before a constant stream of ants would be coming through the window, down the wall and across the floor to pick up what I had dropped. I also learned that fish oil attracted ants from a greater distance and at an even greater speed than sugar. Occasionally we would have sugar for breakfast, and if you spilled just a few grains, the ants would be after them.

Sometimes we managed to save a piece of bread for another, hungrier time. We'd wrap it and lay it on our nets to keep it away from the rats and the mice. The ants would smell it, despite the fact that it was wrapped as tight as possible. They would come in through the window searching until they found the string that suspended the net on the wall. Then they would come down the string, across the net, through the folds of the rags or the shirt or whatever we had the bread wrapped in, to the bread.

If you decided to eat the bread in the dark the first thing you knew, you'd feel the things crawling across your hands and sometimes across your lips. Or if that didn't warn you the crack between your teeth and the metallic taste were good indications. I would take the bread, and even if I couldn't see, thump it on the end of the bed near the stocks, and just keep doing that for maybe ten minutes and most of the ants would be gone.

The ants were a nuisance, but they also furnished a lot of diversion. They would eat nuts and go after peelings or almost anything. We used to put something out for them, to find out how the scouts worked, how long it would take them to find it, to send the word out, and whether or not they could call. It seemed as though they could actually signal in some fashion, for there would be others appearing very shortly. We watched them by the hour as they traveled along, going in both directions, and marvel at how they would mark a trail. I still don't understand how their scouts worked. Attracted by particles of food, the scouts would search until they found them. Returning to where they had come from, they would leave some sort of trail, so after only a few minutes the ants would start appearing in greater and greater numbers, coming down the trail. Soon, it would be an established path which every ant would come down and return on, just as if they had laid a cement highway.

Once I watched them pull a huge moth across the floor. The moth had come in to die, evidently, and was hanging up on the wall until it fell off from weakness. Maybe it was too old, but it was not yet dead. The ants had come in such numbers that they managed to drag off the moth while it was still fluttering. If a big roach, two inches long, was injured, the ants would drag it away while it was still flopping around.

At the Zoo, below the floor, was a six-inch by twenty-four inch opening through which, by lying on my stomach, I could look out. I developed a habit of getting up about five o'clock or earlier. I would lie down and start looking out this vent. Sometimes I watched it turn daylight and observed the ants and insects crawling up the blades of grass. During this period I would usually practice the Morse code because it was faster than what we were using, though not as accurate if you had to go through more than one wall.

One morning for practice, I was saying my prayers in Morse code. I had a piece of rock and the "Da Da Dit's" and "Da Da Dit Da's" were echoing around my cell. I said the Twenty-third Psalm in code and when I finished, Ed Davis in the next cell tapped out in Morse code, "Say it again."

Diversions such as these were lifesavers for most of us. But within the same cells in which we watched the insects and animals play, a more serious and deadly game was constantly being waged—the stance we took toward the Vietnamese using us for propaganda. For three men, their stance resulted in death.

XXIII

Three Who Paid with Their Lives

In late 1969, following the death of Ho Chi Minh, conditions began to improve. At about the same time in America our government made a policy switch regarding POWs. Until then we had been played in low key by the United States government, which hoped to keep us from being used as bargaining tools. But when the word got out that we were being treated like animals, the Administration felt that the only way to get our treatment improved was to focus world attention on the North Vietnamese brutality.

They did this in all kinds of ways, and it wasn't solely the government. There were people like Texas millionaire Ross Perot, a truly great American and red, white and blue down to his toes, Bob Hope, all those who wrote letters, wore bracelets, used bumper stickers, the wives who went on tours appealing to the various heads of governments throughout the world—all of these people had a tremendous impact.

We started getting out for exercise in October. At that same time everyone got a new blanket and an extra mat. Instead of two meals a day, they added a piece of bread for breakfast and a cup of hot water. And sometimes we would get a little salt or sugar. Additionally, they gave us a bamboo basket that was padded inside which just fit our little teapots and kept the water hot. We were also given a handkerchief and were permitted to write a Christmas card home. By 1970, everyone had a roommate. But for three American POWs, it was too little, too late.

In the meat-hook room in New Guy Village, Swede Larson and I made a little hole through which we could see into the main prison courtyard. This was where the civilian workers entered and departed. We were also able to observe the arrival and departure of civilian prisoners—sometimes even nine- or ten-year-old little girls, brought in handcuffed.

Around July or August in 1970, an American stumbled out of Heartbreak in his shorts. He was so emaciated that he looked like one of the Dachau inmates. Though over six feet, he weighed about a hundred pounds. He staggered with weakness and could hardly maintain his balance. After he walked up and down in the sun for a while, the guard took him back in. He was followed, one at a time, by two others who looked the same way. The third one was not only emaciated, like the other two, but he appeared to be in a trance. Looking only at the sky, he kept his arms in identically the same position at all times, rigidly pressed to the sides, never moving. It was as though he were hypnotized, just walking around and around. Sometimes when he went to the wrong place, the guard would come and get him as you would a little child, and head him back.

The next day we saw the same three men again, only this time the Vietnamese had not let them walk out without shirts on. It was obviously an attempt to hide their emaciated state from the Vietnamese civilians.

Later, when Swede and I were in the courtyard for exercise, we managed to signal Major Bud Day in Heartbreak and inquire about the three men. One was a Navy commander and the other two were Air Force captains.

According to Bud, in order to prevent the Vietnamese from using him for propaganda the Navy commander had starved himself until he was so weak that he could not write and too emaciated to appear before a delegation. He had been solo for five years, ever since his capture, and was terribly, terribly frail. By this time he so mistrusted everyone that when Bud tried to communicate with him, he didn't want to talk. Then Bud when to the Scar, the camp commander, and asked if he could visit him, and surprisingly, the Scar answered yes.

They unlocked Bud and took him to the man's cell. He still didn't trust Bud and thought he was one of the patsies for the Vietnamese. Bud told him they were no longer torturing for propaganda, but he wouldn't believe him. When Bud told him things were better, he laughed. He was not eating his food but throwing it down the drain, and throwing away his clothes—anything to inconvenience or make it hard for the Vietnamese and to keep himself in bad physical shape.

When Bud reported his condition to me, he asked if I would order the commander to eat. So I sent a direct order for him to start eating all his food and to begin exercising to build himself up. Conditions were better, I told him, and I expected them to continue to get better. Further, I said he would be in better condition to combat the Vietnamese if he was strong and healthy.

He sent back a "Wilco." The next day Bud was in his cell when they brought the food. It was probably one of the best meals we had—green salad, potato soup and some liver. The guy felt Bud was tricking him because my order coincided with the good meal. He thought he was getting special treatment and decided not to eat. Bud reminded him of my order, and he ate it all. But he had gone so long without eating that he threw it all up!

The next day they let him out for exercise. He tried to jog-trot twice around the courtyard. Although hardly able to walk, he was trying to show me that he was obeying orders. It tore my guts out, watching him. I was full of anger, tears and sympathy, all at the same time.

As for the second man, he had begun to break when they first started to torture him. He was linking everyone together as his enemy, not trusting even his friends. The Vietnamese thought he was putting on an act and showed him no mercy. They hit him in the face with fan belts, and literally beat him senseless at times. It made him imagine everyone was against him, and even from a strange planet. During this period he was in a room with several other POWs. Some of them had to hold him, and the others force-fed him. They kept him alive for a long time this way until he finally began to eat by himself. But in 1970, when I saw him, he was as emaciated as the other two, but he was not as rational as they were.

The third man was still communicating well during 1970, but he was putting on quite a show for the Vietnamese. The last time they tortured him, he had lost the complete use of his hands for an extended period. To keep from having to write statements, he pretended that he never regained use of his hands, never using them when they could see him. Additionally, he had starved himself until he was skin and bones. In his mind, this was the solution to the problem of foiling their efforts to use him for propaganda. He refused to let it happen to him.

Not long after they had been brought to Heartbreak, the men were moved again. They were a heartrending trio. We begged the Vietnamese to let them live with us. Given time, food, exercise and contacts with their friends, they could, we knew, be brought around.

We conjectured that the Vietnamese thought the three were unbalanced, although only one was in really serious condition mentally. But the Vietnamese had a very strange attitude about mental cases. They seemed to think it was communicable.

When the final POW tallies were made in 1973, these three, like Ron Stortz, were listed as having "died in captivity."

XXIV

"Who Is In Command?"

Establishing who was the senior ranking officer was no small task as the number of POWs increased through the years. There were several factors which complicated this. Some of us were given promotions while we were in prison. Yet, verification of the effective date of the promotion was almost impossible. Conceivably we could hear about a recent promotion almost at the time it occurred. But due to bombing pauses or the lack of pilots being shot down, we might not learn of another promotion until months or years after it was effected. To solve that, we went by the rank at the time of shoot-down. Mine was lieutenant colonel. Although I became full colonel in less than three months after shoot-down, in the POW chain of command I remained a lieutenant colonel until 1971, when an exception was made by the SRO, Colonel John Flynn.

In addition to promotions making it difficult to establish who the ranking officer was, it was made more difficult by the North Vietnamese's refusal to recognize rank in their relationship with the prisoners. They realized the military chain of command was a strong factor in discipline and morale; consequently they were always trying to undermine us. Many times they would attempt to use the most junior officers in command positions.

A third obstacle was the geographical location of the various cellblocks within a given prison, as well as the number of different prisons. Many men were constantly being shuffled from one cell to another or even from one prison to another.

Finally, the most difficult obstacle was simply the process of communications itself. For instance, when I first went to the Zoo in 1965, I was able to contact all of the people in all of the buildings. I could get a message to them and an answer in a maximum of two days. The Vietnamese started cracking down on this and made it more difficult. When I was moved into isolation, I only had intermittent contact for the next few years.

In December of 1969, when Swede Larson and I were put in one cell, both of us had been in isolation for a long period. Though we were now together, we were isolated in the meat-hook room from the rest of the camp. Then, in November 1970, they moved us back to Vegas into the building we called Thunderbird.

We had just put our gear down and our bedding on the bunks and the guard had been gone about a minute, when a big loud voice came through the window. "Hey, do you read me in there?" We looked all around, and I jumped up on the bunk and said, "Roger." He identified himself, also gave the name of the senior officer in the building and asked our names. I answered, "This is Robbie Risner and Swede Larson." He said, "Rog, I'll be contacting you later. The signal will be two coughs."

We were really surprised at the boldness of this guy to jump up on his bunk and talk out loud. I could just imagine guards running from everywhere, but these guys had lived there long enough to know where all the guards were. They had been tracking them and knew what they could get away with.

The first thing the next morning, we heard a double cough. I hopped up on the bunk to answer. Our windows were hidden by bamboo screening a foot or two from the window, so we couldn't see out. The voice told me that we would establish our next contact by tapping on the wall.

That same day they took Swede and me out to exercise. I heard a cough from the other side of the bamboo fence that enclosed our exercise pen. There was another exercise area on the opposite side for another building of American prisoners. Some water had accumulated in a little pool under the fence. The POW who had coughed walked up, and I could see his reflection in the water. He began to signal and to talk with his hands in the reflection of the water.

He told me I was the senior officer and asked what my orders were. Since I had only been in Vegas two nights and a day, I didn't know what the situation was. I asked him some questions and told him I would be in touch.

When I went back inside, the men in the next cell contacted me through the wall. One of them was Ernie Brace, a civilian pilot flying for Bird and Sons, a freight-carrying outfit. He had been captured by the North Vietnamese in Laos when he landed on an airfield that he did not know had been taken by North Vietnamese troops. They had held him at Dienbienphu for two or three years in leg stocks and in a bamboo cage. He had escaped three times. Once when they caught him, they buried him up to his neck for several days as a lesson. Despite a tremendous amount of torture, privation and humiliation, he was still a gung ho ex-Marine.

In with him was Steve Bettenger, a young redhead who was really a ball of fire—a Navy lieutenant (j.g.). He, too, had been captured in Laos—one of the last pilots captured in 1968.

These two men were doing a lot of communicating, with the guards almost on top of us at times. They actually sat outside our doors on a stool or walked up and down the hall.

When I started tapping through the wall to Ernie, since I had just learned I was the senior ranking officer, I felt it necessary to establish command and to put out a few brief directives. I assumed that the previous senior officer had been Commander Jim Stockdale.

To make sure all the basic loopholes had been covered in case there had been a period without a senior officer, I put out three items: I ordered no taping, no writing and no public appear-

ances. In the meantime, a question had been put to me to determine what my policy would be this year on going to the special
North Vietnamese church service at Christmas.

Since 1968 they had taken some people from each of the
camps to a church service administered by the Vietnamese. Apart
from the spiritual benefits that might derive from these services,
it also allowed us to pass information between camps. We had
begun to realize, however, that we were simply providing propaganda. I felt they had hidden cameras from which they were taking pictures that they sent around the world which, in effect, said,
"Look, folks! This is how we treat the American prisoners. Here
they are in a church service being administered by one of our own
ministers. Isn't this nice?"

That was the biggest bunch of malarkey possible, so the question was reduced to whether the benefits outweighed the propaganda material the Vietnamese would get.

While I was debating this decision and waiting for my initial
directives to circulate, a communication came asking my date of
rank. A couple of days later I learned I was outranked by Lieutenant Colonel Vern Liggon. I immediately sent a message to the
whole camp saying, "Hold my policies pending approval of
Colonel Liggon, who is SRO." I didn't know that Vern had just
taken over the reins from Jim Stockdale, who had been running
the camp while Vern was out of communication. Our policies had
differed only slightly. I then sent a message to Vern saying, "I'm
at your command."

In only a few days I received a message from Colonel John
Flynn saying, "I assume command," and giving his code name
(each of us had one). This meant there were four SROs in a matter
of a few days. Needless to say, there were a lot of code names
going around and quite a bit of confusion.

We were just getting this ironed out when one of the most
morale-building events of the war occurred—one which so scared
the Vietnamese that our whole pattern of prison life was altered.

XXV

The Move to Camp Unity

On Christmas evening, December 25, 1970, Swede and I heard doors opening and shutting with a lot of people moving around. Soon they opened ours and said, "Pack up. You're moving." We rolled everything up in a blanket, slung it over the shoulder, tucked our mat under the arm, and picked up our bucket. They moved us from Thunderbird over to the south side of the Hilton, where they had always kept the Vietnamese civilian prisoners. They put two of us in each cell and left.

Major Bud Day and some others had been living in this area for some time. They reported that the same night we moved, there was a big emergency exodus of the civilian prisoners in order that all the POWs be put together in one place, which we called Camp Unity. We learned later that there had been an American commando raid at Son Tay, a POW camp less than thirty miles away. Unfortunately, all of the POWs had been moved out previously. It had its impact on the Vietnamese, though. They were afraid there would be such raids on all the camps, so they began bringing in the POWs from the outlying areas into one central camp, which they could better defend. The raid may have failed in its primary objectives, but it boosted our morale sky-high! It also put all the POWs captured in North Vietnam together for the first time. This would have a major impact on us.

The next day a guard came to our cell and told us we were

moving again. We walked across the courtyard to a large building. I opened the door, and I cannot express the feeling I had when I saw who were inside. There appeared to be hundreds of POWs—actually we were only forty-six altogether—laughing and shouting, grabbing one another, hugging and shaking hands. It was absolute pandemonium. People were helping each other with their bedding and trying to get situated. Some were trying to move next to each other.

The first person I saw was Air Force Major Larry Guarino, a good friend of mine who had been in a sister squadron at Kadina in the 18th Tactical Fighter Wing. He is a little volatile Italian with a bristling mustache. He had been SRO over a camp longer than any other man. Larry had taken over when they moved Jerry Denton out from the Zoo. He threw his arms around me and mine went around him. We were trying to talk and people were trying to push by us and others trying to get to us. Everyone had bedrolls under their arms and buckets in their hands.

A few minutes later I spotted Lieutenant Colonel Fred Crow, who was an old friend from Germany where he had been in my squadron. I was trying to find a spot to bunk, and he helped me find a place next to him. Swede put his bedding down beside me.

I almost immediately found Commanders Jim Stockdale and Jerry Denton. We had been in prison together from almost the first at Heartbreak Hotel and then at the Zoo. We were the closest of friends, although we had never shaken hands. We had prayed for one another, sent encouragements when we could, and grown very close. It was a joyful reunion. Names, faces and voices all came together. Stories we had heard of each other, accounts of prayer and concern made the time fly.

The Vietnamese made us get under our nets, but that didn't matter—we talked the night through. It was the most exciting time we had had. It was so great to actually touch people, to put your arms around them, to sit and relate past histories.

Our quarters was a large, open room about forty-five feet long and probably twenty feet wide. In the center was a raised cement platform about a foot high. This was where we laid our mats. By putting them head to head butted up against each other, and side by side touching each other, we could get forty-six men on the platform. Around it was a roughly two-and-a-half-foot alley to walk in.

We estimated that there were now 350 POWs in the Hilton's Camp Unity. There were ten buildings in the compound surrounding the courtyard which was walled in by bamboo fences.

In the excitement of the first few days, we almost forgot our duties' of establishing primary command and control. Regrettably, John Flynn and the other three officers shot down as full colonels (Dave Wynn, Norm Gaddis and Jim Bean) were still being kept isolated, two to a cell in another building. We determined for the time being to leave the rank structure as it had been: namely, shoot-down date of rank. Since we had no contact with the four full colonels, that meant Lieutenant Colonel Vern Liggon was the commanding officer, and I was next in line as the deputy for operations, with Jerry Denton and Jim Stockdale helping me.

The men started referring to the top-ranking men in the building as the wise men (maybe a bit wryly). They included the flight commanders, who had "flights" of eight men, basically for doing the daily chores. The duty was rotated among the flights.

After a week or so, we received a short message from Colonel Flynn. His policy agreed exactly with what we had already put out. We formalized our organization and buckled down to the task at hand. It looked as if after more than five years we were finally going to be afforded appropriate POW recognition. Unfortunately, that was a delusion.

We had good communications throughout camp except for the one or two buildings with only a few men in them such as Colonel Flynn's. Now that we were together in a camp where we could communicate, we were getting stronger and more capable. Soon this new strength began to rattle the Vietnamese cage a little bit.

The men were not taking as much from the guards, and the Vietnamese were still trying to deal with us on an individual basis and prevent us from using our command organization. They didn't want it; in fact, they were afraid of it. They also knew that it was in the code of conduct and that we were obligated by military law to establish such an organization and use it. They didn't want an SRO giving orders and all those under him taking them.

In every way we had been told we were criminals; preventing us from doing anything that smacked of the military was one way they tried to convince us of this. They had several ulterior motives, of course. They wanted to keep us from deriving strength and support from the military organization which we had been in so long, and also convince us that we were not obligated to the military law or to the code of conduct.

Along with this unity and strength, the frustrations and anger harbored by the men began coming out. We started having problems controlling our own people. As has always been true, it is more difficult to discipline yourself, quite often, than it is to fight the enemy in a prisoner-of-war situation.

We were trying to maintain control. At the same time we recognized what was happening. The men had every justification in the world to be angry and frustrated. They had spent years in solo, had been tortured, deprived of necessities, and even the minimum privileges that should have accrued to prisoners of war. POW-Vietnamese friction increased.

For instance, the guards would issue a razor blade to an individual and tell him he was responsible for the razor blade. It had to be used by from four to seven people. That individual was expected to keep track of it and turn it back in. It had been determined earlier by our command that this was the flight commander's duty, which the Vietnamese refused to accept. So some of the men refused to take the razor blades.

As another example, the Vietnamese wanted to appoint our work details and our "flights" (of eight men per flight). We refused and set them up ourselves. They even tried to show us where we had to sleep. The camp officer would come in and read off a list: "You will sleep in this order, and this will be your duty section." We refused if it was not convenient.

There were some who were giving the raspberry to the Vietnamese who would never have thought of doing it before. Now that they were lost in the crowd, they could get away with it. The group had given them false confidence.

The Vietnamese were apprehensive, not having had to contend with this behavior before. I'm convinced they didn't want trouble; in fact, I think the camp commander was removed because of this trouble. Everybody was walking on pins and needles—except us.

Something almost comical was our baths. We washed in a small courtyard ringed by a bamboo fence. It was ten feet high and no one could see through it, except that the Vietnamese guards and officers could walk through the gates. There was a large cement horse trough in the courtyard from which we got all our water to wash our clothes and our bodies. Naturally, when we washed we stripped. The Vietnamese had a thing about nudity and the guards wanted us to wash with our shorts on!

One day the guard took me to a little shack outside our building for a quiz with the Bug. (We named the shack "The Bug House" in his honor.) He told me that since I was responsible for the behavior and conduct of all the prisoners, I would be punished for any misbehavior. Then he laid down a bunch of rules that we couldn't possibly follow: Go to bed when the gong rings, and keep quiet. Don't talk loud, laugh, sing or whistle. It was ridiculous. After years of being alone, not to be able now to talk, joke and laugh was absolutely impossible. I let it ride for a few days, and then I had about three more quizzes. I finally asked Vern, "How do you want me to handle this? It doesn't seem right to let them get away with using me as SRO, when you are." He said, "Next time, tell him I'm SRO."

The next time out, the Bug said, "You are responsible for the misconduct going on and now we're going to punish you." I felt that this was a poor time to say, "Look! I'm not the SRO; Vern Liggon is. Punish him." But I felt sure that I was not going to be punished for anything. He was just mouthing. I had received the same threats for three days running.

A few days later he said, "If you don't obey what I am telling you, I will not only punish you, but I will release the statements you have written and the tapes you have made. I will show them to all the men."

That really made me boil. I answered, "Look! You have already used them to the maximum amount possible, not only among the men but to the whole stinking world. If you want to release them to the men, you just feel free." Then I told him, "I am not the SRO; Vern Liggon is." He was somewhat surprised, because they don't go exactly by rank in their army. When he asked, I told him Vern's date of rank and my own. The next time someone had a quiz, it was Vern. They asked him a lot of questions about how we decided who was senior officer, and he told them it was by shoot-down date of rank.

On occasion the guards were completely unreasonable. When that happened, the men would often turn around and use a four-letter word or tell them to cram it. The guards didn't like it, naturally, but they didn't know exactly what to do. Apparently they were under a different set of orders and a different policy. For the first time they were nonplused. They would take the problem to their officer, and the officer would call Vern or maybe the man involved and chew him out or threaten him.

One man had a fracas with a guard, and began to *"Bao cao!"*

at the top of his lungs. It frightened the guard and I think it frightened the officer who came running. The guy was shouting so loudly that it was going over the wall to the people in the city. They yanked this man out and put him in solo in Heartbreak, where he stayed for a month or two. This happened to two or three other individuals.

A major problem was the Vietnamese's refusal to let us have a mass meeting, even in our own building. They were still trying to maintain control of everything. We were bumping heads with them every day. They said we could have a maximum of twenty people in one group. We didn't argue with them about twenty men in groups for classes, but we were determined not to follow that in other areas.

They were really getting skittish now—watching us almost constantly through peepholes, putting a guard on the roof of the adjacent building, and sometimes a twenty-four-hour watch. It was almost as though they felt they were sitting on a volcano.

The tension was, in fact, building. We had daily problems about razor blades or who was going to dish up the food. The Vietnamese would say, "You, you and you—come empty the waste buckets." Since they would not be the flight we had designated as duty crew that day, we'd refuse to let the men do it. There would be a big confrontation and harangue. Sometimes we would back off a little, but sometimes we would hold our ground.

One day we lost a razor blade. It probably washed down the drain, but we were accused of stealing it. "Until you produce this razor blade, nobody else gets to shave." All of us went for maybe a week without shaving because one blade had been lost. And yet it wouldn't have happened if they had given the blades to the flight commander.

There were a certain number of men who absolutely refused to wash with their shorts on. As soon as the guard's back was turned, they'd strip down and start washing. They would soap themselves all over, and then the guard would see them. He'd run toward them, screaming all the time and telling them to put their clothes on. First, though, they had to get the soap off, and that took a few minutes.

This kind of thing went on day after day with constant friction. It looked as if we were headed for a big confrontation. Those of us in the command structure were discussing the rule which we had not been keeping about going to bed at nine-thirty when the gong sounded. There were some men who wanted to go to sleep at nine-thirty; they had become accustomed to it and wanted to continue. There were others who wanted to stay up and talk until two or three in the morning. Finally we made the decision that everyone would go to bed at nine-thirty.

It caused a lot of hard feelings. We talked about it and decided to temper it a little bit. Those who wanted to stay up after nine-thirty would have to go to a certain section of the building and talk in low voices. Even this did not go over too well with some. They had been resisting the Vietnamese on an individual basis for so long that it was difficult to come into a room with forty-seven Americans, with a command set up, directives and certain restrictions.

As deputy for operations I called them all together, despite the Vietnamese ruling that we could not have a full assembly. I reminded them that we were all military men and that ours was a military organization. They were expected to act like military men and comply with all directives without quibble. If they had any questions or matters to discuss, they should take them to their flight commander with whom we met daily. He would bring it to the staff, and we would make the final decisions. Once the decision was made, the discussion period was over. We expected the orders to be complied with to the letter—the talk seemed to help.

The confrontation that busted everything wide open was the Vietnamese refusal to let us have church services. We were determined not to back down on this issue. I felt it was especially important. Because of it, I would be thrown back into solitary confinement for much of the remaining time.

XXVI

The First Church Service

On the first day we were all together, several of the men had asked
me about having a common church service. I had dreamed about
this for a long time, so naturally I was extremely enthusiastic. We
had all been brought together on Saturday, December 26, 1970, so
there seemed to be no better way to start this new phase of our
imprisonment than with a common church service the next day.

Once we made the decision to proceed, our first task was to
find a chaplain. Navy Lieutenant (j.g.) George Coker said he had
never conducted church services, but would count it an honor until
we found someone better qualified. George was one of those who
had escaped and been recaptured. He was tough, knew quite a
bit about the Bible, and was a good speaker. (We were split pretty
evenly between Catholics and Protestants, with a sprinkling of
other denominations. If we hadn't learned it before imprisonment,
we knew by now there is no dividing line between faiths. God
listens to every man regardless of his church choice.)

Next, we started talking about a choir. I appointed another
man to help George—a Marine, Major Howie Dunn. He was very
interested and had musical ability. Between them they found some
people with musical backgrounds who volunteered to form a small
choir. Their director was Colonel Tom Kirk, who at one time had
had a band of his own.

There was a great deal of determination and feeling about

having a service, once the idea was broached. We knew the Vietnamese would be upset, but we decided to do it anyway. And it was going to be a very special and symbolic event. For that reason we wanted everyone to participate. Since we had a few agnostics, we decided to make the service both patriotic and religious. The first part would be patriotic and the rest religious.

The choir of six began rehearsing quietly in a corner. By everyone pitching in, we put together the words of three songs, "America," "The Old Rugged Cross" and "In the Garden." We wrote out two copies on toilet paper.

When Sunday morning rolled around, while the guards were at lunch, Vern assembled the men. They spread out over the room in a kind of semicircle. Most were standing on the platform in the middle of the room. George took over and asked Vern to lead in the Pledge of Allegiance. This was followed by one of the men who had volunteered to lead the opening prayer. The choir sang, followed by a scripture "reading." (Since we didn't have a Bible, "reading" the scripture meant having someone quote a portion of it. I'm sure there was some paraphrasing done!) Then we all said the Twenty-third Psalm together, which was kind of the prisoner's psalm. Through the years we had given this to nearly everyone who came through Heartbreak. George gave a short talk, then followed another song, and at the end of the service we said the Lord's Prayer together. I gave the benediction.

The Vietnamese didn't know we were having a church service until toward the end. Someone looked in and saw what we were doing. Monday morning the Bug laid down the law. He told us we weren't permitted to have mass meetings. If we did it again we would be punished. "How would you like to go back to the 1967 treatment?"—a favorite threat of theirs.

We talked it over and decided we would continue. We really didn't think they would do anything about it. It was our feeling that our having been put together meant something big was coming up. Some speculated we were approaching release and others that we were going to be moved to a large camp where we would have outside privileges. Consequently we felt quite confident and our actions reflected it.

So as not to aggravate the Vietnamese any more than we had to, we decided to keep the service down to about fifteen minutes. We were not deliberately baiting them, for we knew it was in our best interest not to.

It was our feeling that the decision to have church services in our building was not one that should be put out in the form of a directive. We passed along to the rest of the camp what was going on and left it up to them whether they would follow suit.

On the Sunday prior to the 7th of February, 1971, things came to a head. In order to smooth the way as much as possible and to preclude retaliation by the Vietnamese, Vern went to the Bug and briefed him as to what we were doing. The Bug had already been told that the church service was something the men would have as long as we were together, and there was no force that could stop us. Vern gave the impression that even if he, as the SRO, wanted to stop them, he could not. Further, he would not try, but would join them.

The Bug was incensed and threw a lot of threats around. It looked as if they were getting serious. We talked it over in the staff. I felt very strongly that it was our right, and they had no cause to deny it, especially when we were doing all we could to prevent friction. The service was short, and we were using only six men for the choir. There was no loud singing and not even a whole lot of noise when we united for the psalms, prayers and the Pledge of Allegiance.

At the meeting with the flight commanders, a decision was made that we would have church service regardless of the consequences. The next task was to predict what the Vietnamese reaction would be, as well as develop some contingency responses on our part. We thought we knew how the Vietnamese operated, and we expected to have some losses. First of all, we expected they would start pulling out the leaders and putting them in solitary confinement. The intent would be to keep pulling out the leadership until the losses became too great, and the remaining men acquiesced.

To combat this we planned it so that no one would be highlighted as the individual leading the service. Every portion of the service was to have different leadership. The opening prayer would be said by one man, the choir of six would sing, the scripture was to be given by a different person, and the thought for the day by yet another person. We also had a contingency plan: to prevent violence Vern, if he felt it best, could call the whole thing off. If they pulled out the leaders, we agreed that we would continue until the last junior officer was left alone.

However, a favorite saying of ours was "Don't anticipate the V." It proved to be wise and sound. On Sunday morning, February 7, they were ready. A number of guards and turnkeys were right outside the door. Toward the latter part of the service, the Bug entered and directed the action from the back. The Hawk, a turnkey who was one of the two men we respected, came in and told the choir to stop singing. The choir continued until their song was finished. When George Coker started to speak the Hawk told him to hush, but George finished anyway. He told him two or three times, "No talk." He turned to the men and told them to sit down or disperse; they said nothing and kept standing.

No one obeyed anything that the Vietnamese said. Then he went back to the door and talked to the Bug. Meanwhile, Commander Howie Rutledge was quoting some scripture; his part lasted several minutes. The Bug sent Ick forward, one of the English speakers, who told Howie to stop talking. He continued, of course. The service was over, except for the benediction. As I gave the benediction, another guard came forward and told me to stop. Ick went back to the door and the Bug sent the Hawk back down when I finished.

At a prearranged signal, Vern said, "Dismissed," and everyone started to disperse. The Hawk came forward and told me to go out with him. Two other guards came in; one took George Coker and the other Howie Rutledge. As we were walking out the Bug said, "Now you will see that my hands are not tied!" They stood us on the sidewalk with our backs toward the building, right under the windows with the guards in front of us. One of our men climbed up in the window and asked, "What's going to happen?" I answered, "They are waiting on the Bug."

It was only a few seconds until Major Bud Day, one of the toughest men I know, started singing "The Star-Spangled Banner," with everyone joining in. I have never heard a sound like it. We had not heard "The Star-Spangled Banner" during all those years, except in our own minds or under our breath. Now, though, it was ringing throughout the camp, over the wall and into the city of Hanoi. It lifted up everybody in the whole stinking camp! As they sang, I think George, Howie and I stood a little taller, a little straighter, and never prouder.

Soon the communication line in the prison was running like wildfire. The word went out that they had tried to kill our church service. It really fired up the troops.

They took the three of us over to Heartbreak and put us in the room next to the wall of Building Seven, in which we had been living. Since there were only two bunks, one of us had to sleep on the floor.

That afternoon, just before dark, singing started again from Building Seven. They sang other songs in addition to "The Star-Spangled Banner." To top it off they concluded with:

"This is Building Number Seven, Number Seven, Number Seven
This is Building Number Seven
Where the Hell is Number One?"

That started a chant around the camp. Every single building, some with which we had had very limited or no contact, picked it up until the whole camp had joined in. It so shook the Vietnamese that they called out the riot squad!

When everything was quiet again, the atmosphere was charged with tension. The Vietnamese could feel it, and so could the men.

The reaction started. For a week they pulled men out and put them in leg irons in Building Zero, where Colonel Flynn was. They put three to a room: two in one set of irons, and the other in one set. That meant one had his right leg in stocks, the other had his left, and the third man had both legs in.

The resistance continued. Every time a man was called out to a quiz he informed his interrogators how unjust, unfair and cruel it was to disturb our church services. He would tell them how much God meant to us and that they had lied to us about their having freedom of worship.

The men then started marching everywhere in military formation. For work detail, flights of eight would fall in single column, march out and march back. For the outside exercise, it was being done now in formation led by a single individual. The Vietnamese were getting the message.

They continued to pull out the leaders. By the end of the week they had Vern Liggon, Jim Stockdale, Jerry Denton, George Coker, Harry Jenkins, Jim Mulligan, Herv Stockman, Jim Lamar, Jack Finley, Pete Schoffel, myself and others. And there were still several commanders and lieutenant colonels left.

A riot squad was now on hand at all times—forty to fifty armed guards in helmets, carrying tear-gas grenades and the whole bit. To add fuel to the fire, Building Seven had a birthday party for Bob Schumaker, the second prisoner shot down. Bob, who was highly respected, was given a party with singing, a little show, and a skit. Harry Jenkins, the SRO in Building Seven, had planned it. They pulled him out and those who had assisted.

Those left decided to have a bridge tournament. (The Vietnamese had distributed playing cards to some buildings.) Evidently it was a real show, well planned and organized. Those who had been running the bridge tournament, the emcee as well as the participants in the birthday skit, were put in stocks for thirty-seven days. They let them out once a day to use their bucket which is very difficult when you have been tied in one position for twenty-four hours.

Following the seventh of February, the Vietnamese acquiesced and said we could have the services. To save face they said, "But you must write down what you are going to do, write the words in the songs, the scripture verses, everything!"

This came back to me while I was still in Heartbreak. It was left up to the individual building to decide what course of action to take, but one thing we did say, "Don't write the songs. Don't write the scriptures. You can give them the names, the schedule and the program. But do not write out the words." Much of what was said was extemporaneous. Besides, we felt they were being much too restrictive and everyone was fairly angry. We weren't about to buy it. We were not going to write it down, and we didn't.

Up to then we had never been permitted to have any part in any of the decision making. We were controlled like animals—when we went to bed, when we got up, when we ate, when we finished, when we went to empty our buckets, when we bathed—everything was controlled by the Vietnamese. Now they felt they were losing this control. We were a military organization and we were going to act like one, according to the Geneva Convention.

Howie Rutledge and I had been blindfolded, taken up to Building Zero and put in one of the rooms, but we were not put in stocks. George Coker was left in Heartbreak. After a couple of weeks Vern Liggon had been taken out of the stocks he had shared with Jim Stockdale, and moved to solitary confinement. Stockdale now had both of his legs in stocks.

Though it had to be done covertly, we had services each Sunday in Building Zero, each of us listening to the other from within our cells. I conducted the first few. An unusual part of our service was the whistle solo. One of the men with us, Lieutenant Colonel Jack Finley, was a tremendous whistler. He serenaded us almost every week in the last year because everybody requested it. I can still hear the beautiful clear notes of "The Lord's Prayer" or "Ave Maria."

The struggle over the church services was to be remembered for as long as we were prisoners, not only by us, but by the Vietnamese.

The Vietnamese told those of us who had been pulled out of Building Seven and put in Building Zero that they held us responsible for what they called the riot, which was only our enthusiastic songs. Because of this, we were kept in punishment and separate from the other POWs until a few days before release.

XXVII

We Will Talk Regardless

It was not long before virtually all the senior POW officers had been moved to Building Zero. There were still a few in some of the other camps, but for the most part Building Zero was loaded with brass.

One of the benefits from this was that it gave us the opportunity to establish an effective organization for the whole camp with the real SRO, Colonel John Flynn, in command. John had been isolated for a great part of his imprisonment, but soon there was an efficient and fairly sophisticated command structure in control. And since most of the others were in stocks, Howie Rutledge and I were able to serve as a communications post for the whole camp. When the stocks were removed, Colonel Flynn chose to follow this same structure and appointed me deputy for operations. Since I had been promoted to colonel in 1965 he chose to make an exception in our rank structure by date-of-shoot-down rule.

As command tightened, the sophistication of our resistance increased. We were working to control individual acts of resistance (which were sometimes counterproductive to the welfare of all) and to develop overall resistance to effect change. One of the keys to this was the recognition by the Vietnamese of Colonel Flynn as SRO. They refused to do this except when trouble broke out. Each time we told them that the Geneva Convention on Prisoners of War called for recognition of the SRO, they replied that we were criminals, not prisoners of war. We continued to push it, but they wouldn't deal with him. They attempted to belittle or harass him by trying to show that he had no authority. Many times they would try to give orders through a junior man. We had a running battle on that score right up to release.

Not only did we seek to have the articles of the Geneva Convention followed and our SRO recognized, we very much sought to have the outrageous treatment stopped. Thirty-seven days in leg stocks was gross inhumanity. Some of the guy's ankles wouldn't fit in the stocks, which were designed by the French for small Vietnamese ankles, so when they were closed it would cut off the circulation, break the skin and cause infection. Jack Finley, particularly, had bad scars as a result. As a last resort Colonel Flynn wrote a letter to the camp commander asking for recognition of the SRO, which would help provide the stability they were looking for. Further, according to the Geneva Convention, the SRO should be allowed to meet and talk with the camp commander and air grievances, make requests, and so forth.

We anticipated a retaliation, and it was not long in coming. Two guards and an English-speaking turnkey came in and told John Flynn that the camp officer wanted to see him. After John had left, the guards returned for his gear (we had thought he was going out for a quiz and would be coming back). They also told Colonels Dave Wynn and Norm Gaddis to pack up. We were watching from our secret peepholes and as they passed we said, "God bless you." The guard said, "Shut up." After ascertaining that Colonels Flynn, Wynn and Gaddis were not in camp, I sent out a message stating that I had been assigned as vice commander by Colonel Flynn and was assuming command. Jim Stockdale, who was the ranking Navy officer, was my deputy for operations.

In the fall of 1971 Jack Finley became my roommate, and they moved several men over to Building Eight, including Colonel Flynn, who had been missing for months. Our command structure was intact once again.

Gradually the Vietnamese were being forced to deal with the senior ranking officer in the buildings, which made things run a lot smoother. We were able to get some improvements. They started giving out some textbooks, some of the buildings had playing cards and chessboards, and there was an occasional Russian novel in English which either knocked our society or built theirs up.

During this period they tried to keep those of us in Building Zero from talking. I had made the decision that we were going to talk despite their orders. I felt very strongly that it was not only unjust from the very first, but even more so now. All the men in the other buildings were living together, yet they were denying us the right to even talk to each other. We weren't supposed to laugh, sing or whistle but to live like mute animals. I decided it was time for that policy to go, and instructed everyone to start talking. When the guard told us to shut up, we did—at first. After a while we escalated. When he told us to shut up, someone else would start talking from another cell. When they began harassing us quite heavily, I told the men that if one of them was told to shut up, everyone in the building should start talking into the hall.

In December they caught us communicating out the window to another building. In retaliation our windows were covered with blankets. Though the nights were cold, there were days that were extremely hot and muggy. The blankets over the windows made it quite uncomfortable. They also wouldn't let us go outside to exercise. In addition, I was told in front of everybody that I was responsible for all the additional hardship and that I was the one who had been doing the communicating. In reality, they had caught the room next to mine, but I had given the order. Now they attempted to put all the blame on me to cause the men to resent me.

I am sure there were a few who wondered why I had been so bullheaded. Some probably wondered if it was a wise decision. This was the same question many of us had faced from the very first. Whatever your attitude was toward the Vietnamese, you had problems. The only way I was able to live with myself and with others was to determine what was best for all or the majority and then proceed. There was no question in my mind that not being able to communicate openly was inhuman and unjust. I regretted that our windows were now covered and that we had no exercise time, but we could live with that. We kept communicating. I felt it that important to morale.

Periodically a guard or one of the turnkeys, or even the Bug himself, would open the vent on my door and ask, "Are you talking?" I wouldn't try to hide it. "What are you talking about?" I would tell him if the subject was innocuous, and I would even tell him to whom I was talking. The others were doing the same thing; in fact, everybody would increase the tempo when we were told not to talk. So, finally, they stopped telling us not to.

The morning of December 10 the senior turnkey had stuck paper in the crack down the middle of my door and had tried to repair the transom cover, which I had shredded in order to see into the hall and to get more air. That made me a little suspicious. At noon, during the nap period, my vent flew open and it was Hack, an English-speaking turnkey. He asked, "Were you talking?"

"Yes."

"What were you talking about?"

"I was talking about Spanish."

"Do you talk other times?"

"Yeah, I talk all the time."

With that he closed the vent. When he walked away, I noticed that he made no sound. One of the other men told me he was barefooted. That was typical; they were always trying to sneak up on us by walking without their Ho Chi Minh sandals. But it hadn't been necessary; I wouldn't have stopped talking even if I had known he was there.

Hack was back in about three minutes with the Bug, who was fully dressed in uniform, which meant that he had been waiting, prepared. He motioned for Jack Finley to fold up and move. He put him in with Vern Liggon, who had been living solo for several months. He motioned for me to get over on Jack's bunk, opened up the stocks and put both my legs in. "You have been warned about communicating and now you will be punished. If you continue, you will be punished harder."

As soon as he left I began to tap on the wall to the next room, where Lieutenant Colonel Carl Crumpler and Commander Ken Kosky were. I told them I was in stocks and that they had moved Jack. While I was tapping, Hack slipped back and caught me in the act. He said, "Oh ho! You know you will be punished for this." He left and I continued tapping.

On December 16, the Bug came in and said, "Today is the People's Army Day. Because of our humane and lenient treatment and because the people are celebrating Army Day, I now will let you out of the stocks." He told me what would happen if I didn't stop causing trouble and quit communicating. I was out of stocks, but I was still in punishment. I was not allowed to wash at all for several days. When they let me start washing, I was allowed only five to ten minutes to wash and empty my bucket, but no outside time. I could not be with any of the others. They even brought my food to my door.

On Christmas Day they allowed the other prisoners to be together for about two hours in the evening, and they brought them some candy and tea. My Christmas gift was a letter from my wife. I knew something was up because no one else had gotten any mail, and I was in punishment. I was glad, of course, to hear from Kathleen. But the reason they had given it to me was that it told of my mother's death. I didn't want to believe it. Just that morning I had prayed for her, little knowing that she had been dead for several months. At her advanced age, I realized her health was probably failing. But suddenly to be told on Christmas Day that Mother was gone was a heavy blow. No good-byes, no last word or prayer—especially no prayer.

It was a desolate feeling. My little cell became flooded with her memories. I could almost feel her presence: the image that came to me repeatedly was of Mother on her knees praying. When she prayed, she always chose a clothes closet in our old home in Tulsa. While still a boy, many is the time I can remember hearing Mother in the closet as she prayed. For us children to hear her mention our name in prayer only deepened the love we had for her because of her special concern.

If I had been by her bedside, her passing would not have been so hard to take. But no matter what the geography or time, to realize that Mother was no longer alive was difficult. For me to accept it while living in a Vietnamese prison cell was even more difficult. And the reason was the special place that prayer had come to have for me. I could not have existed if I had not been able to pray. To be able to mention in prayer the names of my wife, children, friends or relatives, or one of my fellow POWs who I knew was being tortured or mistreated, brought us together. The thousands of miles, the walls of my cell, the guards, were all transcended by this dimension of communication.

This was especially true of Mother, because it was from her that I had learned to pray. There had been such a special comfort in being able to pray for her. And each time I did, it reminded me that without a doubt, Mother had prayed for "Jamey" several times that day, as she had every day.

My wife, Kathleen, told me after I got home that she had gone to see Mother before she passed away. A lot of people were doubtful that I would ever return, and even some of my brothers and sisters had wondered aloud. Katie said she had gone to Mother's bedside and Mother had taken her hand and given it a weak squeeze and whispered, "Sugar, don't you worry, Jamey's coming home." Mother never doubted it. There is no way to express how much I wished she could have lived to see my return.

To give me the letter telling me of Mother's death was standard operating procedure with the Vietnamese. Bad news you could depend on getting. They had held it for just the right moment. Anything to demoralize you, to make you bitter. I stayed in punishment for another thirty days.

Despite the Vietnamese reaction to our communication, we continued to create methods and systems for utilizing the time. At first we developed study courses, book reviews, entertainment, and language courses, which we held covertly by talking from our separate cells. (By mid-1972 we were allowed to hold these together.) Every Saturday evening we would have a "movie." We had two guys who were especially gifted at describing the movies they had seen. Sometimes they would even give us movies that they had never seen but someone else had told them about. This provided about an hour and a half or two hours of entertainment. We'd lie on our stomachs and listen under the door. *Doctor Zhivago* was one of the better ones. It took about two sessions—around four hours—to tell. Outstanding. We even had a musical.

And if one of us had an interesting adventure to tell from the past, that would be the entertainment for the day. Naturally, there was quite a bit of embellishing of the heroes in these stories.

For our language studies, Tom Kirk served as supervisor and as one of the instructors. He was highly motivated, a good instructor and a hard taskmaster. Helping him was Dat, a Vietnamese prisoner who had been brought up in French schools. French was almost as natural to him as Vietnamese. He knew English well, and was learning Thai, Laotian and Spanish. In fact, he was as good or better than any Spanish student we had. His Spanish vocabulary ran into the thousands of words. I did not participate in the language studies for a while because I had no glasses. I couldn't see the vocabulary list on the toilet paper we passed from room to room. Each man would get to keep it for a certain period of time.

We also had a crafts program. Dat taught us to make crayon-type pencils. We would take our bread, dampen and roll it up just like a pencil. Then we would take a small wire and run it down the middle and allow the bread to harden. Next we would mix charcoal and soap to the right consistency and roll it out with our hand on the bunk and let it harden. Then we would insert it in the dough "Eversharp."

Dat was as ingenious a person as I have ever met. His full name was Nguyen Quoc Dat and his code name was Max. When we were first put in Building Zero we tried to bore a hole through the wall on one side but couldn't. One day we heard a sound in the wall from Dat's side. It continued for two or three minutes. Finally a little bit of plaster fell off and through it came a piece of brass half as thick as a pencil. My gaze through the tiny hole was met by an eyeball. I put my ear up against the hole and someone asked, "Can you hear me, Kornel?" (He always said "Kornel.")

I answered, "Yeah, Dat. What did you do?"

"I have just put a hole through the wall so that we can talk. Isn't this much better?"

"Yeah, but how long did it take you?"

"Oh, about three or four minutes."

I thought to myself, "That little liar." Three of us had been trying to get through the other wall for several days. "What did you use?"

"Here, I will give it to you. Would you like to make one through the other wall?"

I hesitated to tell him we had been trying for days. I told him, "Yeah, let me look at it."

He shoved through a little piece of brass about as big as a welding rod. I couldn't believe it. "Did you go through with this?"

"Yes, Kornel."

We took the little brass rod and ran it into the other wall as he had told us to, and the same thing happened as before. We kept hitting brick. We asked him again, "How long did it take you to get through?" He insisted, "Three or four minutes." I just knew he was lying. There were three of us, all senior officers. Although we considered ourselves fairly intelligent, we couldn't get through that other wall after days of trying with a sizable steel rod.

One day he called and said, "Kornel, did you ever get through to Kornel Kirk?" (Tom Kirk was living in the other cell.) I said, "No, Dat. Our hands are blistered, and we are still not through." He said, "Oh, that is too bad." He was always so polite. After only a few minutes there was a knock on the wall. We pulled the plug, and through the hole came a piece of paper with a diagram of the wall showing the layers of bricks, how they were constructed, and how to go between them. I took the little brass tube and searched for the right spot. In five minutes I went through.

In 1967 the Vietnamese had started to recognize our Fourth of July as a holiday in the prison camps for the purpose of relating American Independence Day to theirs. They wanted us to believe that we were both on the same side fighting for independence. On July 4 they brought us some liqueur. Dat, being Vietnamese, got none at all. But somewhere he had found several pieces of green plastic tubing about as big as spaghetti. We called it his Snake. He used it delivering notes and exchanging items; now we found a new use. We said, "Hey, Dat! Pass the Snake through and keep one end of it." He put it through the hole in the wall. We poured the liqueur into a cup and stuck the tube in it like a straw. We knocked on the wall and told him there was something to drink on the other end. He sucked it right down to the bottom, then knocked on the wall with big thumps: "Kornel, what was that?" We asked, "How'd you like that, Max?" "Oh, Kornel! That was wonderful!"

One day he tapped and said, "Kornel, do you need a pencil?" I said, "Lord, yes, we need a pencil." He gave us the wait signal and in a few minutes we got another tap on the wall. "Look under your door, Kornel." I looked and there was the Snake sticking under my door and tied to it was another green piece of plastic attached to a string. He directed, "Take off the pencil." I didn't know what he was talking about, but I took the small piece of plastic and saw that it was like a pencil. It had a piece of homemade lead that fit just inside the plastic, and as you used up the pencil lead, there was a piece of wood on top with which you pushed out the lead.

Dat was not only invaluable to us; he was a great source of morale. He claimed to be a Buddhist/Confucian but he always told us he enjoyed our church services, the singing and the "wise words."

Eventually they moved us from Buildin, Zero to Building Nine, a large barracks-like building, and Dat was there with us. The Vietnamese made him work in the courtyard every day. Dat would come in, make his report to me, and then flop down on his mat, arms and legs outstretched as though he were totally exhausted. When I'd ask him, "What did they make you do, Dat?" he'd answer, "Oh, Kornel, I went over to the gym and took a nap." He was a riot.

The French students were after him constantly. The Orientals are accustomed to a siesta, as much or more so than the Latin Americans. Dat really needed it and expected it. When he didn't get it he was washed out. I would have to ask the guys to cool it and let him take his siesta.

The Vietnamese told him not to make friends with us. They would come to the door and there would be four or five guys around Dat. They would all be laughing, talking and living it up. The Vietnamese would have him to a quiz and remind him that he should not get too friendly with us. They told him we were only using him and that we were sneaky, cunning and devious. Dat would get the biggest kick out of that. He was a very sharp individual and handled the Vietnamese with real poise.

With all that was being done to occupy the time, still the restlessness of some of the men became more pronounced with intimations of peace.

XXVIII

Intimations of Peace

It was in September of 1972 that they moved all of us in Building Zero (twenty-one prisoners) into Building Nine, which we called the Mayo. Previously it had held people who needed special medical attention, who might be suffering from asthmatic attacks, heart trouble or stomach ulcers. There were cement platforms along three walls; in the middle was a walking area of about seven feet. For the first time we had an indoor toilet—the old French type with a place for your feet but no stool or flushing apparatus. We had a small courtyard, perhaps twenty feet square, in which to bathe, wash our clothes and try to catch a little sun. It was so small and the wall so high that the sun shone in only two or three hours a day, and that was normally during the nap period. To get in the sun sometimes, the guys would get a stool or a bench and stand on it or sit on the low wall around the bathing area.

During this period our planes were coming over, sometimes at low altitude. The sonic boom would catch everyone by surprise. Several times a photo reconnaissance drone—an unmanned plane —came right over the camp. We figured they probably got our picture. The morale picked up. There was a lot of talk and laughter. We knew we weren't forgotten. We wondered if some of the pilots might even come over the camp on purpose just to say hello.

President Nixon's blockade of the ports, and the mining of the harbors and the river mouths had been in effect for some time. Our planes had also been bombing the railroads. This was evidently effective. The Vietnamese used it as the excuse for the lack of improvement in our food. We also noticed a great decrease in anti-aircraft and SAM fire. They were evidently running low on ammunition.

We had long since ceased to listen to the twice-a-day Voice of Vietnam broadcasts, so when they told us on October 26 that there was a special radio broadcast we were to listen to, we all thought it was only more propaganda. To get whatever information possible from the broadcasts, we had appointed a task force to interpret them. These included an American Domestics Expert. He would analyze the political and economic picture in the United States. We also had a Foreign Relations Expert, a Ground War and an Air War Expert. These people gave us a weekly comprehensive briefing. They were the ones who would listen to every broadcast.

On October 26 came the announcement of the peace-agreement negotiations in Paris by Dr. Henry Kissinger. When they started reading it, we all looked at one another. It sounded as if we were going to be home in sixty days. No one said anything, though, for everybody mistrusted the Vietnamese.

When they finally got to the end, the Vietnamese said, "The United States was supposed to have been in Hanoi to initial this today. On the twenty-eighth they were supposed to go to Paris to sign it. Had this happened, some of you would have been home for Christmas. But the United States has now gone back on their word." On it went, denouncing America and the "puppet" government of South Vietnam. It was all down the tubes. Everybody said, "What can you expect from the Vietnamese?"

During the broadcast several Vietnamese officers and some English-speaking turnkeys had been at the door watching. I guess they thought we were going to do back flips and handsprings or holler. Instead the men continued doing what they were doing before the broadcast. Some were playing bridge, others were studying mathematics or some language. They were listening, of course, but we had an unwritten standing rule never to let the Vietnamese know if we were interested. Besides, after years of hearing their garbage we didn't pay a whole lot of attention to the radio.

When they got to the end, everybody went on about their business. Nobody got in groups or in a big huddle. It was treated as normal, run-of-the-mill Vietnamese propaganda.

The Vietnamese watching were amazed. They called me to the door and asked, "What do you think of that?"

"What?"

Rather heatedly, they replied, "What was on the radio?"

I pretended to be dumber than I was and said, "Yeah, we heard it."

One of them asked, "Well, were you disappointed?"

"No, we expected you would do something like that when serious negotiations started."

The next morning, the executive officer came to the building. He wanted to know what had happened and how the men felt. Weren't they awfully disappointed? Didn't they really long for home? Were they sad and unable to sleep? He went through all kinds of mental gymnastics trying to find out if this hadn't had a terrible impact on us.

Then the camp commander called me out for a quiz. He went through the same line. Finally I said, "I would like to try to make something clear to you. You don't understand Americans and you never will. We have been here so long that what comes out of that radio is meaningless. When we walk out of here free men, that's when we'll become excited. Until that day you won't see any excitement, because we don't believe you.

"You can say anything you want to on the radio or tell us anything you want to and it will be just like all of the misinformation, the deceit and trickery that we have undergone for all of this time. You can't undo that. Regardless of whatever you say, the men will not pay any attention until we see it demonstrated in fact!"

They were flabbergasted. That people would go on playing bridge—and a couple or three people were practicing a song for the Christmas program while the agreement was being read—was unthinkable to them.

They continued to inquire in the other buildings to see why there wasn't a big commotion. People weren't crying in sadness or laughing, and there was no emotion or reaction. I think it really impressed the Vietnamese.

"I don't believe you," the camp commander told me. "I think you all are really upset."

"Well, do we look upset?"

"You are all very good actors. You yourself are a very good actor. That's the reason we don't trust you."

After October 26 we received a day-by-day description of what was happening. Of course, we got their view of it. They were always saying the United States was standing in the way of peace negotiations. Regardless, there was additional optimism in the buildings, but for the most part people were reserving judgment. We knew not to trust the Vietnamese or become optimistic and build our hopes only to have them fall again. We adopted a wait-and-see attitude.

On December 18 we were lying on our bunks when we heard aircraft engines. There hadn't been any bombing for a long time. It sounded like a squadron of airplanes at a great distance. We heard them for a long time. We thought they must really be moving slow or there were at least three or four squadrons. Then, shortly after we started hearing engines, the ground began to shake. We thought perhaps it was antiaircraft guns. Then the plaster started falling from the ceiling. Now we knew what was happening.

Everyone was kind of wide-eyed at first. We couldn't believe it. Then we jumped up and started cheering, clapping each other on the back. There was a regular hubbub. The guards ran over to the door to see what we were doing. They told everyone to lie down on their bunks. Some were not doing so. One of the guards got excited and called for an officer. While he was on his way to our building this guard asked me, "Are you afraid?" He was brushing debris out of his hair where something had fallen on him.

"No, we're not afraid." Everyone was laughing, talking and cheering.

He became very excited and said, "They are trying to kill you."

I said, "No, they're not trying to kill *us*."

The officer who came was the camp commander. The guard told him I had said the planes should kill all the Vietnamese women and children, which I hadn't said, naturally. The next morning I had a quiz with the camp commander. He was somewhat up in the air.

By the second night we were sure the planes were B-52s; we knew they were flying at a high altitude. And we could see a definite change in the attitude of the Vietnamese. Before, they had been defiant, because the fighter planes would come in so low that they could shoot at them even with their rifles. Of course they didn't hit many of them. But it was something they could get hold of. They weren't afraid of them. They had been taught that it was a total disgrace to turn from the enemy. They would stand right out in the open and shoot. They would laugh, talk and holler at each other when they were fighting the airplanes.

But it was a totally different situation with the B-52s. They not only came in at night but so high that it was impossible to see them. All you could hear was a faint drone of the engines and then that *womp, womp, womp, womp* of the bombs hitting the ground. The ground would shake and quiver. All the bridges were knocked down and a lot of damage was done to the railroads and highways.

What made us so enthusiastic about the bombing was the fact that the Vietnamese had been dragging their feet on the negotiations for years. All they had done was use the Paris Conference as a propaganda vehicle. Every single week we got a partial transcript of those meetings. It would state: "And as usual, the United

States negotiator, Bruce, made his normal slanderous allegations . . ." Then they would give us the verbatim text of the speech given by the Communists. It was the same old garbage with not one single bit of difference for years.

The bombing stopped on Christmas Eve but started again the twenty-sixth of December. It accomplished its objectives. Shortly thereafter, we were read an agreement plus the protocols. They said, "You will receive these in writing." They brought one over to us that night. For the next day or two they continued to bring them as they ran them off on a mimeograph machine until we all had a copy of the agreements and copies of certain of the protocols.

At this time the optimism was quite high. We were beginning to see the light at the end of the tunnel. Within sixty days we would all be home, according to the agreements.

The Vietnamese had one last present for us before we left. The report came in that they had taken some of the men downtown to a museum of horrors. It had pictures of all kinds of mutilated bodies, dead babies and deformed embryos. Every weapon they could pick up alleged to be American was displayed. The whole building was filled with these. The men that were taken didn't want to go and tried not to go.

The next night they tried to take some others. The men refused and were carried, pushed and shoved into the truck and taken through the museum.

Our building was expected to be next. I put out the order that we should resist. We should tell them that we weren't going, demand to see an officer, repeat that we would not leave the camp voluntarily, and finally, make them use force on us.

That evening it was as expected. The first few men were taken out and they did just as I had said. They demanded to see an officer, refused to go, refused to leave the camp, and really made a big ruckus. As a result, they were brought back and left in the courtyard. Then I was taken out. I started talking to the men and the guard made me shut up.

I was led to the camp commander, who had an interpreter with him. He said, "Why don't you want to go?" I explained to him that we had been used as tools for propaganda, we had been tricked, cheated, lied to and tortured. We were not going to give them any more.

"I will personally conduct you through the town and let you see it," he said. "We want you to take some culture home with you. We want you to understand the Vietnamese."

"I don't want to understand anything more about the Vietnamese than I understand," I replied. "If it's so important, why haven't you been this kind throughout the years? Why now?"

"Because we want you to understand and see the way Vietnamese live."

"We are not going," I said. "We know that it is purely for propaganda purposes."

Then he got hard-nosed. He said, "Look, you are going, and you are going to see what President Nixon has done to the Vietnamese people. You are going to see the instruments of death that he has used. And you are going to see the death and destruction we have suffered."

At first he had said he wanted to conduct me on a tour of the parks, the city, the cathedrals, and all the landmarks. When I told him we weren't interested, he came to the truth of the matter. He was going to make us go to this museum of horrors.

"You have tried for seven or eight years to change our attitudes," I said. "What you're going to show us is nothing new from what you have been showing us all this time. Nothing you can tell us now is going to change our minds or our hearts. You'll have to torture us to get us down there."

He said, "You are going!"

I was taken back to our building. The other men had been

returned also. We didn't know if we had won a battle or if it had just been postponed. It was only postponed.

The next night they came for me. I didn't know exactly where we were going, but I suspected what was up. The Vietnamese had the right to move us from camp to camp. If they ordered you to go someplace, there was very little you could do. I didn't want to refuse to be moved.

When I asked where we are going, they retorted, "None of your business." I said, "I'm not going to leave this camp until I talk to the camp commander."

They took me out the gate, pulling me by both arms. When I saw the bus I said, "I'm not getting on. I want to see the camp commander." I began to make a fuss. They got a man behind me and one on each arm and propelled me toward the bus. I stuck my feet in the ground. They pushed and dragged me. When I got to the bus I tried to put my arms against the door frame to keep from going in. One of the guards got inside and they passed my arm to him. With one dragging and some pushing they put me in the bus. The same thing happened to the other men. Some of them were lifted up, bodily carried in and plopped down in the seats.

Downtown we refused to get off the bus. They pulled us off and told us to march inside the museum. We wouldn't move. They had to push and pull us inside the building. Then one of the guards started giving us a running commentary on all the displays. We refused to look. We would stare at the floor or the ceiling.

This upset them, to say the least. The guards came over and tried to turn our heads with their hands. It started getting pretty rough. They jerked, pushed, twisted and poked us around. During the whole time they had to physically propel us. When they turned our heads with their hands, we would close our eyes.

After we got back to camp, the next group to go was the nine senior officers billeted in Building Eight. They were told to get dressed, and they refused. They were in their shorts. The guards had to throw them down and dress them. One of them had to be dressed in the bus. Another was taken off the bus and dressed in front of the museum.

They came back bruised, cut and bleeding. Their clothes were torn. They had really put up a wrestling match. They didn't raise their hands against the guards, but they resisted in every way they could to keep from being put in that bus.

After that first night another batch was taken down, but they discontinued before everyone had gone. This was no more than a month or so before release.

Now that release was imminent the Vietnamese camp staff began to deal more with the senior officers. They let the senior officers run the buildings and began to talk to them for the first time. They also began to talk to John Flynn, since they knew he was running the camp; they had monitored enough of our communications to know John was calling the shots. Yet we coded the communications so much that they could never tell for sure what was happening. They had gotten the tap code many times, but it was used in so many different ways it was hard to grasp. And when we talked we noticed how surprisingly effective Pig Latin could be.

Since release was to be in order of shoot-down, the men were brought back from Dog Patch, a camp near the Chinese border. (Even while they were up there, they had been put in buildings according to shoot-down date.) Two weeks before release they moved some people over to the Plantation, including Colonel Flynn. That left me as POW camp commander. During this period I talked to the camp commander every day. He let me start going around talking to people in all the rooms. The last few days I had all of the men out together for the first time in POW history. Without asking for permission, I addressed them in the courtyard. It was really funny. The guards' eyes nearly popped out. I wanted to see if we could get away with it. I also wanted to tell the men what to do in case cameras came into the camp. They had wanted to show us playing ping-pong and volleyball on tables and courts that had not been used the previous seven and a half years.

Before they moved Colonel Flynn, the camp commander informed him that there would be a live show and asked if the men would attend. He told them no. When they took John out, they approached me. I told them no also. When they persisted, I went through the same reasons I had given them before as to why we weren't going downtown. I said, "We don't trust you. The only reason you want to bring live entertainment in is to get pictures of it and show how nice we are treated. I'm not buying."

They brought it in, anyway, and set it up in the courtyard. It was a live troupe. There were a lot of good-looking girls, some song-and-dance acts, juggling and musicians, etc. When it started, as per instruction, everybody went inside. No one appeared at the doors or the windows. The guards went around and talked to them and tried to get them to come out. Not a soul did.

The Vietnamese said they were going to have another show the next day, for the Vietnamese. We could come if we wanted to. Everyone said "No go!," so they disassembled their equipment and disappeared.

We had talked to the camp commander about cameras. To prevent incidents we asked him to keep correspondents and cameramen away from the men on the day of release, including the time we would be en route or when we got to the airport. I told him there'd be bad trouble if he let correspondents or cameramen in camp. He said, "I can control them inside the camp but I cannot control them en route. They will be lining the streets and they will be at the airport. But I will tell them to keep a respectful distance and not to bother you." We said, "Okay." He added, "I guarantee there will be no cameras in this camp and no correspondents."

I told the men what he had said. If the reporters did show, I told them to notify me.

Sure enough, three or four days before the release a whole battery of French correspondents and photographers walked through the gate with cameras going. We were all out in the courtyard and I saw them almost as soon as they came in. I gave the signal for the men to go to their rooms and pull the doors closed after them. They were not to pose for any pictures. Everyone picked up and started to go in, but several men were photographed on the way in.

The French journalists wanted to ask questions. The men referred them to the senior officer and when they came to me, I was somewhat aggravated over the camp commander's broken promise. My answers to a few of their questions were printed and misquoted in a couple of instances. They were still trying for propaganda in the last few days.

They issued some very brightly colored sweaters for us to wear. We wouldn't accept them, for we did not want to appear like civilians coming out of prison. First, we were going to demand to go out in prison clothes. Then we decided that might not be helping the release. We decided to be more flexible. We would take what was reasonable, no loud clothes, no suits or ties. We would go out in shirt and pants provided by the Vietnamese, and if the weather was cold, we would wear a jacket.

Release time began to approach. As it did I reflected a lot on what had happened to me during my stay in the Democratic Republic of Vietnam. I'm awfully glad I didn't know seven and a half years before, when I was shot down in a rice paddy, what was ahead of me. In my wildest imagination I had no idea American prisoners of war would be treated as inhumanely and cruelly as we were. But that long night was almost over. We were going home!

XXIX

Free At Last

On the day of release we left the Hanoi Hilton by bus in order of shoot-down. There were four groups of us, with about 120 men in each. Ev Alvarez was number one. Bob Schumaker was next. I was number twenty-seven now, since Ron Stortz had given his life in prison.

We went to Gia Lam, three miles from Hanoi, and were held there for a few hours. While sitting in buses on the ramp, we saw three C-141s make a circle. It was so beautiful. We couldn't believe a bird that big could be so graceful. Along the sides of the fuselage was painted UNITED STATES AIR FORCE with a big red cross on the tail.

The planes landed one by one and taxied up, and we got out of the buses. There were a lot of photographers, but the Vietnamese wouldn't let them come close. Then we formed in columns of two. The Rabbit was in charge. As he called our names we stepped forward to shake hands with the American representative. In our case it was Air Force Colonel Al Lynn, an old friend of mine. He was dressed in a beautiful blue Air Force uniform. I was overwhelmed with emotion. The moment I touched his hand, I knew I was free. I couldn't restrain myself. We threw our arms around each other and embraced in front of all the people.

Escort officers took us by the arm and steered us onto those beautiful airplanes. The crews, the wonderful nurses, the escort officers—everybody was so great. However, when we boarded we discovered there were litters for everyone in case we were sick—since they didn't know what our state of health would be. There was no brandy or steak or any of what the guys had been expecting. I asked the physician on board, "Doc, what happened?"

"Well, we knew you have been on such a bland diet for so long that we were afraid to upset your stomach, and that you would be sick before you reached the hospital." Then he said, "You'll be on a soft diet for a few days."

I was convinced that would have to be changed, but right now we were leaving North Vietnam—a feeling I didn't want to miss.

We had always said we wouldn't really trust the Vietnamese until our wheels had left the ground. Our plane taxied out and waited for clearance. Then the pilot threw the coal to it. Everyone was kind of tense and unmoving. We hadn't ridden in a C-141 before and we didn't know how long the takeoff roll would be. It didn't take long. We surged forward, the nose came up, and we were airborne.

As soon as we felt the vibrations stop and knew the aircraft had lifted from the ground, a wild cheer swept the airplane. Everyone shouted, clapped their hands and laughed. There were a lot of released emotions at that moment. Some people were taking pictures, the nurses were getting a lot of hugs and kisses—all very circumspect, of course—and everyone was plain happy. The captain of the airplane, a lieutenant colonel, came on the intercom system and said, "For everyone's information, I am empowered to perform weddings." The nurses gasped, "Oh, no!" (At the banquet for the Son Tay Raiders, sponsored by Ross Perot, one of the nurses came with one of our bachelors in a leopard-skin formal! She was really something to see.)

During the four-hour flight I continued to insist that the doctor get the diet changed. He asked me what we had been eating. "Well, the last few months we've had a lot of pig fat and grease," I said.

"If you can digest that, you can eat anything." He radioed ahead to change the diet to the normal one.

On the way to the Philippines we received a radio message from Clark Air Force Base saying that they would want the senior officer to say a few words when we disembarked. I said I would, and then totally forgot about it. There were so many exciting things going on that it was impossible to keep track of what was happening.

It was a grand flight out. We got the names and addresses of all the crew members and later wrote them a letter of thanks.

Our minds were running like a fast-speed motion picture. A million things flashed through our minds: When would we get to see our wives and families? What were we going to buy? How soon could we get back on flying status? What would our reception be like? How would the American public feel about us? How long would we be at Clark? Where would we go next? But no one was sitting lost in reverie. Everyone was either talking, reading or moving about. The time was filled to the hilt.

As we approached Clark, the pilot received a radio call from a commercial airliner that was departing. They said, "Is Wes Schierman on board?" The pilot called back to find out. Wes went scuttling up to the cockpit and the airline pilot identified himself. It was a friend of Wes's who had flown with him while he was with the airline. The pilot told him, "Wes, just wanted to tell you that we're waiting for you to come back. Your seniority has continued and you are less than 300 out of 1500!" Wes really got a charge out of it.

It was one great feeling to touch down at Clark; we knew now we were in friendly territory. I had been at the base lots of times and had many friends there, both military and Filipino civilians. As the plane drew to a stop, we looked out the window and saw quite a few people. On the way over, we had been told by our escort officer that the President himself, out of consideration for us, had requested everyone to allow us the maximum amount of privacy. We were informed there wouldn't be very many people present, for they had been told not to come. We would proceed quickly and quietly to the hospital.

But as we taxied in, we saw that the ramp was surrounded with American flags, banners, signs, and thousands of people were there. They were so emotionally caught up with our homecoming that they refused to stay away. When the door to the aircraft opened, there were people waving and shouting. When we got close enough to see them—our own emotions were already near the surface—it was just more than we could take.

As we taxied up, my escort officer had reminded me that I was supposed to say something. Absolutely no one had suggested anything to say or not to say, but we were not unprepared for being released. We had been making plans for years. We knew there was an area about which we could not talk without jeopardizing those that remained—no one had to brief us on that. And we knew what we felt. When I stepped off that airplane, I knew that the men with whom I had shared more than seven years of hell felt as I did. They were thankful to God, to the American people, and to their Commander in Chief, President Nixon.

As the door of the plane opened, I was the first one to leave, followed by my very close friend Navy Captain Jim Stockdale, who is now an admiral. As I walked down the ramp on the red carpet they had spread out, Admiral Noel Gayler, Commander in Chief Pacific, was at the end of the ramp. I saluted him, shook hands, and he welcomed me back. Next was General Joseph Moore, commander of the Thirteenth Air Force. He said, "Welcome home, Robbie."

After I shook a Marine master sergeant's hand, General Moore directed me toward a microphone that had been set on a stand. As I turned toward the microphone, I caught my first real look at the people. They were cheering, and I had some friends who were shouting my name. My eyesight had deteriorated so badly in prison that without glasses I couldn't identify anyone, but I could see some big signs, "WELCOME HOME, ROBBIE." I saw people wiping their eyes, but I didn't realize they were crying until someone told me later. All of us were overwhelmed at the reception. There had been a lot of questions about how we would be received. But the sincerity and feelings in the welcome was beyond anything we had imagined.

After I said a few words into the microphone, we got on the bus for the ride to the hospital. Both military and civilians were lining the streets. Some were crying, many waving flags; they were just like our family.

At the hospital it was the same way. The nurses and staff on the floor we were assigned cried and hugged us. Every minute detail was taken care of. There wasn't anything we needed or wanted that we didn't get. People were bringing in fruit, cookies, candy, books, games, harmonicas—you name it and it was available.

At six-thirty the entire first contingent on the three aircraft ate dinner together. This was supposed to be the regular diet to replace the sick diet they had planned. It was unlike any regular diet that I had ever seen: we had our choice of steak and fish, and the desserts were fantastic. They had an ice cream bar with eight or ten kinds of ice cream, all sorts of syrups, dressings and peanuts. Everyone had dreamed of steak. We hadn't had any the entire period except for one piece of water buffalo. We were starved for beef. And the ice cream bar really took a beating. Some guys went back four or five times. Some of them must have eaten half a gallon of ice cream the first night.

The salad bar was tremendous. That was something else we had missed in particular—green vegetables. Several took a whole dinner plate full of salad with salad dressing all over it.

Instead of bread I ate two or three pieces of cake. That was one of the foods I had missed most. Through all of it the dietician, a female black major, just smiled and made any combinations we wanted.

They waited on us as if we were bed patients. They had our schedules arranged with a trip to the base exchange. After the BX was closed, they took us back at night and all the personnel came back on duty voluntarily.

Some guys did not go to bed the first night, they were so excited. They talked and talked to the nurses. They called home, went by each other's rooms, and partied. It was hard to unwind.

I was doing a lot of administrative work trying to square things away for the people going back to the States, and also to smooth over the release of the next POW contingent. They were doing such a bang-up job at Clark that all of us wanted to give them any information they did not previously have that would make their jobs easier.

Once at the hospital we shucked the clothes we had been issued by the Vietnamese, never to put them back on again. Some of them went to charitable organizations, to schools and boy scout troops, and even the Smithsonian Institution. Until we could get uniforms, we were content with hospital pajamas and robes. The very first day the military tailors began to fit us with a Class A uniform, two Class A shirts, two short-sleeved shirts, a couple of sets of underwear, handkerchiefs, socks and shoes. They had all of the ribbons that we were entitled to mounted, fixed and ready to go. Although I had been a full colonel for seven years, this was my first time to wear the eagles.

When I got everything on, I felt like a new man. It had been so long since I had had any decent clothes on. Besides being dressed, I was in a uniform that reflected something of which I was very proud—the United States Air Force.

The only thing that bothered me were the shoes. The bottom of my feet were like the pads of an animal—thick and calloused from going barefooted so much of the time. And I had run a lot in place barefooted. But the tops of my feet had hardly been touched for seven and a half years and were extremely tender.

Next we flew to a tremendous welcome in Hawaii at Hickam

Air Force Base. I had been stationed there before going to Kadina. There were banners, "WELCOME HOME, POWs," and I saw some, ten or fifteen feet long, saying, "WELCOME HOME, ROBBIE." It looked as if there were several thousand people.

Admiral Gayler was present again, and some of my very old friends. Major General Smokespanger of the Marines, who had flown with me in Korea in F-86s as an exchange pilot, was there, as was Dottie, the wife of Boots Blesse, deputy for operations at Pacific Air Force headquarters and the author of the U.S. Air Force's primary manual on fighter tactics, *No Guts, No Glory*. Boots was on a trip and couldn't make it. Also, General Tim O'Keefe was in the terminal. The protocol officer took me to see some old friends, Mr. and Mrs. Yasahari and Mr. and Mrs. Tam. They were Hawaiians. Mr. Yasahari had been the assistant pastor of the church we had attended during my three-year tour there from 1961 to 1964.

I said a few words into the microphone and then we flew to Travis Air Force Base near San Francisco. The welcome was just as enthusiastic as in Hawaii. In the terminal I was surprised right off of my feet when my brother, Grover, and his wife, my sister, Peggy, and her husband, and my niece—all of whom lived in California—were all standing just inside the door. It was a wonderful surprise. Some of my old classmates and friends were there. I was taken by the base commander to make a telephone call to the Pentagon. When he brought me back, I hadn't had any time to visit with my relatives. He let me visit with them fifteen minutes longer while they held the airplane.

It was one grand feeling to be in the continental United States. But I could hardly wait to see Kathleen. She would be waiting for me at Shepherd Air Force Base in Wichita Falls, Texas.

XXX

My Candle in the Window

Letters and packages from home had been great morale boosters in prison—which was the reason the Vietnamese seldom let us receive them. Most men received little mail until 1969. If we were in punishment at the time they were being distributed, they kept them. They usually rifled the packages so that we averaged getting less than half of what had actually been sent. And for some perverse reason, they refused to let some of the men receive any.

The packages were like a life line with our family. I can remember picking up each item, no matter how small, holding it and looking at it. Then I would smell it, and hold it to my face, just because I knew my wife and children had sent it and touched it. That was a link that was sacred.

I remember the first package I received was delivered in the winter of 1969. I was in solitary confinement. The Cat himself gave it to me. I could carry it in one hand. There were two packages of gum, two packages of mints, a plastic bottle of deodorant, one of after-shave lotion, and some family snapshots. I was so thrilled to get it I didn't think to ask him what happened to the other 11½ pounds of items.

I made the gum last three months by just chewing a piece every week. The same way with the mints. I kept the deodorant and the after-shave lotion until 1971. It was a tangible memento of my family.

The same pattern applied to letters. We averaged receiving two letters a year. Some men not only did not receive their first letter until after more than five years of captivity, but they also were not allowed to write their first letter until then. Normally, if the Vietnamese wanted a man to record or write something to use for propaganda, they would let him write a letter first. Then after they had tortured a tape or statement out of him, it would be more credible when they presented both.

The letters that we wrote were restricted to six lines (it increased to seven in 1971) on a narrow piece of paper. We would write out a draft on a brown piece of paper. We would have to put the address and our name and everything on it just as if we were going to send it. It would then go to the censors. When it came back it would have words marked out, circled in red along with comments. We would have to rewrite it, take out all the objectionable words and phrases, and very seldom would we be allowed to put anything else in.

One time the Vietnamese were angry at me but they had an order that all the prisoners would get to write a Christmas letter home. I wrote one and when it came back from them, they had taken nearly everything out but "Merry Christmas"!

We learned to put a lot into those six or seven lines. Sometimes we would work on them all month. We would have them composed in our minds so that when they offered us the opportunity to write, we could sit down and scribble it out. I was getting as much as 130 words to a letter. Then the Vietnamese complained that I was writing too small and they couldn't read it.

We also debriefed each time after our approved letter was written to find out what words and phrases had been objectionable to the Vietnamese. This way we were able to sterilize our letters ourselves so that we could get the maximum amount out.

I remember one time thinking for days of a suitable phrase that would convey to Kathleen how much I loved her and missed her. I knew if the words I chose were not very clear, the Vietnamese would take them out. Finally I hit upon it. It expressed my feelings perfectly and I felt confident the Vietnamese would let it pass. When letter-writing time came, I wrote among other things, "Kathleen, you're my candle in the window."

When the letter went to the censors, I felt safe with my choice. And I knew it would convey to Kathleen how very much I was thinking of her. When the letter came back the sentence was deleted and they had me in for a quiz because of it. They were sure it was some code or phrase with a double meaning.

Kathleen was an anchor to me all the time I was imprisoned. Many a time while in stocks or solitary confinement, I would picture in my mind my lovely Kathleen. I wanted to see her so badly I could hardly stand it.

While we were at Clark my new escort officer, Colonel Fizzell, arranged for a telephone call the very first evening. After dinner he took me to the Red Cross and placed the call and got Kathleen on the line. He had talked to her several times before. When I said, "Hello, Kathleen," she said, "Robbie, is that you? You sound just the same." We talked and laughed a great deal. I asked about each of the boys. I dreaded to for fear one of them had died or was in the hospital. She said, "Oh, they're fine." Then I named them one by one to get reassurance. She told me Jeff and Paul had an old van, which I found hard to believe. She said vans were very popular. They just threw a mattress in the back seat and picked up a whole load of kids on the way to school. However, right then it was out of commission in the front yard.

She said the boys were apprehensive about their hair. She asked if I knew that they had long hair. I said yes. I didn't tell her that I had read it in *The Christian Science Monitor*. She said they wanted to know how short they should get it cut. I said, "Sugar, you tell them not to worry about it. Tell them to use their own discretion." She said, "They'll be relieved." She said I looked good and talked strong when I came off the plane. She wondered if I knew that my mother had passed away, which of course I did.

I asked her, "Would you like to meet me alone, or do you want to bring the children?"

"What do you want to do?"

"I'd like for you to meet me alone."

She said, "I was hoping you'd say that."

At Shepherd I left the aircraft and went directly to a car where my new escort officer was waiting. He took me to the quarters arranged for us and left me at the door so that I could meet Kathleen in privacy. It was a wonderful meeting. We just held each other for a while and Kathleen cried out of happiness and relief. Then we sat down on the divan to talk and it lasted almost all night. We finally went to bed but didn't go to sleep. I would ask her questions about anything bad that had happened; I guess I wanted to get it over with. She would start telling me some things about Jeff having plastic surgery after a motorcycle accident, or one of the motorcycles being stolen, and the car being crumped. I would say, "Oh, oh, wait a minute, that's enough for now." She was feeding me a little bit of bad news at a time. Then came a big blow. Paul, my brother, my fishing and hunting buddy, the one who loved horses and motorcycles as I did, had died before I was released. There would be no more bass fishing on quiet lakes, or trout lines across muddy rivers, no more glorious exhilarating motorcycle rides along winding roads. Our knees would never touch again as we rode loose-reined quarter horses along moonlit trails. Someone I loved very much was now missing from the picture I had mentally painted while in prison.

After we had been together almost a week, Kathleen had to go to Oklahoma City for a day to do some things for the children. When she left I called my eldest son, Rob, who was working on his master's in criminology at Sam Houston State College in Huntsville, Texas. I asked him if he could come up to spend the night with me.

Rob had been in the news quite a bit while I was in prison

because of his support for Senator McGovern for President. I had learned of it in prison. In 1972 before the elections, the Rat, one of the camp officers, came to my building. He brought a copy of a recent *Christian Science Monitor*. He called me to the door and said, "This has an article in which you will be interested." It was circled in red on the front. The headline read: "POW's Family Split on Politics."

It was a UPI story about my family. The Vietnamese gave it to everybody in camp. The text of the article was that my wife and son Rob had been interviewed in our home and that they did not agree on politics. It said my wife backed President Nixon to the hilt. She was quoted as saying, "It's the only way to get the POWs home." She advocated leaving troops in Vietnam until we were out, to continue the bombing and the mining. I was so very, very proud of her.

Then it said Rob was driving a green Volkswagen with a McGovern sticker on it. He had been campaigning in East Texas for Senator McGovern. I must confess I was shocked and a little sick. I couldn't help it. I guess I had banked on President Nixon so heavily that I had assumed my entire family would do the same. It just shows how unbalanced a person's thinking can get in such an environment. I knew that Senator McGovern had appealed to the young people in the United States but I didn't know that Rob was for him.

After I got over the shock of the article, I realized that in the land of the free we have a choice. That also meant my son. My family had always been Democrats. As I read and reread the article, I could see Rob's reasons for supporting Senator McGovern. He felt President Nixon had had four years to get the POWs home and they were still in prison. He said, "I've got to try something different, the only alternative is Senator McGovern. I like what he's saying. I believe that he can and will get my dad out." He not only supported the senator on Vietnam, but on most other issues preferred him over the President.

I liked some of the things Senator McGovern was saying. But I simply couldn't buy his foreign policy. I didn't know how he could say the things he did about the war, although I felt sure he was absolutely sincere, a fine man and a good statesman.

After digesting the article, I didn't condemn Rob. I loved him too much. I respected him and I knew that anything that he was doing had my best interests at heart. He was doing his level best to get me out of prison. I couldn't do anything but love him more for it.

Also, I had always wanted my boys to stand on their own two feet, to make their own decisions. Rob had done that for sure. I respected him even more to think that he would go against the tide to do something that he felt very strongly about. And I learned after I came back that some of the younger boys felt the same way as Rob.

I had just returned to quarters from the hospital when Rob drove up. I was still standing on the sidewalk and I recognized his green Volkswagen. I wasn't sure I recognized him. He had a mustache and his hair was almost to his shoulders.

When he had told me, "Good-bye, Daddy," seven and a half years before, he was a month short of seventeen years old. He was driving my little white TR-3 around the base when I wasn't using it. Once a month he could take it off the base at night for a date. He was mature for his age, dependable, trustworthy and honest. I went around to the driver's side of the car. He got out and said, "Daddy," and put his arms around me. We just squeezed each other and stood there for a few minutes until we regained our composure.

Rob is small, perhaps five foot eight and weighs 150 pounds. When I left him he was perhaps five foot four and weighed about 125. He felt as hard as a rock. His arms were larger than mine. I pushed him away from me so I could look at him. I said, "Where'd you get that mustache?" He laughed and said, "I thought you'd like that."

I helped him unload his stuff. He'd brought a couple of tennis rackets. He'd asked me on the phone if I wanted to play a little tennis.

That night we sat down and talked about politics. I had not told him about having read the *Christian Science Monitor* article. I tried first as best I could to explain my position regarding the war, as well as President Nixon and Senator McGovern. I said that in the prison we came to the conclusion that the Vietnamese understood and respected force. Many times when we were reasonable, they would assume it was weakness and took advantage of us. They respected strength. They respected a person who was unyielding, who upheld those things that he believed in, who did not yield, who did not weaken, who did not compromise. They may have hated and mistrusted President Nixon, but I honestly believe that he had a greater respect in their eyes than those who might have been a little more tractable.

President Nixon had presented a strong stance all through his term in office. It was not just words, for he backed up each position with action. He would make public his plans for ending the war. In so doing he would spell out to the North Vietnamese the parameters of acceptable conduct. He always explained that overstepping of those boundaries would result in retaliation. And he kept his word. The Vietnamese respected that. They knew he meant what he said.

Each time the Vietnamese violated tacit agreements, such as coming across the DMZ in force, shooting down a reconnaissance plane or making rocket attacks on the population centers in South Vietnam, he would hit them in force. Not only did he respond with strength, but there was always sound military logic and strategy behind his moves. The Vietnamese knew this better than anyone.

When he went into Cambodia he proved to them that not only

did he have guts, he was smart. He continually attacked their major supply lines into South Vietnam for the Viet Cong. When he mined the harbors and the river mouths, it was a drastic step. But it had its effect.

When they began pussyfooting around at the negotiating table, in effect playing with the lives of thousands of American fighting men, he bombed the stuffings out of their highways, bridges, factories and railroads. They finally got the message. They recognized they couldn't hold out. Either they negotiated or committed national suicide.

Rob seemed to understand my position better. Then he told me quite frankly what he had been doing. He was very honest about it. He said, "Daddy, I felt the only way to get you out was to get McGovern in." I said I understood. We talked on a great deal. When we had finished he said, "I'm glad we had an opportunity to discuss this. You know why I was campaigning for McGovern. Now I understand your thinking and I have a better picture of President Nixon." He had not changed in his respect and admiration for Senator McGovern—this had not changed and it probably never will—but he did understand President Nixon better and the reasons for his moves. He was able to appreciate my admiration for President Nixon's personal courage.

Later a reporter from *Time* magazine who had talked to Kathleen off and on down through the years, spent a couple of days around the house. During this period the reporter talked to the boys as well as to Kathleen. She almost became one of the family, she was there so often. She had breakfast with us occasionally, saw all the ins and outs and got a pretty good feel for things. The only thing she misunderstood was what had happened between Rob and me. She thought that Rob had changed and was now a Nixon man. When an issue of *Time* came out with this story, it upset us all. She had Rob switching from McGovern to Nixon due to my influence.

Rob prepared a letter to the editor to correct it. He was a

little apprehensive about what I would think of it. When he came up from Huntsville one evening, he showed it to his mother and asked, "What do you think Daddy will say to that?" She just laughed and said, "Why don't you show it to him?" With a kind of cute apprehensiveness about him, he said, "Daddy, would you read that?" I read it and really got a charge out of it. I said, "Why don't you send it?" He was so relieved he said, "Dad, I'm glad you said that." Rob's letter was reprinted in *Time* (April 23, 1973) and read as follows:

Non-Support

Sir/ In your story on the P.O.W.s [March 19] you said that as a newly returned prisoner of war, Colonel Robinson Risner had even talked all of his children into supporting President Nixon, although they all had supported Senator McGovern in the presidential campaign. I am Colonel Risner's oldest son, and I do not now support, nor have I ever supported President Nixon.

When Senator McGovern campaigned in Oklahoma City last summer, I explained in his presence that I believed President Nixon had failed at any attempt to end the war and free the prisoners; and that I believed Senator McGovern was sincere in his efforts to end the war and bring the prisoners home.

ROB RISNER
Huntsville, Texas

After I had been at Shepherd for seven days, I had seen Rob, but I had not been with the other four children. My good friend at Shepherd, Colonel Frank Snyder, volunteered to drive Kathleen and me to Oklahoma City. Before we left I had a call from the Warr Acres Police Department, the suburb in which we lived, saying they would like to have a little parade for us when I came into town. I agreed and the Warr Acres Police Department met us at Chickasha, about forty miles out of Oklahoma City, and escorted us in. We picked up another police car or two on the way.

When we began to get into Warr Acres, we saw some street decorations. There were flags lining the streets and signs saying,

"WELCOME HOME, COLONEL RISNER" or "WELCOME HOME, ROB-
BIE!" Once in Warr Acres, we pulled into a side street and there
was a band in front of us.

We got out of the car and I saw some of my old friends and
one of my nephews. People were shouting "Hello!" and "Welcome Home!" On the bandstand the mayor read a proclamation
and presented me with the key to the city. Then Miss Oklahoma,
who was from Warr Acres, kissed me and presented a bouquet to
Kathleen. I said a few words of appreciation to the crowd.

Then they took me home. My brothers, sisters, and kinfolks
had sort of told Kathleen they would not be present when I
arrived so I could have a reunion alone with the family. Somehow
or other they couldn't wait. They were there, also some newspaper
people, and a man whose son was missing in action was waiting
to talk to me. When I arrived and got out of the car, the first person I saw was Jeff, my eighteen-year-old. He ran up to me and we
embraced. Then the others descended on me—Paul, sixteen, Tim,
fourteen, and Danny, twelve. It was a real thrill. They had grown
so much, I don't know if I would have recognized them.

We had a wonderful reunion. Someone was taking pictures.
The bakery had sent a two-foot-square cake frosted with an American flag and "Welcome Home, Robbie" on the bottom. The table
was completely loaded with all kinds of seafood. Everything was
there.

I was home. There was no longer any need for a candle in
the window.

XXXI

Home

The next evening for the first time we sat down at the dining room table alone together. I had anticipated this for so long, for one of the things that I had thought about most was the family around the dining table. I always wondered what they thought of as they asked the blessing, and I remembered wondering how it would feel to put my feet under my own table again and to look around at the faces I loved. Now it had come true at last. It was a very special moment. Everyone was rather quiet. I asked the blessing and their quietness evaporated. It was a regular hubbub with everyone talking at once. It was a wonderful, wonderful meal.

I noticed that the children were very complimentary to their mother. After the meal was over we just sat there. We talked for hours and hours. Finally Kathleen cleared the table so we would have more room. It was a very special time.

In prison I remember thinking that one of the things that hurt most was my children growing up without me. I was missing a critical time of their life. That thought had tortured me. I would talk to my roommate about it. We discussed how the older children would have grown away from us, and that we could no longer expect a lot of affection from them because that's the way young people are. I thought perhaps the two younger ones might still be small enough to pull down on my lap occasionally or kiss good night or put my arm around, but not the older three.

It turned out to be just the opposite. The two younger ones are still becoming accustomed to me, I guess, although they show signs of affection. They tell me good bye when they leave, and they're glad when I come back home from a trip. But the three older ones are very affectionate, even though there may be a stranger in the house. When they go to bed or when they leave to go somewhere, they normally put their arms around me and give me a kiss and tell me they love me. It's something I wouldn't trade for all the tea in China.

If I am critical of something they do or might not do, I always return to the fact that we love each other and we are a close-knit family. Kathleen did an absolutely miraculous job in keeping our family together. None of the boys are hooked on drugs. They are alive and healthy. They're honest. They're loving. And I feel that we all have a great future.

That first full day at home was all I had dreamed of. Replacing taciturn guards were my sons. I had silverware instead of a spoon, china instead of a metal dish, plenty of water and plumbing facilities.

That day the beautiful sun shone. I could stay in or go out as I pleased.

I didn't have to dream of someone to touch, to kiss or caress. My wonderful wife was near me.

The musty, dank smell of small enclosed cells was forever gone. The air was fresh and free for the taking.

I could go where I wanted, talk to whom I wished, read—with glasses—whenever and whatever I wished. I was being treated as a man again and not as a caged animal.

Our house, though very modest with one story and four bedrooms, was a beautiful mansion compared to Hoa Lo. I was grateful for everything there. For my clothes, razor blades, towels, hot water, soap, everything.

My dread was gone. The future was before me. The doors that were locked and closed were now unlocked and permanently open. The darkness of that long unbelievable night had finally passed.